AF621911

Dictionary of
ECONOMICS

nary of

OMICS

Pokriyal

wealth Publishers

Dictionary of Economic

© P.K. Pokriyal

ISBN : 81-7169-658-9

Edition : 2026

Published by :
COMMONWEALTH PUBLISHE
4831/24, Govind Lane,
Ansari Road, Darya Ganj,
New Delhi - 110002
Ph. : 23272541, 23242541
e-mail : commonwealthpublishers2

Distributed by :
ARJUN PUBLISHING HOUSE
4831/24, Govind Lane,
Ansari Road, Darya Ganj,
New Delhi - 110002
Ph. : 23272541, 23242541
e-mail : arjunbooks2001@gmail.com

Laser Typesetting by :
Dimple Computers
Delhi

Printed at :
Divine Digital Press
Delhi

Preface

Economics is a vast field of social science. Its specialised branches have gown tremendously in the present century. Economics studies how mankind organises productive resources like land, labour and capital; how and why production of goods and resources takes place and in what manner these are ought to be distributed among different sections of people.

The study of economics helps us to solve all the basic problems of the society, rather of the whole mankind, particularly those pertaining to human needs in day-to-day life, at all levels—individual, social, national and international.

This illustrated dictionary has been specially prepared for students of economics. It is the result of a careful analysis of the needs of such students and should be an invaluable aid in their day-to-day learning and in their preparation for examinations. It will be useful for laymen also, in their daily life.

Editor

A

Abatement Cost: The cost of abating a nuisance like pollution or congestion.

Ability to Pay: Everywhere the government try to make the taxation system a equitable and just as possible. The equitable taxation system is possible only when persons are taxed in accordance to their ability to pay. The university accepted measure adopted to know the ability to pay is the income of the individual. Higher the income normally ability to pay the tax increases.

Ability and Earnings: Measures of ability and levels of education ('schooling') are highly correlated; raising the possibility that much of the estimated return to education is in fact a return to ability. Until recently, however, it was not thought that allowance for ability much reduced the *rate* of *return* to education. But studies of identical twins, who presumably do not differ in ability, have yielded much reduced estimates of the rate of return to education; the true *rate of return* may be as low as 5 per cent rather than the usual estimate of 10 per cent and above, although there are disputes over the findings. Persistence of schooling expenditures in such circumstances might be attributable to the consumption value of education.

Absenteeism: Failure to report for work although the

terms of the labour contract require the worker to do so and the contract is still operational. The *over-employed worker will* resort to this where control of the terms of the labour contract is lax or where sanctions for noncompliance are negligible. In particular employers who are currently experiencing labour shortage may be reluctant to use the ultimate sanction of *sacking*.

Absentee Landlord: An owner of land or property who lives away from his estate, collecting rents and administrating his business through some intermediary or agent.

Absolute Cost Advantage: A concept referring to those advantages possessed by established firms who are as a consequence able to sustain a lower average total cost than new entrants irrespective of size of output. Examples of sources of absolute cost advantages are: control of the supply of key factor inputs, patents and superior techniques available only to established firms.

Absolute Income Hypothesis: This hypothesis states that consumption expenditures (C) are a function solely of current personal disposable income (Y): C = C (Q. This view of the determinants of consumption was detailed in the general theory by *Keynes* who hypothesized that consumption would be functionally related to income in the following way.

Absolute Prices: *Money prices* as opposed to *relative prices;* that is the price of goods and services expressed directly in terms of a quantity of the monetary unit.

Absolute Value: (also known as modulus). The value of a variable ignoring its sign. Thus the absolute value of a positive number is just that number, while the absolute value of a negative number is itself multiplied by minus one.

Absorption Approach: A method of analysing the effects of a *devaluation* or depreciation of a country's exchange rate on its balance of trade. The approach focuses attention on the relationship between *national product* (Y) and national absorption (A), where the latter is defined as the use of goods for the purposes of *consumption* and *investment by* the private and public sectors of the economy. The balance of trade *(B)* can only be positive (i.e. in surplus) if Y exceeds A. Thus in its simplest form the relationship may be written as $B = Y - A$.

If the balance of trade is to improve then devaluation or depreciation must raise (Y) relative to A. In an economy with unemployed resources this is possible, since the decline in the exchange rate should be a greater stimulus to Y than A. At full employment, however, Y cannot be increased, so that B can only improve if A falls. The merit of the approach is that it draws attention to the need for complementary action, e.g. some degree of *deflation*, if a decline in the exchange rate is to improve the balance of trade in conditions of full employment.

Abstinence: A term which describes the necessity of foregoing present consumption in order to allow capital accumulation. It was first used by *Nassau Senior* in his theory of the *rate of interest.* For Senior, the creation of *capital goods* involved saving from current income in order to augment the *capital stock,* and create a greater future stream of consumption goods, As such it implies that a reward for such behaviour is required if capital accumulation is to continue.

Accelerating Inflation: An increasingly sharp rise in the rate of *inflation*. If government attempts to hold unemployment below the natural *rate of unemployment* this will result in accelerating inflation.

Accelerator Coefficient: The multiple by which new *investment* increases in response to a change in income. New investment is hypothesized to be some multiple greater than one of the change in income because the value of a machine is usually well in excess of the value of its annual production.

Accelerator Principle: The theory that the level of aggregate net *investment* depends on the expected change in output.

Acceptance: Strictly the act of 'accepting' a *bill*, performed by the person or body on whom the bill is drawn, consists of signing it, usually across the face. However, the term is commonly used to mean a bill of exchange that has been 'accepted' by an accepting house or bank on behalf of a customer who requires *credit* to cover a purchase of goods, or to enable him, as a seller, to extend credit.

Accepting House: One of a group of London-based *merchant banks* which, for a commission, 'accepts' *bills*, that is, engages to meet payment of them on maturity. The house accepts on behalf of customers whose transactions, e.g. importing, give rise to bills, and from whom it eventually recovers payment. Bills accepted by a recognized accepting house may be discounted at the finest rates in the London bill market, and if they carry another 'good' British name are eligible for rediscount at the *Bank of England*.

Accessions Tax: A tax levied on gifts and inherited property. Such receipts are not usually classified as income but as they confer spending power they are arguably a legitimate subject of taxation. An accessions tax is levied on the recipient and, as it is related to his economic circumstances, is superior from an *equity* viewpoint to the UK *capital transfer tax* where liability is on the donor, Proponents of an accessions tax normally argue that it should be levied at *progressive rates* on the lifetime cumulative amount of gifts received, This is to prevent the situation arising where one person receives a very large sum in small, annual parcels and pays little or no tax because the receipts are spread over a long period.

Access/Space Trade-off Model: A theoretical model used (principally) in the analysis of residential location in urban areas which explains location pattern the outcome of a trade-off between accessibility of a site to the centre of the area and the spaciousness of the site. The model assumes that all employment is at the centre of the area, thus sites close to the centre can command a higher price than those further away since travel costs are reduced by locating near the centre. In *equilibrium,* the price or rent of land will fall with increasing radial distance from the centre, the difference in rent exactly reflecting differences in travel costs.

Accommodating Transactions: A type of international transaction implemented in order to offset a net credit or debit situation arising from *autonomous transactions.* They are dependent on these credit/debit situations which occur because international payments and receipts will not always be in balance. Examples are, stabilization *of exchange rates* by central banks; changing international loans, paying foreign debt with short-term domestic liquid claims. Accommodating transactions share the characteristic of being purely monetary there is no accompanying movement *of goods,* services or *fixed assets,* only money and short-term liquid claims.

Account: 1. A running record *of* transactions between two transactors, who may be two departments of one business, and a basic element in all systems of recording business transactions. In retail trading the term is widely used to denote the *credit* facility automatically extended to a customer with whom an account is operated. In banking, customers' accounts have a particular significance in that some or all of the outstanding credit balances in them are regarded as forming part of the *money* supply.

2. The periods, normally of two weeks' duration, into which the business year of the London and other UK *stock exchanges is* divided, and over which the settlement of all transactions except those in *gilt-edged securities is* deferred. Unless there is an arrangement to carry it over to the next Account, a settlement must be concluded on the fifth day, called Account Day, after the close of the Account.

Accounting Standards Committee: An independent body set up initially in 1969 by the Institute of Chartered Accountants in England and Wales in response to demands for the accounting profession to develop and improve a set of consistent standards in financial reporting.

Across-the-board Tariff Changes: A situation when all *tariffs* in a country are increased or decreased by an equal percentage.

Action Lag: The lag between a policy decision (particularly in macroeconomics) and its implementation. The action lag is usually preceded by a *decision lag. Also* a component of *inside lag.*

Active Balance: In monetary theory, some models postulate a division of the money supply into active balances, which are money stocks that turn over actively within periods determined by the in travels between payments; and *idle bal*ances, which are money stocks not employed in the circuit of regular payments. In the quantity theory of money, changes in the velocity of circulation, in conditions other than hyperinflation, are conceived to occur mainly through transfers between active and idle balances, and only to a lesser extent through changes in the rate at which money moves round the payments circuit. Empirically, the distinction between active and idle balances is elusive since the 'activity' of money is a matter of degree. But for practical purposes active balances are frequently defined as *currency* in circulation plus *current account* deposits in *banks.*

Additional Worker Hypothesis: On this argument, the fall in family real incomes during a cyclical down-turn will exert an *income effect:* additional workers from the family will enter the labour force in the hope of finding a job so as to maintain family income. Thus *labour force participation rates will* move countercyclically. In fact, the evidence reveals that on balance labour force participation rates move pro-cyclically (see *Discouraged Worker Hypothesis).* However, the added worker effect is discernible among certain low income groups for whom need is more important than price.

Addition Rule: A rule for the determination of the derivative of a function with respect to a variable, where the function consists of the linear sum of two or more separate functions of the variable.

Adjustable Peg System: This was instigated by the *International Monetary Fund* (IMF) at the *Bretton Woods* conference and refers to a set of fixed, or pegged *exchange rates* which are basically static, but allowed to adjust or change by small amounts in either direction. Adjustable peg systems have three main problems; finding the necessary reserves to meet short term fluctuations in foreign receipts and payments to keep the rate fixed, and compensation for long run trends and crises due to speculation.

Adjustment Lags: The time taken for a variable such as *capital stock* to adjust to changes in its determinants.

Administrative Lag: One of the lags in time between the implementation and resulting effect of *a monetary policy*. It is the time between the recognition by the authorities that action is necessary and the actual taking of the action. Its length depends on the efficiency of the authorities and whether they believe in prompt action or infrequent but more major changes.

Ad Valorem Tax: A tax based on the value of a transaction. It is normally a given percentage *of* price at the retail, wholesale or manufacturing stage and is a common form of sales tax.

Advance Corporation Tax (ACT): When a company in the UK makes a distribution of dividends it has to pay advance corporation tax at the rate of 3/7 *of* the distribution. As the name suggests it is an advance payment of corporation tax and is credited against its liability for that tax. It is a device to collect some corporation tax earlier than otherwise would be the case. It is noteworthy that when taxable profit is not big enough to 'cover' all dividend payments ACT cannot be fully recouped against corporation tax, The existence of ACT in this situation means that imputation credit cannot be claimed by shareholders without corporation tax being paid by the company. The maximum ACT which can be set off against corporation tax liability is the amount which after being added to the dividend equals the taxable profit. The rules allow a surplus of ACT to be carried backwards for two years against taxable income and forward without limit.

Advanced Countries: The dividing line between advanced countries and *developing countries is* usually based on per capital income.

Advertising: Expenditure incurred by a firm to promote the sales of its products, the basic aim being to increase the number *of* consumers who prefer these products to those of its competitors. This can be achieved in two different ways. Firstly, advertising can be used to inform consumers of the existence and location of the product(s) to which it is directed. Secondly, advertising can influence the nature of consumers' preferences to the benefit of the firm's products. It has been argued that advertising is a source of *market imperfection,* in particular, by contributing to *barriers to entry* and *product differentiation,* established firms arc, given an element of discretion over price. In this way, advertising can sustain existing levels *of* concentration within the industry.

Advertising- Sales Ratio: The ratio of firms' advertising expenditure to total sales revenue. Rivalry in more highly concentrated market structures tends to take the form of non-price competition, hence we can expect centeris paribus the intensity of advertising (as measured by the advertising- sales ratio) to increase as we move from a perfectly competitive market structure to oligopolistic market structures.

African Development Bank: A regional development bank established in 1964 to accelerate the economic development and integration of independent African countries through the evaluation, coordination and financing of development projects.

African Development Fund: An inter governmental institution created in 1972 to assist the *African Development Bank* in effecting the economic development and integration of its members. The fund, originally established to allow capital exporting countries control over their contributed funds, enables the bank to include non-African funds in its investment portfolio.

Africanization: A term used with reference to employment in Africa to describe the changeover from non-Africans (usually Asians or Europeans) to Africans in any type of employment.

Age-Earnings Profile: The relationship between earnings and age. The simplest age earnings profile would be a horizontal line stepping up from zero at the age of leaving school with the size of step being determined by the quantity of schooling. In fact the typical post-school age earnings profile is more complex than this: the pattern for annual earnings is for a steep increase on leaving school followed by a slower increase until a plateau is reached in the mid-forties, after which a slow and then a faster descent occurs. The modern explanation of the parabolic path of earnings is that after leaving school the individual does not cease to invest in his *human capital*. He is still willing to forego a certain fraction of his potential earning power, thereby reducing current earnings so as to accumulate capital and raise his earnings at later stages of his life cycle. Because the period over which the investment can be amortized becomes shorter as the individual approaches retirement, he will devote a smaller and smaller proportion of his potential earnings to investment and his stock of human capital will grow at an ever decreasing rate. Eventually investment will no longer exceed *depreciation* and the stock of human capital will actually shrink and subsequently observed pay will decline.

Agglomeration Economies: Cost savings in an economic activity which result from enterprises or activities locating near one another. Examples of such savings include the clustering of retail establishments which permits consumers to make price comparisons without multiple journeys, the efficient use of information where contact between buyers and sellers is facilitated, the spreading of costs of public services and the development of specialized input suppliers serving a number of consumers in the surrounding area. In the last case, cost reductions arise through economies of scale and specialization in the supplying firms, thus they are said to be internal to the firms. Agglomeration economies are an example of external economies where one firm's activities confer benefits on other firms.

Aggregate Concentration: The degree to which production within a sector of the economy or the economy as a whole is centralized around the largest few corporations.

Aggregate Demand Curve: The schedule detailing the quantity of net national *product* that would be purchased at each general price level as shown below. The combinations of output and the price level at which the commodity and money markets are simultaneously in equilibrium. In contrast to the individual demand curve the aggregate curve does not reflect the ordinary substitution effect of a rising price reducing demand. Rather in this case the rising price reduces the equilibrium level of output demand by reducing the real money supply and thus raising interest rates and lowering investment.

Aggregate Expenditure: The sum total of (nominal expenditure on goods and services in the economy. That is consumption (C), *investment : 1)* and *government expenditure (G)* together with *exports, less imports.* In the simple *income-expenditure model* the volume of aggregate expenditure determines the volume of output and employment. The volume of these expenditures may vary systematically with changes in the general price level.

Aggregate Production Function: A functional relationship between the flow of output in the whole economy (Y) and the total labour (L) and total capital (K) inputs, actually engaged in production.

Aggregate Supply Curve: The schedule detailing the quantity of *net national product* that would be supplied at each general price level given constant price expectations as shown below. In the short run the positive slope derives from the hypothesis that workers do not adjust their expectations about the future level of prices to take account of the current movement in prices. In consequence the rise in nominal wages that accompanies the rise in prices is mistaken for a rise in real wages and hence more labour is offered and more output produced. The rise in nominal wages follows from the increase in the *marginal revenue product* of output due to the rise in prices which encourages employers to increase output.

Aggregation Problem: The problem of deriving predictable *macroeconomic* behaviour from the behaviour of the underlying *microeconomic* units. Any attempt to derive macroeconomic or aggregate consumer behaviour from individual consumer preferences runs into problems treated by the impossibility theorem, while attempts to derive aggregate firm behaviour encounters the problems associated with the *aggregate production functions*.

Agricultural Earnings: The earnings of those engaged in the *agricultural sector;* in developing countries there is a major disparity between urban and rural wages. The problem of large numbers of people moving away from the rural areas can be largely explained by the very low agricultural earnings compared to urban wage levels. Often agricultural earnings cannot easily be quantified, especially in subsistence agriculture or where earnings are paid in kind, i.e. in agriculture produce or livestock.

Agricultural Exports: Agricultural products produced specifically for export and not for subsistence purposes or home markets.

Agricultural Lag: This is the gap between actual and potential agricultural productivity. With an increasing number of people in *developing countries* moving to the cities, the supply of food and other agricultural raw materials has to expand in order to satisfy the needs of the increased urban population. If there is a shortfall, food will have to be imported, increasing the burden on the industrial sector and constituting a lag in the development process.

Agricultural Reform: One of the major obstacles to *economic development* is the use of primitive and inefficient methods of agriculture. The rural sectors in less developed countries have to support an increasing urban population in terms of supplying basic foodstuffs. The old primitive methods are inefficient, yet new modern mechanized techniques are usually unsuitable, so one type of reform is the implementation of an appropriate style of agricultural technology. For example, handdrawn ploughs, though widely used are very inefficient, yet the small farmer cannot afford a tractor and even if he could he does not have the knowledge or equipment to maintain it. However, bullock-drawn ploughs have been introduced as *a* kind of intermediate level of technology; with great success in many situations.

Furthermore, there is great need for reform in the system of land ownership, where often one of two extremes can exist: the land is sometimes too fragmented in terms of ownership, with no-one owning enough to implement any efficient production methods or produce food for marketing in excess of his subsistence requirements. The other extreme is the situation of excessively large estates, sometimes owned by absentee landlords so that arable land is not even being utilized. Useful reforms here are the setting up of cooperatives in the first instance, and setting ceilings on landholding in the latter case so that the available land becomes more equally distributed amongst the population.

Agricultural Sector: The sector or part of a population that is involved in agricultural work, providing food; or other raw materials such as cotton or timber for home consumption or export. There is a tendency, which although present in some *advanced countries,* is much more marked *in developing countries* for this to be the lowest paid sector of the economy, or to consist of subsistence agriculture to a major extent.

Agricultural Subsidies: Payments made to farmers for the purpose of encouraging food production and supporting the incomes *of* farmers.

Agricultural Wages Board: Statutory bodies which establish basic rates of pay for agricultural workers in Scotland, England and Wales, in the same manner *as Wages Councils.*

Alienation: A term used by *Karl Marx* to describe the mental condition of workers in a capitalist system. Marx suggested that. In industrial society characterized by capitalist ownership and organization of the tools of production would inevitably instill in workers a sense of isolation, self-estrangement and apathy. This aspect of Marx's theory has been emphasized by a number of modern Marxists particularly Marcuse, Paul Baran and Paul Sweezy.

Allocation Function: That part of government tax and expenditure policy which is concerned with influencing the provision of goods and services in the economy. The allocation function of government is usually said to be necessary because certain goods, known as public *goods,* cannot be provided by private markets and because of the general problem of *externalities* where one individual's action creates costs or benefits for other individuals. This function is one of the three identifiable economic functions of government suggested by, among others, R. A. Musgrave; the other functions are the *Distribution Function* and the *Stabilization Function.* Although the division of functions is analytically convenient, we should recognize that these functions will, in practice, impinge on one another.

Allocative Efficiency: The production of the 'best' or *optimal* combination of outputs by means of the most efficient combination of inputs. 'Optimal' output might be determined in various ways but in *welfare economics* it is generally held to be that output combination which would be chosen by individual consumers responding in *perfect markets* to prices which reflect true costs of production. The efficient combination of inputs is that which produces output at the least opportunity cost and the use of inputs in this manner is sometimes referred to as technical efficiency.

Allowances and Expenses for Corporation Tax: Certain allowable costs which, when deducted from revenue, yield taxable income.

Allowances and Expenses for Income Tax: Income tax systems contain a system of allowances and expenses. These are subtracted from gross income to determine taxable income.

Alternative Technology: One of the names usually given to a type of technology which has some or all of the following attributes: minimum usage of *nonrenewable resources;* minimum interference with the environment; either regional or local self-sufficiency; and the absence of exploitation or alienation of individuals,

Altruism: Concern for the well-being of others.

Amplitude: The term used in a *trade cycle* to describe the distance between the *peak* and trough of any one cycle. Amplitude may be constant in successive cycles, may diminish, in which case the cycle is said to be damped or it may increase, when the cycle is said to be explosive or antidamped.

Analysis of Variance: (also known as ANOVA). The breakdown of the total variation in a dependent variable (with total variation defined as the sum of squared deviations from its mean) into the proportions which are accounted for by variation in individual, or groups of *explanatory variables*, and the unexplained or *residual* variation. This can provide the basis for testing hypotheses about the significance of either individual, or subsets of explanatory variables in regression analysis.

Anarchy: The theory that social and *economic* affairs of individuals ought not to be restricted by any government interference. It is a more extreme view than that of laissez-faire or liberalism which allow the usefulness of authoritarian power to regulate those activities which individuals cannot accomplish efficiently by themselves.

Anchor Argument: One of the *issues* relating to freely fluctuating *exchange rates* is the argument that to advocate free exchange rates implies an absence of foreign payments deficits and hence monetary authorities would no longer have an anchor' to hold down monetary expansion. The other side of the argument is that to remove this monetary anchor of fixed exchange rates is a good thing as it only hinders newly elected policy-makers by not allowing them complete freedom with monetary policy.

Animal Spirits: An explanation of *investment* which rejects mathematical models as of little use, and instead analyses investment as deriving from the animal spirits or whims of entrepreneurs.

Annual Capital Charge: A technique of appraising capital projects which employs *discounting* and recognizes that the use of capital involves interest on the amount employed and depreciation. To discover whether a project is acceptable it is necessary to discover whether the net cash flow cover both the minimum required interest, cost or *cost of capital* and the *depreciation* of the asset. The method involves the calculation of the average annual charge or depreciation plus interest and comparing this with the annual net cash flow. If the net cash flow is greater than the capital charge the project is acceptable.

Annuity: A promise to pay a given sum each period over a number of periods, the sum in each period being constant.

Anomalies: A break in the formal linkages between the pay of different bargaining groups as a result of the introduction of an *incomes policy,* e.g. the imposition of a freeze may prevent some occupations in *a job cluster* from achieving a settlement in line with the *key rate* because their settlement date falls after the starting date of the new policy.

Antilogarithm: The inverse function of a logarithm, simply the base of the *logarithm,* raised to the power of the number whose antilogarithm is required.

Anti Trust: An American term for legislation to control the growth of market power exercised by firms. The term relates not only to anti- monopoly policy but also to restrictive practices operated by individual firms, groups of amalgamated companies (trusts) and groups of cooperating firms *(cartels).* In the US the intent to possess monopoly power by means of merger and acquisition, and its exercise through non-normal business practices is declared illegal. Non-normal business practices *or restrictive practices* include such behaviour as *price discrimination, price leadership,* and exclusive dealing.

Appreciation: A rise in the value of an *asset,* the Opposite of which is *depreciation. An* asset may appreciate in value because its *price* and hence its market value has risen because of *inflation* or a change *in demand* for the asset will lead to increased scarcity value.

Appropriate Products: Generally discussed with reference to products which are appropriate for use in *developing countries.* It is argued by some economists that through *international trade* and multi-*national companies* inappropriate products are often introduced into less developed countries as well as inappropriate technology. Multinational companies will have developed products suitable for the conditions pertaining in Western economies. They tend to use the same materials in developing countries where they will often be inappropriate.

Appropriation Account: Businesses keep accounts showing how profits after taxes are allocated or appropriated. Normally the bulk of such funds will be paid out in *dividends* and/or transferred to reserves, This account indicates how net profits are utilized.

Approval Voting: A form of decision making in which each individual votes *for* each of a set of alternatives of which he approves. The alternative which receives the highest number of approval votes is then chosen. Approval voting is one of a number of mechanisms of' collective *choice* which have been proposed as alternatives to the simple system of majority voting in which any alternative obtaining more than half the number of possible votes is chosen.

A priori: A term which describes a process of reasoning deductively from initial premises to conclusions. Such an approach may be contrasted with one based on induction from observed facts. In some cases, the results of a priori reasoning may be compared with empirical evidence in order to test a hypothesis.

Arbitrage: An operation involving simultaneous purchases and sales of an asset e.g. a commodity or currency, in to or more market between which there are price difference or discrepancies. The arbitrageur aims to profit from the price difference, the effect of his actions is to lessen or eliminate it.

Aristole: Greek philosopher whose work also covered economic matters and in whose writings can be found analyses of production, distribution and exchange. In analysing exchangeable value and offered a theory of money as a conventional device for indirect exchange.

Asian Development Bank: The United Nations Economic Commission for Asia and the Far East recommended the creation of this bank to encourage economic growth and cooperation in Asia and the Far East and to accelerate economic development in the developing countries in the area.

Aspiration Level: A desired level relating to some objective such as price. The individual seeks to achieve this level.

Asset: An entity possessing market or exchange value, and forming part of the *wealth* or property of the owner. In economics an important distinction is made between 'real' assets, which are tangible resources like plant, buildings and land yielding services in production or directly to consumers; and financial assets, which include *money, bonds* and *equities,* and which are claims or titles to receive income, or to receive value from others.

Asset Stripping: A company carrying out a successful takeover bid may be able to make significant *profits* selling the valuable *assets* of the company taken over if they have been undervalued by the stock *market.*

Assignment Problem: The name given to the question of whether it is possible always to assign one policy variable, e.g. *monetary policy,* uniquely to the attainment of one policy end, e.g. foreign balance, under all *exchange rate* regimes.

Assisted Areas: Regions of a country within which economic activity is supported by government tax and expenditure policies which do not operate in nonassisted areas. The, operation of such discriminatory policies is known as *Regional Policy.* In Britain, assisted areas have generally been designated as a result of such areas having *unemployment rates* significantly above the national-average, but other criteria may be and have been used, such as income per head or rates of economic growth.

Association of International Bond Dealers: An institution founded in 1969 which compiles and publishes current market quotations and yields for Eurobond issues.

Assurance: A type *of insurance* relating to a situation where the cover is against an event that is inevitable. This can be because the contract is related to paying the specified sum on a particular date or on the death of the assured.

Asymptote: A value to which the *dependent variable* of a function tends as the *independent variable* becomes very large or very small, but without ever reaching it.

Asymptotic Distribution: The *probability distribution* to which a *statistic* tends as the sample size approaches infinity. The concept is useful in assessing the large sample properties of econometric *estimators.*

Atomistic Competition: A market structure in which the number of firms is very large and hence each firm competes independently.

Attribute: A feature or 'characteristic' of a good. Thus a house may have as its attributes the number of rooms, the presence of a garage, central heating, proximity to shopping or business districts, a clean environment and so on. Note that attributes extend beyond the features of the good itself and can include features of

Attrition: In labour economics the wastage of a labour force that occurs naturally as a result of voluntary quits, retirements, discharges for cause, and deaths. This is one method of dealing with excessive manpower levels resulting from labour-saving technological change without unduly exacerbating the unemployment position.

Auctioneer (General): An agent who is employed to facilitate the establishment of a mutually acceptable price between buyer(s) and seller(s).

Auctioneer (Walrasian): This fictitious character, sometimes described as the 'Walrasian' auctioneer, is a necessary part of the tatonnement process by which Walrasian general equilibrium is reached. His role is to call out the various sets of prices in the market place and then allow trading to take place until an equilibrium in which supply equals demand is reached.

Auction Markets: An organized *market in* which prices adjust continuously in respect to shifts in supply and demand, Key features of auction markets are standardized items or products, anonymous trading, and sufficient numbers to insure competitive behaviour. This is the textbook model for competitive supply.

Automatic Stabilizers: Relationships which reduce the amplitude of cyclical fluctuation in the economy without any direct action by government, *firms* or individuals. One of the major benefits of automatic stabilizers is that their *inside lag is* zero. One of the most important automatic stabilizers is a proportional *income tax;* which stabilizes the economy by reducing the *multiplier* of any *exogenous* changes in *aggregate demand.*

Automation: While used in various ways, the term automation' is generally regarded as being synonymous with the displacement of labour by some automatic process, e.g. handling of machine parts by other machines, automatic paint spraying and so on. Automation is typically associated with *technological unemployment,* but no such direct linkage need occur if automation permits increases in *labour productivity* which in turn permits the generation of *economic growth.*

Autonomous Expenditures: Expenditures which are considered to be independent of the level of income in the income expenditure model. Government expenditure, investment expenditure and expenditure are the principal examples.

Autonomous Investment: Capital investment which is unrelated to changes in income levels. Public investment, investment which occurs in direct response to inventions, and much of 'long range investment which is only expected to pay for itself in the long run are examples.

Autonomous Transactions: A term used in the theory of the *balance of payments* to define those transactions, which take place spontaneously for reasons of gain or profit on the part of firms or increased utility on the part of individuals, e.g. the import of a foreign good, the taking of a holiday overseas. These transactions are contrasted with *accommodating* or compensatory transactions, which follow from autonomous transactions. If as a result of all autonomous transactions, the foreign expenditure by a country exceeds foreign income, the difference will have to be met by a compensatory transaction such as running down foreign exchange reserves or the arranging of foreign loans.

Availability Effects: The effects of changes in the quantity of *credit* available, other than those effects operating through prices, i.e. rates of interest. These effects occur when for institutional reasons or other imperfections in the *capital market* the availability of credit (loans) is regulated by non-price means, e.g. by banks restricting their advances by rationing or similar means. Monetary authorities may make use of such institutional factors to affect credit conditions in important sections of the capital market.

Average Cost Pricing: A pricing rule which postulates that firms add a mark-up onto *average variable costs* (A VC) so as to cover its *average total costs.*

Average Fixed Cost (A.F.C): Fixed cost is the cost that remains fixed.

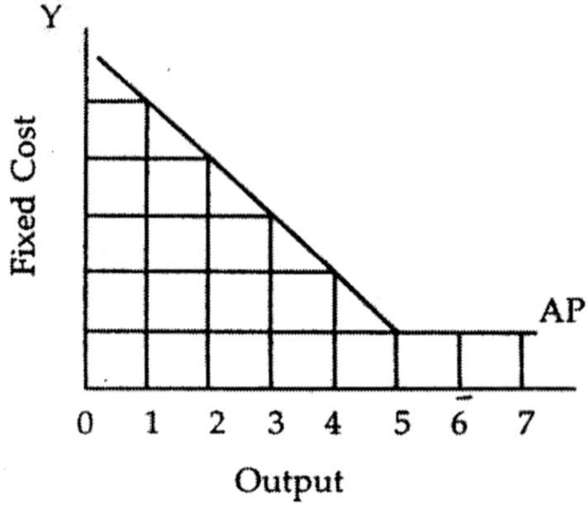

It does not increase when more is produced and likewise it does not fall when less is produced. A.F.C is worked out by dividing the total fixed cost. With total units manufactured A.F.C initially is high with higher production. It tends to fall and later it tends to become constant. A.F.C. is illustrated above by help of a diagram.

Average Propensity to Consume: The proportion of income, Y, that is spent on consumption, C. The average propensity to consume = Cl Y It can be stated as a propensity to consume out of either national income or disposable income.

Average Propensity to Save: The pro portion of income, Y, that is saved, S. The average propensity to save = S1 Y It may be stated as a propensity to save out of either *national income* or *disposable income.*

Average Revenue (AR): AR is worked out by dividing the aggregate sale proceeds by the total units sold. AR under perfect or imperfect competition or monopoly conditions equals the price of the product. So AR curve is also known as the price curve. While under perfect competition. AR curve is parallel to OX. Under imperfect competition or monopoly AR curve slopes downward as illustrated below—

Perfect competition

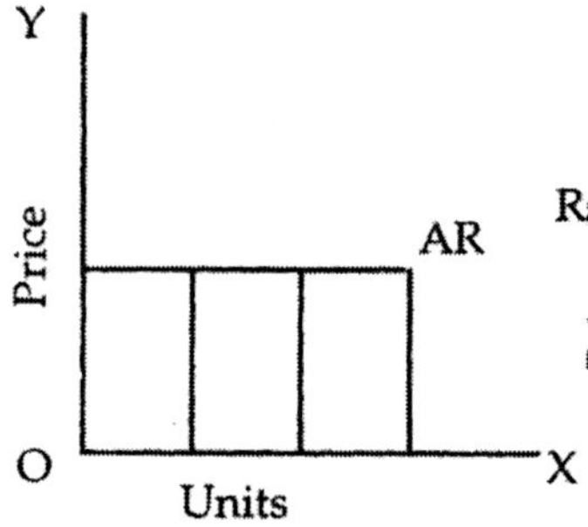

Monopoly/Imperfect competition

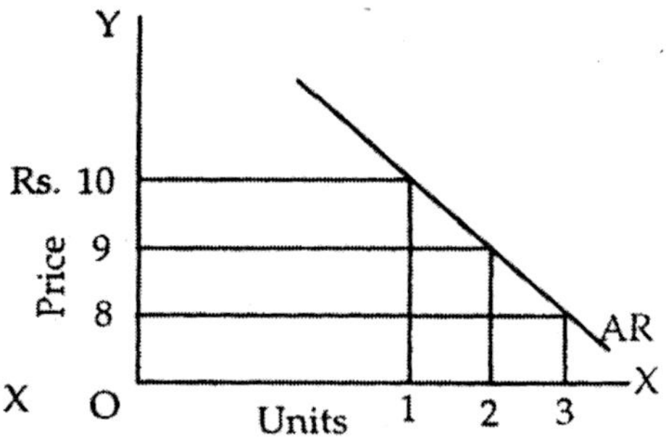

Average Revenue Product: The average physical product of an input factor of production) multiplied by the, *revenue*.

Averch-Johnson Effect: Refers to the profit-maximizing response of regulated firms who in facing a given allowed rate of return on capital, have the incentive to choose input combinations which are more capital intensive than would have been employed in the absence of a set rate of return.

Avoidable Cost: Prime cost may be called avoidable cost unlike the Supplementary cost that is unavoidable. With the stoppage of production, the prime cost need not incurrent. So it is avoidable.

B

Backward Integration: When two independent working concerns combine themselves into one, it is called integration. Integration may be of the concerns which are at the same stage of production of the same product. Integration of the first category (same stage of production) is called horizontal; the second and third category is called vertical (different stages). Vertical integration may be forward or backward. When the merger is with the succeeding stage. It is called backward integration in contrast to the forward integration which is of the aforesaid last third category.

Backward Bending Supply Curve of Labour: A negative relation between the supply of labour, however defined, and the real wage. The outcome may be viewed as signifying the dominance of the negative *income effect* over the positive *substitution effect* (with respect to the particular supply measure). Historically, the supply curve of hours has followed this configuration. Even though at first sight it might appear that hours of work are largely influenced by institutional factors in the shape of trade unions and labour standards legislation, the latter may be thought of as being the institutional impediments through which the preferences of the work force are registered.

Backward Linkage: The relationship between an industry or firm and the suppliers of its inputs. A change in the output of the industry will be transmitted backwards to the supplier of its inputs by a change in demand for inputs.

Backwash Effects: Backwash effects are said to operate where the economic growth in one region of an economy has adverse effects on the growth of other regions. These effects are said to consist principally of flows of *factors of production* (usually labour and capital) from slow growing to fast growing regions. The *cumulative causation* approach to regional economic growth argues that if one region's growth rises above that of its neighbours, backwash effects will reinforce the initial advantage, resulting in a widening gap between regional growth rates. Backwash effects are claimed to result from increased efficiency in production arising from the geographical concentration of activity.

Balanced Budget: Current income exactly equals current expenditure. Most frequently used to describe the situation where government income, *tax receipts* exactly equals *government expenditure*.

Balanced-Budget Multiplier: The ratio of the change in real income to the change in *government expenditure* when government expenditure and *tax revenues* are changed by equal amounts. Thus where increase of $1,000 in government expenditure is financed by an extra $ 1,000 in taxes and this leads to an increase in national income of $1,000, then the balanced budget multiplier is 1. In general, however, we might suppose that the act of transferring $1,000 from the private sector to the government would, in the framework of the simple *income-expenditure model,* lead to an increase in national income, since some of the $I,000 'that was previously in the hands of the private sector will have been *withdrawn,* saved, and not passed on in the *circular flow, of income.* In contrast the government has spent all of the $I,000 and it is therefore a net *injection* into the circular flow.

Balanced Economic Development: The idea that all sectors of an economy should be developed simultaneously to achieve a balanced type of development. Some argue that it is not easy to define what constitutes the correct balance and that planned, careful but unbalanced development is more appropriate.

Balanced Growth: In *growth theory* a dynamic condition of an economy where all real variables are growing at the same constant proportional rate.

Balance of Payments: This term is used in more than one sense, the two commonest interpretations being the 'market balance of payments' and the 'accounting balance of payments'. Used in the sense of a 'market balance' the term signifies the current or ongoing relationship between the two flows of payments, one coming in, one going out, in which a country is continuously involved. Much theoretical analysis of the balance of payments is concerned with 'balance' in this sense. It should be noted, however, that by its nature the 'market balance' is observable only in its effects, e.g. on the *exchange rate* or the level of *external reserves.*

As an accounting balance the balance of payments is a statistical statement summarizing all the external transactions in which a country is involved over a given period of time, say a year. They include 'visible' trade transactions, and 'invisibles' which, broadly, cover payments for services like insurance, shipping and tourism; transfers of interest, profits and dividends currently earned on assets held abroad, and other transfers such as gifts and migrants' remittances. Investment and capital transactions' include all payments arising from transfers of capital or *assets* (plus all extensions of' credit), official or private, which-roughly speaking-arise from considerations unrelated to the position of the balance of payments as a whole, e.g. profit possibilities and relative interest rates. Leaving aside for the moment an item called 'balancing item', at this point in the accounts a 'line' is usually drawn, the balance of all transactions current and capital is struck and the outrun, surplus or deficit, is described as the 'balance for official financing'.

The third and final section of the account then shows all those official transactions., including use of, or additions to, external reserves and the use of funds borrowed from the IMF or from other governments, the purpose of which is to 'accommodate' or finance the balance on the current and capital items. To return to the 'balancing item': this is shown above the 'line' referred to and indicates the discrepancy between the out-runs on the current and capital accounts, as statistically recorded, and the actual total of official financing undertaken.

The item arises from unrecorded transactions and from timing discrepancies between the recorded movement of goods (from which the trade items in the account are derived) and the actual payments for them. But it also points to the fact that since the accounts are constructed on the double-entry principles, so that every transaction is—in principle—recorded in two accounts, once as a debit, once as a credit, they must, given complete and accurate recording.

Balance of Trade: This normally means the balance on 'visible trade, that is trade in goods, over a given period. Thus if exports of goods exceed imports the trade balance is said to be 'favourable' whereas an excess of imports over exports yields an 'unfavourable' trade balance. In fact the balance of trade is only one element, albeit major one, within the 'current balance' which is itself only one part of the total *balance of payments* of a country.

Balance Principle The: This refers to a basic method of Soviet planning, which involves double-entry bookkeeping in physical or price units. There are material balances for the production and distribution plans, labour balances for the labour plans, energy balances for the energy sector and financial balances for the financial plan. The purpose of the balances is to ensure consistency in the plans. The balances, which are less sophisticated than *input-output* tables fulfil a role in planning similar to the latter.

Balance Sheet: This is a statement which shows the *wealth* of a trader or company at a given date. Traditionally, a balance sheet was set out in two halves, the *assets* on the right and the *liabilities* on the left. However, a more common format today is the single column presentation showing the net asset position, followed by the method of financing 'that position. The example given below shows this. The 1981 Companies Act, in order to incorporate the EEC Fourth Directive, has a requirement for companies to produce accounts for shareholders in a specified format, with fuller disclosure than in the past.

Bancor: The name given by *Keynes* to an international currency which he proposed should be created by an international bank, used for settling international debts and which would constitute part of international liquidity. These proposals were part of the *Keynes Plan* for international monetary reform which were put forward at the *Bretton Woods* Conference in 1944.

Bank: A financial intermediary which takes in funds, principally as deposits repayable on demand or at short notice, and which it employs to make advances by overdrafts and loans, and by discounting bills, and to hold other, mainly financial assets such as marketable securities. An important banking function is to maintain a money transmission system by accepting deposits on current account and operating a system of transferring funds by cheque or giro, transfer. Other important banking activities are providing foreign exchange services for customers, financing foreign trade, operating in wholesale money markets and providing a wide range of financial advisory services. In a developed financial system only certain institutions cover all or most of these operations.

The regulation of the banking system in the sense of sustaining the strength and soundness of banking institutions has recently become a matter of heightened concern, following the 'secondary banking crisis' of 1974-6.

Bank Advance: A general term for any form of bank lending. The term does not normally include bill finance, though bankers do extend some *credit* through this medium.

Bank Bill: Traditionally, in the London bill market, a *bill* which has been accepted by an *accepting house, a clearing bank,* or one of a group of other British or ex-Dominions banks on behalf of a customer for whom an acceptance credit has been opened, By accepting a bill the institution concerned engages to pay it on maturity and because of the acceptor's standing such a bill may be discounted in the London market at the most favourable rates. Bank bills have also traditionally constituted *eligible paper in* terms of the operation by the *Bank of England* of its *lender of last resort* function.

Since the new monetary control arrangements, introduced in August 1981, greatly extended the list of banks whose name on a bill established it as eligible paper, to include all the major overseas banks operating in London, bills carrying their names must now be classed as bank bills.

Bank Charter Act: Usually refers to the Bank Charter Act of 1844 passed under Sir Robert Peel's administration, While renewing the Bank of England's charter this Act introduced a major reform of the currency based on the monetary principles of the *Currency School. The* Bank's activities as a banknote issuer were separated from its other banking business, at that time extensive, and its powers of issue were limited to the amount of a fixed *fiduciary issue* plus notes equal it, value to the gold held in the Issue Department which was set up to administer its issuing business.

Bank Credit: Lending by the banking system, by whatever means: bank ad*vances, discounting bills* or purchasing securities. In the theory of banking and money supply a change in the amount of bank credit outstanding produces a change in the same direction in bank deposits, the size of this effect depending on the scale of 'leakages' of reserve assets from the banking system induced by the credit and deposit change itself. Such 'leakages' arise, for example, through increased demand for currency in circulation, or an increase in imports.

Bank Deposits: In the popular view, funds deposited in bank accounts. In reality they are simply records of indebtedness of a bank to the depositor, and they arise from the character of banks as *financial intermediaries*. Deposits are held in various types of accounts, involving varying conditions of use or withdrawal. Current account deposits are universally regarded as forming part of the money stock, and in financially developed countries are the major component of it.

Bank for International Settlements: An intergovernmental financial institution originally established in 1930 to assist and co-ordinate the transfer of World War I reparations payments among national *central banks*. Although a moratorium on reparations payments emerged soon after the bank began operations, it continued to provide facilities for international financial transactions and gradually emerged as a bank for central banks.

The creation of the *International Monetary Fund* following the *Bretton Woods* conference in 1944, however, constrained the subsequent expansion of the bank's international monetary role and activities. Nonetheless, the increasing reliance on *swap arrangements* by the US to finance *balance of payments* deficits and the growth of the *Eurocurrency* market increased the importance of the bank as an international financial institution. Current activities of the bank, in addition to its traditional role as a bank which assists central banks in managing and investing their monetary reserves, include acting as agent for the *European Monetary Co-operation Fund* and the Committee of Governors of the Central Banks of the Member States of the European Economic Community. The bank is also the official depositary for the European Coal and Steel Community.

Banking Panic: An episode in which a failure of confidence in one or more banks produce a sudden and widespread 'run' by the public on banks in general, to withdraw *deposits,* or on times when private *banknote* issues were common to demand payment of such notes in another medium.

Banking School: A body of opinion concerned with the debate over the regulation of note-issue by the Bank of England in the first half of the nineteenth century. In opposition to the Currency School this group argued that regulation was largely impossible and any attempt to limit the issue of banknotes would have undesirable effects on the financial system. The banking system itself, they argued was the best judge of the needs of the economy for banknotes.

All that was strict convertibility of notes into gold, arid this would automatically ensure that banks supplied notes in the correct amount according to the needs of the public and the state of the economy. They placed faith in the competition between banks to ensure that the note issue was kept within these bounds. They further denied that the government could control the money supply since it had no control over bills *of exchange* and *bank deposits.* Their views were not reflected in the Bank Charter Act of 1844 which embodied the principles enunciated by the Currency School.

Bank Loan: This commonly means any advance by a bank, but there is a distinction in bank lending between *overdraft* terms and loan terms. A *bank advance* specifically in the form of a loan is credited in full to the borrower's account at the outset and the interest liability may be a fixed sum calculated on the initial loan and its duration. In some cases, e.g. personal and term loans, there is provision for repayment by regular instalments.

Bank Note: A form of currency issued by a bank, and in essence a 'negotiable' (i.e. transferable simply by delivery) evidence of the bank's indebtedness to the value of the note. The banknote developed from the *bill,* and is in principle a bill payable at sight' (on demand) in some other medium. Originally the other medium was fullbodied *coin* (silver or gold coin), or in practice, Bank of England notes which were themselves so payable.

Bank Rate: Before September 1971, the minimum rate at which the Bank of England would rediscount eligible paper brought to the Discount Office by the institutions to which this facility was available, namely the Discount Houses. The need for such rediscounting arose when there was a general shortage of liquidity in the banking system, and the banks were calling (i.e., recalling) money lent at call to the houses If the position was not relieved by the Bank itself, operating through the 'back door', the houses were compelled to turn to the Bank as lender of last resort.

Bank rate was an administered rate which the Bank moved as its policy needs directed Such movements were significant in that they influenced other short-term rates through their effect on the rates at which the discount houses were prepared to deal; but also, more directly, in that under the pre- September 1971 arrangements the clearing banks altered their own deposit and lending rates in step with Bank rate, a practice which had wide effects on financial institutions and markets In 1971 Bank rate was replaced by Minimum Lending Rate, a rate which fulfilled some of its functions but which for a time at least was operated in a different way and was itself suspended in changes introduced in August 1981.

Bankruptcy: A legal proceeding under which the property of an insolvent debtor is taken for the benefit of his creditors generally In the UK control of a bankrupt's property is initially in the person of the official receiver who is an officer of the courts. Subsequently a trustee is appointed and it is his duty to realize the property and to distribute it among the creditors in proportion to their claims and in accordance with certain priorities laid down by the taw. Ultimately the bankrupt may be granted a discharge which, subject to certain exceptions, releases him from his past debts and liabilities.

Bargaining Theory of Wages: Wages are commonly fixed in a collective bargaining process; an arrangement that differs mechanically from the orthodox demand-supply adjustment process. The bargaining theory of wages refers to model building exercises of the bargaining process applicable to union-management relations that seek to proceed beyond the bilateral monopoly model in which the final outcome of bargaining is indeterminate.

A variety of bargaining models exist, in most of which it is assumed that the union and employer sides attempt to maximize some utility or objective quantity. For the union, this could be the discounted value of membership wage income over contract length and, for the employer, the discounted value of the future profit stream. The desire Of each party to concede or hold out would then depend upon, firstly, a set of objective factors such as the state of product demand and, secondly, a set of subjective factors such as the perceived bargaining strategy of the other party. Since it is conventionally assumed that a settlement achieved after a stoppage is non-Pareto optimal the orthodox bargaining models argue that there will be a tendency for the bargaining parties to reach agreement without recourse to a stoppage. In other words, most bargaining models consider the determinants of a no-stoppage solution. Such stoppages as are observed in practice are thus attributed to mistakes or even irrationality.

Three main types of conventional bargaining models may be identified. De Menil builds upon game theory to provide a deterministic theory of wage bargaining. On the assumption that both the firm and the union are rent maximizers, it is possible to derive the prediction that they will act so as to maximize the surplus of enterprise revenue over competitive wages and capital costs, dividing the surplus between them in certain proportions. There emerges a model of profit-sharing unionism.

An alternative approach is that of Zeuthen. This model emphasizes the problem of risk. During the bargaining process, the parties continually compare the options of immediately accepting the opponent's offer or of holding out at the risk of stalemate. The probability of a stoppage works out to be the ratio of the benefits of disagreeing relative to the costs of disagreeing. Zeuthen describes an atonement process whereby the party with the lowest 'propensity to fight' always reduces his demand. This concession in turn causes the other party to make a concession since he now has a lower propensity to fight, and so on in a limiting process. This is shown to occur at the point where the joint utility of both parties is at a maximum. A further group of bargaining theories follow J. R. Hicks and adopt a cost-benefit analysis approach. Hicks argues that both the employer's propensity to make concessions and the union's resistance depend positively and negatively respectively on the expected duration of a strike. Either party will choose, or threaten to choose, a strike in preference to a concession only if he expects the strike to cost him less than the con cession.

Hicks argues that there is some unique wage rate that both parties as society with a strike of a given length, this representing the highest wage that the union could obtain from the employer. (It is assumed that the employer's wage offer increases with strike duration and the union wage claim diminishes with strike length.) But since both parties know this wage rate in advance there is no resort to a stoppage provided that there is adequate knowledge.

Whatever their form, all the above models attribute strikes to mistakes, or irrationality. More recently, however, research has shifted to model building exercises that in a sense hark back to less sophisticated interpretations of the bargaining process. Thus the political bargaining model of Ashenfelter and Johnson is based on the notion that there are not two but three parties involved in labour management negotiations, namely the employer, the union leadership and the rank and file membership of the union. The alms of the leadership are said to diverge from those of the rank and file.

Moreover, the leadership is more acutely aware of the bargaining possibilities than the rank and file who have unrealistically high expectations, These can only be eroded by a strike and attendant loss of income. The leadership goes along with the strike so as not to appear to be selling out to management. As the strike proceeds workers will reduce their wage aspirations and so the firm is faced by a concession curve that is assumed to be convex. The firm for its part seeks to maximize the discounted value of its profit streams: it will choose the optimum trade-off between foregone profits during the strike and increased labour costs after a strike subject to the concession curve. There is shown to be a determinate wage and strike length outcome.

Barriers to Entry: Factors which place new entrants at a cost disadvantage relative to established firms within an industry. As long as established firms then price at a level just below the minimum point of the long-run average cost curve of the best placed potential entrant, these established firms can earn super-normal profits in the long run.

Barter: A method of exchanging, *goods,* and services directly for other goods and services without using a separate *unit of account* or *medium of exchange,* A successful transaction requires the existence of *double-coincidence of wants.*

Barter Agreements: Agreements between countries, usually with *balance of' payments* troubles, for the direct exchange of agreed quantities of goods without the mediation of international finance.

Barter Economy: An economy where the exchange of goods and services is achieved by the method of *barter,* which would lead to very little specialization or *division of labour* due to the requirement of *doublecoincidence* of *wants.*

Base Period: A point in time used as a reference point for comparison with some later period. For example, in the theory of *price indexes* the *Laspeyres price index* uses the earlier of the two years over which prices are compared for purposes of weighting the relative price changes. This earlier year is then the base period and the price index is a base period weighted index.

Base Rate: After the abandonment of their agreements on deposit and lending rates in 1971, the UK *clearing banks* adopted the practice of individually determining and announcing a 'base rate' which is essentially a reference rate which forms the 'base' to which the structure of lending rates applied to different classes of borrowers is related, and to which the rate paid on interest bearing *deposits is* also linked.

Basic Exports: The name given to the primary products produced by underdeveloped countries for export; it includes basic raw materials, such as copper, tin, cotton, timber, tea, coffee, etc.

Basic Needs Philosophy: A development strategy which has received much discussion in recent years. It rejects conventional accumulation theories and states that there are a number of targets which should receive priority. These are (1) the provision of basic consumer goods such as food, clothing and shelter, (2) access to basic services such as water, education and health facilities, (3) the right to employment which would yield an income sufficient to meet the basic consumption needs, (4) an infrastructure capable of meeting the requirements to obtain the basic goods and services and (5) participation in decisionmaking. The strategy is production oriented. The philosophy has been supported by both conservative and radical thinkers. It has been criticized as having an inadequate theoretical framework and as saying nothing which is really new.

Basing-Point System: A type of pricing in which the various sellers in a market agree that the price to be charged for a good will be calculated by the sum of a fixed price, and an agreed transport charge which is related to the distance between the consumer and the nearest of' a number of agreed locations known as 'basing points'. The 'basing-point' may be nearer to the consumer than the seller in which case the customer pays less than the 'true' transport cost, or further away in which case he pays more than the true transport cost.

Bayesian Techniques: Methods of statistical analysis (including estimation and statistical inference) in which prior information is formally combined with sample data to produce estimates, or test hypotheses. The techniques provide a way of including subjective impressions and/or theoretical elements in quantitative analyses.

Bearer Bonds: A type of bond which does not require a transfer deed because the holder has legal ownership

Bears: Individuals who believe that stock or bond prices are likely to decline and thus sell expecting to be able to buy them back at a lower price A 'covered' or 'protected' bear is one who possesses the securities that he is selling One selling securities that he does not have is said to be 'selling short When prices are falling, the term can also be applied to the state of the stock market itself, i.e., the market would be described as 'bearish'. A speculator with converse expectations is known as a bull.

Beggar-my-Neighbour Policies: Economic measures taken by one country to improve its domestic economic conditions, normally to reduce unemployment, and which have adverse effects on other economies A country may increase domestic employment by increasing exports or reducing imports by e.g. devaluing its currency or by applying tariffs, quotas or export subsidies. The benefit which it attains is at the expense of some other country, which experiences exports or increased imports and a consequent lower employment level. Such country may then be forced to retaliate by a similar type of measure.

Behavioural Expectations: A view on the formation of expectations based on social and psychological factors. It emphasizes the role of interpersonal contacts and of mass communications. Of its nature, considered less rigorous than rational or adaptive expectations.

Benefit Principle: A traditional theory of *taxation* which states that tax burdens should be allocated among tax payers in accordance with the benefits they receive from the provision of public goods. The aggregated *pseudo-demand* curves of the population along with the supply curve determines the amount of a public good that to be produced and the individual pseudo-demand curves determine the distribution of the tax burden among tax payers. The operation of the theory depends on the willingness of tax payers to reveal their true preferences for the goods in question. As the *exclusion principle* does not apply to public goods there is an incentive for individual consumers to understate their true preferences as this will reduce their contributions while the reduction in supply resulting from a change in demand by one person is imperceptible. In aggregate, however, the consequences are that total output is less than optimal.

Benelux Economic Union A customs union, established initially by the Convention of Ouchy in 1932, between the governments of Belgium, Luxembourg and the Netherlands. The present organization was created by the Benelux Economic Union Treaty in 1958. The union seeks to develop tighter economic and social links among its members by encouraging the free movement of *labour* goods and *capital* between the member countries and establishing a common policy with respect to foreign trade.

Bernoulli Hypothesis: Daniel Bernoulli, a mathematician in the eighteenth century, proposed a solution to a celebrated paradox, the so-called 'St. Petersburg paradox'. The problem was one of explaining why individuals would not pay extremely large sums to play the following game. A coin is tossed until, say, a head appears. If the head appears on the second toss the player receives 2^2 units of reward. If the head appears on the third toss, the payment would be 2^3units, on the fourth toss 2^4 units, and so on. The sum of the probabilities of the prizes occurring must sum to unity but for an infinite number of tosses the expected value of the prize is actually infinity.

Bertrand's Duopoly Model: A model of a two firm market developed by J. Bertrand in 1883. The model differs from the Cournot duopoly model in that each firms is assumed to maximize profits on the presumption that the other firm will not change its price. Bertrand's model results in a stable equilibrium for the firms.

Best Linear Unbiased Estimator (BLUE): That estimator which has the smallest variance of all linear estimators, which are also unbiased (i.e. whose expected value is equal to the true parameter value). This property is usually taken to indicate that the estimator is the most desirable.

Betting and Gaming Duties: There are several forms of taxes on betting and gaming. A general betting duty at the rate of 4 per cent of the stake money for on-course betting and 7.5 per cent of the stake money for off-course betting covers most forms of course betting. Gambling in casinos is taxed through licences related to the rateable value of the premises concerned. Similarly gaming machines are taxed through licences related to the cost of playing and the type of premises. Gaming by machine is also subject to VAT. In Bingo halls duty is levied at the rate of 5 per cent of stake money with a further one- nineteenth of the amount by which the value of the prizes exceeds the duty-exclusive value of the stakes. Revenue from these taxes was expected to be 410 million in 1979-80.

Beveridge System: A term used to describe the principal elements of the British Social Security system. Named after Sir William Beveridge, author of the *Beveridge Report* in 1942, the system was designed to consist of benefits paid in cases of sickness, unemployment and retirement and certain other situations, entitlement to benefits being contingent on the payment of *National Insurance Contributions*

Bid-Rent Function: A relationship which indicates the amount a household or firm will be able to pay for the use of a given quantity of land (the bid-rent) at varying distances from the centre of an urban area while maintaining a constant level of *utility* or *profit*. In general it is argued that bid-rents are higher the nearer one is to the central point. This follows as accessibility is held to be a desirable attribute in terms of utility or profitability while the centre of an area is the most accessible point. If the bid-rent functions of various individuals and activities are known the bid-rent for each activity at each distance can be compared with market rents to determine which activity will occupy each location.

Bifurcation Hypothesis, The: The hypothesis that while the availability and cost of *external finance* are important determinants of *investment* in the *boom*, *retained earnings* are most important in the *recession*.

Big Push: This refers to one of the contributions to a debate which took place in the 1950s and 1960s as to whether balanced or unbalanced growth was the most appropriate development strategy for developing countries to adopt. The 'big push' concept originated by Rosenstein- Rodan supported the balanced growth philosophy and suggested that a large investment programme on many projects would surmount the indivisibilities in demand and supply.

Bilateral Assistance: Assistance or aid which is based on a direct arrangement between two countries; this differs from *multilateral aid* which can come from a group of countries or an international organization.

Bilateral Monopoly: It is a market consisting of a single seller (monopolist) and a single buyer (monopronist) for example, if a single firm introduced all the copper in a country and if only are firm used this metal the copper market would be a bilateral monopoly market.

The equilibrium in such a situation can not be determined by the traditional tools of demand and supply. Economic analysis can only define the range within which the price will eventually be settled.

The precise level of the price (and out put), however, will ultimately be defined by noneconomic factors, such as bargaining power, shill and other strategies of the participant firms under condition of bilateral monopoly economic analysis leads to indeterminacy which is finally resolved by exogenous factors.

It should be obvious that bilateral monopoly is save for commodity mavents, but us quite common in labour markets, where workers are organised in a union and confront a single employer.

The following diagram shows the position.

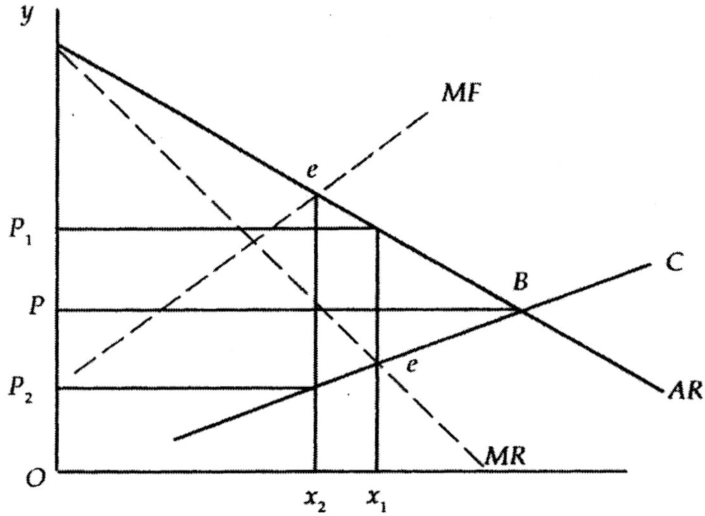

The monopolist wants to change the price OP_1 where as the monopronisst wants to pay OP_2 price.

Given that the buyer wants to pay P_2, while the seller wants to change P_1, there is indeterminacy in the market. The two firms will sooner or later start negotations and will eventually reach an agreement about price which will be settled any where about P_1 & P_2 depending on the bargaining shill and power of the firms.

Bilateral Trade: 1. Trade, usually the subject of government negotiation, between two countries, whereby one exports a given quantity or value of goods to the partner in exchange for an agreed quantity or value of imports from the partner.

Bill: A short-term debt instrument in the form of a document ordering the drawee (i.e. the debtor) to pay the drawer (the creditor) a stated sum at a specified date, or 'at sight' which means on demand. Once accepted, i.e. signed by the drawee (who may be an *accepting house* or bank), and 'endorsed', i.e. signed on the back by the acceptor, a bill becomes negotiable and may be discounted, i.e. sold at a discount on its face value, at a rate which reflects current short term rates of interest. A bill normally has a maturity of up to 6 months and historically was used extensively to finance trade (especially the shipment period of goods) and the work*ing capital* needs of manufacture and agriculture.

Bill Broker: A person who specializes in bringing together, for a commission, buyers and sellers of bills. In the nineteenth century, before the emergence of discount houses, bill brokers performed a key role in the financial system since the initial discounter (buyer) of a bill, frequently a bank, might not have the resources to hold it to maturity, and the broker found someone, frequently another banker, who had surplus funds.

Bills Only: The doctrine prevalent in the US in the 1950s, that in engaging in *open market operations,* the *Federal Reserve System* should operate only in bills. This was based on the view that by concentrating its operations at the short end of the capital market, these operations would achieve their intended effect on bank liquidity with the minimum disturbance to financial markets in general. At the same time the induced changes in short term interest rates would influence other markets through the 'normal' means of portfolio adjustments by *asset* holders.

Bill of Excahnge: Is a bill that is drawn by the creditor on the debtor. When the debtor gives his unqualified acceptance, the paper then takes the form of a Bill of Exchange—specimen of the Bill is as follows:—

Stamp	accepted Hire Lal 10-7-88	D-279, Vivek Vihar Delhi-32 8th Juky 1988

Three months after date,
pay to my order the sum
of Rupees Five hundred only. Sd/- K.B. Lal
Value received Rs. 500/-
Shri Hire Lal
22 D Anand Vihar
Delhi

Binary Variable: A variable which can only take two values (e.g. 0 and 1), normally used to account for qualitative, or non-quantifiable influences in regression analysis.

Biological Interest Rate: A value for the interest rate in *growth theory* where amongst all *balanced growth* paths the highest per capita *consumption is* achieved and sustained by the path on which the marginal productivity of capital (equal to the rate of profit under perfect competition) is equal to the constant exogenously determined rate of growth of the labour force.

Birth Rate: This is defined as the average number of live births per 1,000 of population, per year. Although it appears to be declining in advanced countries, it is a major problem in underdeveloped countries where it is very high, such that very poor countries find it more and more difficult to support an ever-increasing population.

Black Market: Any illegal market established in a context where prices have been fixed at minimum or maximum levels usually by government. Thus, if maximum prices have been fixed, trading may take place at prices above the maximum. Black markets are common in times of rationing or national crises as with the occurrence of war.

Bliss Point: Usually referring to a *consumer equilibrium in* which the consumer experiences total *satiation* with respect to the goods consumed and which point of satiation is within his *budget constraint. Such* point can only occur if the consumer does not act in accordance with the *axiom of dominance* ---*i*.e. if he does not always prefer more and more *of* all goods.

Blue Chip: A term referring to first-class *equities* which have a very low risk of depreciation of earnings.

Bond: Although it has some narrower land more precisely legal meanings, this term is used generally and more loosely to denote any fixed- interest (debt) security, e.g. a *gilt-edged* stock or a *debenture.* The asset negotiable (saleable) and contracts *in* pay the holder a certain fixed money sum at regular intervals (the coupon payments) until maturity, that is until such time as the liability is discharged and 'outstanding sum (the principal repayed.

Bond Market: The term describing any place, or incidence of transactions involving any kind-of *bond* changing hands: the obvious example is the *stock exchange.*

Bonus Issue: This refers to shares issued by a company to existing shareholders not in respect of the subscription of new capital but as a *capitalization* of reserves. The extra shares are issued free on a *pro rata* basis. They should not by themselves confer any benefits to shareholders. They bring the issued capital more into line with the real capital employed by the company.

Book Value: A term used in accounting. To determine the

book value of a share, all the company's assets are added up, all debts and liabilities deducted including liquidation prices of preference shares. This total is divided by the number of ordinary shares issued to obtain book value per share, This value may well have little relationship to market value,

Boom: The *expansionary* ' v phase of the *trade* cycle. The term is usually only applied to particularly fast rates of upward divergence from the *secular trend.* It is usually characterized by a *speculative boom.* Its opposite is a slump.

Borda Count: A system of *collective choice* in which each voter ranks each of a set of, say, *n* alternatives, giving n points to the proposal ranked first down to I point for the proposal ranked last. The points awarded to each alternative by each voter are summed and the proposal obtaining most points is chosen.

Boulwarism: The process of collective bargaining over terms and conditions of employment is normally one of compromise and concession; the two parties bargain and approach one another until a point somewhere between their original or opening positions is attained that is mutually satisfactory to them.

Bounded Rationality: The cognitive limits of human agents in relation to the complexity of the problems with which they are confronted. In essence, economic agents are rational up to a limit because of their limited capacity for computation and information processing. Rules and institutions emerge to reduce the amount of complexity faced by economic agents. These are to be seen as devices that economize on bounded rationality.

Bourgeoisie: A term used to describe that section of industrial society which came into prominence in the course of the Industrial Revolution as entrepreneurs and professional persons.

Box-Jenkins: A forecasting method based on *ARIMA time series* models. The technique does not take causal factors into account, as would forecasts based on *regression analysis* for instance, but relies on being able to capture the trend, cyclic and other systematic characteristics of the time series statistically. It has proved to be a very accurate forecasting method for the short-run (up to 2 years ahead), but this precision tends to decline rapidly thereafter.

Brain Drain: The migration of educated and skilled labour from poorer to richer countries, Education or skill, which represents investment in human capital, is usually cheaper to acquire in poorer, labour-abundant countries, since its provision is usually a labour-intensive activity. Those with the skills or education then move to more developed countries where the return to their human capital is higher.

Break-Even Analysis: The costs of producing a good can be split into two main J parts. *Fixed costs* are those that remain the same for the firm however many goods are produced, i.e. rates, rent, etc.

'Break-Even' Level of Income, The: The point at which consumption expenditures are just equal to income as illustrated by the point at which the consumption function intersects the 45° line in the income--expenditure model. Below this point consumption is greater than income, that is dis-saving occurs, above this point consumption is less than income that is *saving* occurs.

Budget: Since the Second World War it has been accepted that the government budget is a major instrument for regulating the overall economic situation in the economy. Thus if inflationary pressures are thought to be too strong a restrictive budget will be introduced. This means that taxes will be increased and/or government expenditure reduced. It has become accepted that the government could run *budget deficits* or *surpluses to* achieve its objectives in managing the economy. The appropriate level of deficit (or surplus) has become a matter of major controversy in recent years. In the budget the government also makes changes in the structure of taxation and, to a less extent, in the structure of government expenditure. This is to achieve economic goals. For example, income taxes may be reduced to encourage work effort and risk-taking.

Budget Deficit: Current expenditures in excess of current income. Most frequently used to describe the situation where government income, tax receipts, fails to cover government expenditure

Budgetary Control: A system whereby checks are made on expenditure and revenue flow against targets which have been set out in a budget. The purpose is to discover to what extent practice is actually, deviating from targets so that action can be taken in reasonable time to bring tile flows into line with the desired objective. A control system normally involves the regular preparation of statements of these flows.

Buffer Stocks: Stocks of a commodity held in an attempt to even out price fluctuations in primary commodities. The operators use the stock to mitigate fluctuations in prices by selling from the commodity stock when prices are high and by buying the commodity when prices are low. The schemes may be international or run by one producer. The scale of such schemes tends to be limited by the costs of warehousing and of finance, and while they could diminish short-term fluctuations they are powerless against long-run trends, which is often the problem to which a solution is sought.

Building Society: A financial institution which accepts funds in the form of shares or deposits for relending almost wholly to owner-occupiers for the purchase of houses or other dwellings. The modern building society movement developed in the nineteenth century, and the societies were founded as mutual, non-profit making bodies, to encourage and facilitate home ownership, and also thrift, among people of modest means. Building society shares have some slight legal affinities with company shares, but for all practical purposes are much more like *savings bank* deposits. Both shares and deposits in building societies are withdrawable at short notice, and indeed quite large sums can be had virtually on demand. Apart from substantial reserves, mainly of *gilt edged* securities and *Treasury bills* (amounting, with premises, to nearly 20 per cent of total assets), the societies' assets are loans, almost wholly to owner occupiers on the security of the properties purchased. As a matter of policy building societies try to keep to a minimum changes in their interest rates, to borrowers and to shareholders and depositors.

Bullion: Precious metals such as gold silver which are held in bulk in the form of ingots or bars. Gold bullion is used for international monetary transactions between banks and governments.

Bulls: Individuals who believe that stock or bond prices are likely to rise and thus purchases expecting to be able to sell them at a higher price. If prices are rising generally, the stock market might also be described as 'bullish'. A speculator expecting a price fall is known as a *bear.*

Bureaucracy, Economic Theory of: This model assumes that state agencies will behave as budget maximizers. Larger budgets enable bureaucrats to satisfy their preference for salaries, promotion, job security and such non-pecuniary advantages as power, prestige and opportunities to allocate contracts.

The *demand function* facing a bureau is the relation between the marginal value of a service and the level of the service: it is not a relation between price and quantity for the simple reason that the bureau exchanges the service for a total budget and not a per unit rate. Similarly the *marginal cost* function is not a supply function because a bureau does not supply services at its marginal unit cost.

The equilibrium output of a bureau is given by the point of budget maximization subject to that budget covering the costs of providing the corresponding level of the service. Bureaux may thus operate with or without 'fat'. Cost-effective analysis need not, therefore reveal any inefficiency. However, output will always exceed the optimal level.

Bureaux: Non-profit organizations that are financed, at least in part, from a periodic appropriation or grant and which offer a total output in exchange for a budget as opposed to units of production at a price.

Business Behaviour: Those actions or policy strategies pursued by firms with the aim of favourably changing the business conditions they face. Examples of such behaviour are research and development and advertising.

Business Cycles Characteristics: Its one unique features is its cylical nature. It occurs with fair degree of regularity. Jevon calculated its period as 10.46 years. While its duration phase does change, but the regularity with which it occurs cannot be denied. Its all embracive nature is the other important feature. No part of the country's economy—agriculture, trade, industry, consumer goods, transport, services—escapes its net. The two most important characteristics thus can be summed up as (a) periodicity and (b) synchronism.

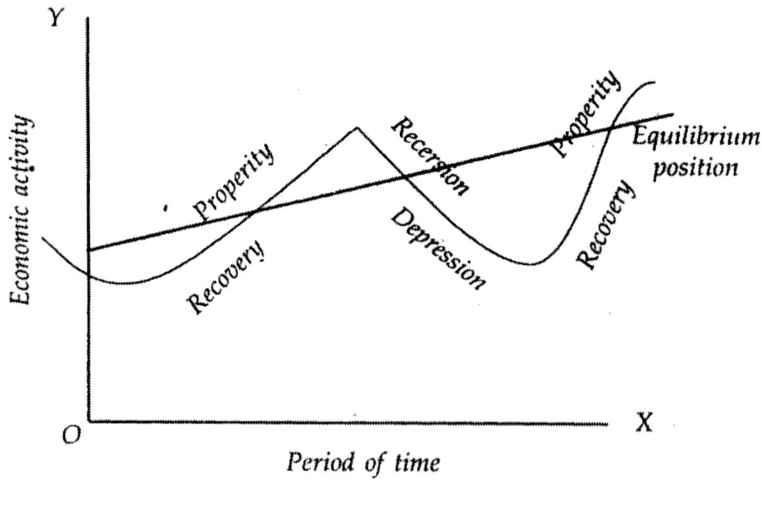

Business Performance: The extent to which an industry achieves the goals or objectives its member firms pursue. Performance is then multidimensional and can cover aspect such as profitability, innovation, product design quality and growth.

Buyer Concentration: Refers to the extent to which total transactions within a market are dominated by the largest few buyers.

C

Call: Is the unpaid portion of a share. Certain concerns realise only a part of the shares value at the time of application and ask the share holders to pay the balanced amount of the share at allotment.

Call-option: A contract giving the option to buy *shares* at a future date within a prearranged time limit.

Cambridge School: A view of economics, deriving from two main intellectual influences

1. J. M. Keynes who may be regarded as the originator of the Cambridge School.

2. Ricardo and Marx of the classical tradition.

It is particularly critical of neoclassical economics and of the work of P. Samuelson and R. Solow of the Massachusetts Institute of Technology (MIT) of Cambridge, USA, who are seen as its main representatives. This antagonism has given rise to a debate between the two Cambridges which has continued from the 1930s to the present with the participants scarcely agreeing on the importance of topics considered or on the techniques of the discussion.

The Cambridge School see an economic model as

encompassing' historical, sociological and psychological notions and facts as well as the purely economic. In its attack on neoclassical economics, a principal target has been the use of the *aggregate production function,* especially in *growth theory.* Some of the more noteworthy members of the school are Mrs J. Robinson, N. Kaldor, Lord Kahn, L. Pasinetti and P. Srafla. The influence also extends to Italy where P. Gareguani, D. M. Nuti and L. Spavanta are associated with the work of the school.

Capacity Model: A model to explain the rate of investment which is closely related to the *accelerator* and *capital stock adiustment* models but especially the latter. It works in terms of ratios where the ratio of *net investment* to *capital stock* depends on the ratio of *output* to *capital stock.* Statistically it has been found to be more satisfactory as an explanation of investment than either the accelerator or capital stock adjustment models.

Capacity Utilization: The ratio of actual to potential output. This can refer to firms, industries or whole economics and gives a measure of the amount of the total capacity that is being used.

Capital: A word used to refer to capital goods in general. Capital is a factor of production in that it represents produced goods which are used as factor inputs for further production. *As such* capital can be distinguished from *land* and *labour* which are not conventionally thought of as being themselves produced by the economic system. As a consequence of its heterogenous nature the measurement of capital has become the source of much controversy in economic theory.

Capital Allowances: These are allowances against

corporation tax related to firm's *capital expenditure*. Generally corporate tax systems provide for the *depreciation* of capital equipment to be allowed as a deduction.

Capital Asset: An asset which is not bought or sold as part of the everyday running of a business. Examples would be property, land, or shares in another company. It is usually held for investment purposes, and has a life of more than one year.

Capital Assistance: Foreign aid is invaluable to the development process when it is used to provide the *capital requirements* for a take-off into *sustainedyrowth,* The domestic capacity for savings and investment is often too low to finance the take off, and so capital assistance vs needed.

Capital Budgeting: Refers to the process of allocating investible funds to capital projects. Many techniques have been suggested for this purpose. There are traditional accountants' methods such as pay*back period* and *rate of return* on capital employed. These are not highly regarded by economists who have suggested techniques such *as net present value* and *internal rate of return* based on *discounted cash flow analysis*. The traditional accountants' methods are not favoured because they do not highlight the timing of *cashflows* from projects. Capital budgeting is employed by all types of organizations but a variety of techniques giving different answers is employed

Capital Charges: These are charges which companies and individuals make in their accounts for interest payments on capital borrowed, depreciation of assets and loan repayments.

Capital Controversy: A debate between the *Cambridge School*

and the Neoclassical School, of the Massachusetts Institute of Technology, Cambridge, Massachusetts; about the validity or otherwise of the neoclassical approach to economics.

Capital Deepening: The process of accumulating *capital* at a faster rate than the growth of the tabour force. The capital/labour ratio is rising.

Capital Expenditure: Expenditure on capital goods by firms, government government agencies or households The *expenditure* may be for purposes of replacing depreciated capital or for creating new capital.

Capital Gain: The difference between the purchase price of an *asset* and its resale price at some later date, where that difference is positive.

Capital Gains Tax: A tax levied on the capital *appreciation of* property. In most Western countries capital gains are not classed as income but it is recognized that they confer purchasing power and so are a fit subject of taxation. In practice it is only *realized income* which is taxed rather than *accrued income*. Generally it is monetary gains which are liable rather than real gains. This has given rise to controversy in recent years when inflation rates have been high. Some other forms of capital gain such as those reflecting falls in interest rates on government securities have also been the subject of controversy.

Capital Intensity: Refers to the ratio of capital to labour employed in production.

Capital Intensive: A technique of production A is said to be more capital intensive than some other equivalent technique B if the ratio of capital to other *factors of production is* greater in A than in B.

Capital-intensive Economy: An economy in which the majority of production techniques are *capital-intensive*. Most advanced countries have this property which has led some people to suggest that this is the only means to growth, but the *correlation of capital-intensity* and advanced countries does not necessarily imply causality.

Capital-intensive Sector: A sector in an economy where the majority of production techniques are capital-intensive in nature. The industrial sectors in less developed countries are usually capitalintensive although there is often a scarcity capitalization issue of capital and surplus labour.

Capital-intensive Techniques: A prodution technique which has a higher proportion *of capital* than any other factor production.

Capitalization: The total amount and structure of shaare *capital of a com*pany. All companies must have owners who own the ordinary *shares* or *equities. A* compay with only one class of share is said tohave a straight capitalization. Many companies have several different types of capital issued and are then said to have a differerntiated or structured capitalization.

Capitalization Rates: This concept relates the proportion of each class of capital in a company to its total market *capitalization.* Many large companies have several classes of *shares,* for example, ordinary shares, preference shares and debentures, and the use of this ratio indicates the relative importance of each in the *capital structure.*

Capital labour Ratio: The ratio at which labour and capital are combined within the production process. Generally labour and capital are measured as flows per unit of time.

Capital labour Substitution: The process of altering the factor proportions of *capital* and *labour* in a production technique; if one factor costs less than the other, there will be a tendency for the expensive factor to be substituted by the cheaper one in a free market situation.

Capital Market: The market, or realistically the group of interrelated markets, in which capital in financial form is lent and borrowed or 'raised', on varying terms, and for varying periods from the ultra-short to long or, as in the case of *equities,* non-specified periods.

There are strong forces causing conditions in one set of financial markets to affect others, notably the propensity of some lenders or borrowers to switch between them as the relative favourability of these conditions changes. This transmission effect is far from perfect, and is subject to complicating expectational effects.

Capital Movements: International flows of funds which may be undertaken by either private individuals or governments. An important element in the Balance of payments,

Capital-output Ratio: The ratio of the amount of capital to the amount of output produced by that capital. A constant capital -output ratio forms the basis of the *accelerator principle.*

Capital Rationing: Generally employed to define a situation where there is a budgetary constraint on the amount of funds available for investment in projects over and above the normal market constraint determined by the relationship between cost of capital and expected returns. Frequently this rationing will be selfimposed. A family firm may be unwilling to raise more *equity* *capital* for fear of losing control or because a quiet life is preferred.

Capital Requirements: The estimation of' capital requirements necessitates the determination of the incremental capitaloutput ratio, that is, the relationship between investment and the consequent increase in income.

Capital-reversing: The adoption of a technique of production when the value of the associated capital stock and the rate of profit have both risen. It implies a positive relationship between the value of capital and the rate of profit. When only two techniques are being considered capital reversing implies *double switching* as the rising rate of profit means that a technique abandoned as the less profitable of the two will be readopted at a higher rate of profit implying a higher value of the capital stock associated with the abandoned technique. If more than two techniques are compared it is possible to have capital reversing without double switching, as a technique once abandoned may never be readopted for higher rates of profit, but techniques considered unprofitable at lower profit rates are adopted for higher rates.

Capital Services: The flow of services over time which stem from a stock of capital equipment.

Capital Stock: Refers to the aggregate or sum of capital goods in an economy. This implies that the stock of capital can be measured by a single number, and requires the heroic assumption that the diverse constituents of this stock can be reduced to a common unit and summed to obtain an unambiguous measure of society's physical stock of capital. *Karl Marx* argued that capital consists merely of past embodied labour and thus can be reduced to the common unit of labour time.

Capital Stock Adjustment Principle: A theory which suggests that the level of *net investment is* a proportion of the difference between the desired capital stock and the actual *capital strick* reflecting tht: possibility of imperfect ad justment to an optimal level in an,,, finite period of time

Capital Structure: This refers to the composition of a company's *capital. A* company must have ordinary *share* capital but it can have several other types such as preference share capital *and debentures* or longterm debt capital. The capital structure refers to the weight which the different classes have in the total capital employed. The question of capital structure becomes particularly significant when a choice between debt and *equitly* capital is made. There is a major debate as to whether there is some optimal debtequity rate *which* minimizes a company's weighted overall cost *of capital.* The conventional view is that at very low levels of gearing debt capital will be cheaper than equity capital because the level of risk is low with debt interest being a prior charge. The overral1 cost of capital is thus brought down wit h the use of debt. As the debt-equity ratio increases, *interest* becomes a bigger proportion of expected profits.

Capital Turnover Criterion: An early investment criterion suggested for use in *developing countries.* The suggestion is that projects be selected in accordance with their *incremental capital-output ratio* and that priority be given to those with the lowest ratio. The argument was that in capital scarce countries a high rate of capital turnover would lead to anefficient allocation of resources. The ust, of the criterion would also lead to utilization *of labour-intensive production techniques* which would be appropriate in developing countries. The use of the criterion has been the subject *of* much criticism. Thus it does not take into account the fact that in many projects, e.g. in the agricultural sector, fixed capital may be a small proportiom of the total investible inputs required and so the use *of* the criterion could lead to projects being ranked in an inappropriate manner.

Capital Widening: The process of accumulating *capital* at the same rate as the growth of the *labour force* so that the *capital-tabour ratio remains* constant.

Capture Theory: This is a theory of regulation developed by *George Stigler. Basic*ally, an industry that is regulated can benefit from its regulation by 'capturing' the regulatory agency involved. This can occur because of political influence; superior technical knowledge that forces the regulatory agency to depend on the industry; appointees being selected from the regulated industry or the possibility *of* future positions in the industry; and the agency's need for recognition and in formal Cooperation from the industry.

Cardinal Utility: Two meaning of this term may be distinguished *The* first and less likely one is that the *util ity attached to* a bundle *of* goods is capable of absolute measurement in terms of some of units such utils'which would be com parable to the units used for height, weight and distance. That is absolute numbers would be placed on 'the utility level and those numbers would be related to a 'real' origin of zero

The second and more widely used concept relates only to the intervals between utility levels. Thus, faced with four situations 1, 2, 3 and 4, if a consumer can say that the difference between the utility levels of 1 and 2 is some multiple or fraction of the difference between 3 and 4, he can be said to have scaled his utility levels in cardinal terms. The difference between this 'interval' interpretation and the absolute interpretation given above is that the 'interval' approach does not require us to attach absolute numbers to levels of utility.

Caribbean Community and Common Market: A common *market,* established in 1973 as successor to the Caribbean Free Trade Organization, which has attempted to encourage economic integration in the Caribbean region. A coinmon external tariff and protective polic for the community were partially agreedy to in 1978.

Cartel Sanctions: Penalties imposed by members of a *cartel* to induce adherence to the joint goals of the group.

Cash: In its broadest sense it simply denotes money including *currency* and *bank deposits.* In some contexts it may be restricted to the most liquid forms of money, i.e. currency and *current account* deposits. In the case of *banks* the term covers currency in tills or vaults plus balances held with the *central bank.*

Cash Crops: This term refers to crops grown by peasant farmers specifically for sale in the market as opposed to crops directly consumed for *subsistence* purposes.

Cash Flow: The sum of retained earnings and depreciation provision made by firms, As such it is the source of internally generated long term funds available to the company.

Cash Ratio: The ratio which banks maintain between their holdings of *cash* and their deposit liabilities, and sometimes referred to as the cash reserve ratio. Historically it was determined by day-today *liquidity* needs, but it tended to become conventionalized and in most banking systems became fixed by law or

Charge Account: A credit facility extended by retail traders to customers. Conditions normally call for settlement within a given period though until recently failure to meet this rarely incurred a penalty. With rising interest rates and inflationary pressures on costs, traders have increasingly begun to include a 'service' or interest charge on outstanding balances owed.

Cheap Money: Denotes a phase in which loans are available at low rates of interest or a policy which creates this situation.

Check-off: The direct deduction by the employer of union dues from the employee's wage, which charge is then paid over to the union. Check-off arrangements require the written assignment of the employee.

Cheque: A document, normally supplied in printed form by a *bank,* ordering the bank to transfer funds from the drawer's *current account* to a named payee. If the payee signs the reverse side of a cheque it becomes' negotiable', i.e. he may assign his claim in it to someone else simply by handling it over. A cheque 'crossed' with two lines and bearing the words 'and Co.'effectivejy can be paid only by being credited to a bank account; it should not be paid in cash over a bank's counter.

Cheque card Cards issued by banks to *current account* customers, which guarantee the payment of' cheques drawn by these customers tip to specified limits. Such cards also permit the holder to obtain cash up to this limit, on demand, from any branch of the issuing bank.

Child Allowance: In most income tax systems an allowance for dependent children is given. The idea is to provide some relief for the costs of maintaining children.

Chi-square Distribution: A probability distribution with parameter n. The distribution is useful in econometric work since the sum of squares of n independent standard normal variables follows approximately a Chi-square distribution with n degrees of freedom.

Choice Variable: A variable in an optimization problem, whose value is 'chosen'so as to optimize the value of the objectiuc function. Choice variables are normally the *independent variables* of the objective function.

CIF: Cost, Insurance, Freight or Charged in Full. A term which describes pricing or valuation of a good to include all of the costs, known as transfer costs, of delivering the good to the point of consumption. It may be contrasted with the f. o.b or free on board method where the transfer costs are excluded. In British overseas trading accounts imports are measured c.i.f while exports are calculated f.o.b. However, for the purpose of calculating the Balance of Payments both are calculated f. o.b. Transfer costs are then counted in inuisibles.

Circular Flow of Income: The flow of payments and receipts between domestic firms and domestic households. Money passes from households to firms in return for goods and services produced by firms and money passes from firms to households in return for the factor services provided by households. The simple notion that the money value of the income of households must equal the money value of output of firms and the money value of households expenditures to purchase this output provides the basis for *national income* accounting.

Circular Flow of Money: It study explains how money constantly keeps an moving from one class to the other and back from the latter to the former. To start with in a society of 2 groups householders (HH) and the firms, agents of production, work with the firms. Money moves from the firls to the householder who spend it on the satisfction of there various wants. Money then gets back into the hands of the firms as shown below:

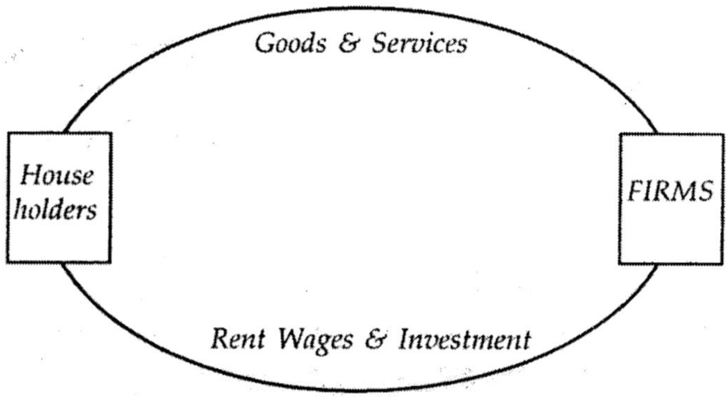

Classical Dichotomy: The separate and independent determination of relative and absolute prices in classical and neo*classical economics.*

In the classical and neoclassical analysis of employment and output all variables are initially expressed in *real* terms and in relative prices. At its simplest output is a function of employment and the technique of production. Employment depends on the real wage, The real wage depends on the supply and demand for labour. To determine the absolute level of prices and wages, the quantity theory of money in one of its forms is introduced separately.

The implication of this procedures that money is neutral and can have no effect on real magnitudes. It is one of the postulates of *Kynesian economics, which* attempts to integrate money and red' variables, that money is not neutral but may be held as an asset in idle balances in the face of an uncertain future. A decision to hold money may lead to a failure in effective demand for sonic good or service with resulting unemployment. This offends the classical conception of the *neutrality of money.*

Classical Techniques: A term normally used to describe standard statistical techniques, in order to distinguish them particularly from Bay*esian techniqucs. The* feature of classical methods is that no information other than the sample data is used to make *statistical inferences,* or in the *estimation* of parameters *of regression* equations.

Clay-Clay: An aspect of the *production function* in *growth theor y which does* not allow the capital labour ratio to he varied either before or after investment is carried out. The term 'clay' referring in particular to capital, is used due to that substance's assumed lack of malleability.

Closed Economy: A concept used mainly in theoretical models to describe an economy with no external trade, which will be completely self-sufficient and insulated from external forces.

Closing-prices: This is most commonly used in connection with the *stock-market* to describe the prices of the *stocks* and *shares* etc. at the close of trading on a particular day.

Club Good: An intermediate case between purely *public goods* and *private goods.* With the club good *exclusion* is feasible but the optimal size of the club is in general larger than one individual. An example would be cinema shows.

Clubs, Theory of: The theory of clubs is part of the theory of *impure public goods.* A club *good is excludable,* but *non-rival* in that the consumption of the good by one person does not reduce the consumption of the same good by other persons. Examples would be swimming pools, museums, beaches and parks. Obviously, the nonrivalry will cease when congestion occurs and the utility of any one individual will therefore be affected by the presence of more members' of the club. The aim of the theory is to determine the optimal size of the club, and the optimal provision of the good.

Coase's Theorem: This theorem is based upon the argument that *externalities do* not give rise to a misallocation of resources provided that there are no transaction costs and given property rights that are well defined and enforceable. Here the parties--the producer and consumer of the externality-- would have a market incentive to negotiate a mutually beneficial trade; that is, to internalize the externality. The neutrality theorem states that the outcome of' this trading process would be the same irrespective of whether it was the producer or consumer of the externality who held the property right of veto over the use of the resource.

Cobweb Theorem: The simplest form *of* a *dynamic model* in which the supply of a good in year *t is* a function of the good's price in year t -1 and where, in any period, price is adjusted so as to 'clear the market'. Such examples may occur in agriculture where the decision to grow a crop or breed certain animals for food may be based on conditions in previous years. The effect can be to generate a process of fluctuating prices, with the fluctuations being 'damped' so as to con verge on an *equilibrium* of prices, or anti damped' so as to continue fluctuating from one period to the next. Indeed, it is possible for the process to be such that the fluctuations grow over time.

Coefficient of Determination: A statistic which summarizes the explanatory power of an equation. It is the proportion of the variation in the dependent variable which is accounted for by the composite variation of the explanatory variables

Coefficient of Variation: A commonly used measure of the degree to which a variable is distributed around its mean value. The ratio of the standard deviation to the sample mean. The advantage of this measure is that it standardizes for the scale of the variable concerned, so that comparisons between the degree of dispersion of variables with widely differing typical values is possible.

Coercive Comparisons: Comparisons drawn between the pay of different groups of workers and used by the representatives of employees as jastification for a pay increase. Such comparisons may result from formal or informal comparability exercises or may be drawn between jobs with a widely differing content.

Cofactor: The cofactor of an element in a matrix is the determinant of the new matrix which is formed by deleting the row and column of the original matrix in which the element is situated.

Coinage: That part of the hand-to-hand currency that consists of metallic coins. Coins are pieces of metal, normally shaped and stamped with a device which is evidence of their value and of their legal status as money. In the case of fullbodied coins which circulate at a value equal to that of the metal in them coining is an evidence of their metallic content. With token coins, the circulating value of which is unrelated to then- value as metal, coining declares value and establishes their legal status.

Coinage Debasement: Historically a reduction in the quantity of the prime metal in a full-bodied coin, without a corresponding reduction in its legal nominal value. Debasemerit occurred in various ways, by clipping and 'sweating', by reduction in the fineness of the metal in nevk coins, and by reduction in the actual weights of coins on recoinage, It was widely practised by rulers and ruled to obtain finance. Theoretically it should have eventually led to a rise in the price of commodities, either by direct markup when debasement was detected and was widespread, or by tire consequent increase in the amount of money in circulation. However, in periods of money shortage its effect could be anti-deflationary rather than inflationary.

Collateral Security: Loosely used it means any security taken by a bank when it makes an advance to a borrowing customer, and which it is entitled to claim in the event of default. More strictly it denotes a non-personal security put up by a third party, i.e. not the borrower, and which offers certain legal advantages to the bank in case of default.

Collective Bargaining: Negotiations between employees and employers about the establishment of procedures and rules to cover conditions of work and rates of' pay. Such arrangements usually involve the joint regulation of agreed procedures.

Collective Choice: Sometimes also called social choice. A decision made by or on behalf of a group. The study of' market .economies is largely concerned with choices made by individuals but in all economies many decisions concerning resource allocation are made by governments or other groups. Economists are interested in the way in which such collective decisions are reached and the allocations of resources to which they lead. In particular, economists have been interested in the pareto optimality of collective choices and the extent to which such choices reflect the preferences of individuals.

Collective Goods: Commodities or services that possess the characteristic of non-excludability alone. In such cases, although it is technically feasible to exclude people from consuming the commodity or service in question it is nonetheless uneconomic.

Collusion: Agreement between firms to co-operate in order to avoid mutually damaging rivalry. The means of achieving such co-operation range from informal or tacit agreement, arising from the pooling of information for instance, to formal arrangement within *cartel* organizations defectors.

Commercial Banks: A general, nondefinitive, term denoting those bank, usually in the private sector which con duct a general rather than a specialized type of business. They accept deposits on varying terms, but including demand deposits; and their lending to private sector business, usually for non-fixed capital purposes, usually accounts for the greater part of their assets. The term distinguishes such banks from savings banks or merchant banks on the one hand, or banking type institutions like building societies and finance companies on the other.

Commercial Bill: A billdrawn to finance trade or other commercial or production activities, It is distinguished from Treasur y Bill or local government bill which are instruments of public financial operations.

Commercial Policy: The rules adopted by a country for the conduct or regulation of its, foreign trade and payments. At one extreme a country may adopt a policy of *.free trade* and at the other one of *autarky* while in between there would be policies of varying degrees of protection by *tariff quotas, exchange control* etc.

Commodities: Objects that are produced as a result of the process of production.

Commodity Money: An object used as money which is also a saleable commodity in its own right: the obvious example is gold. This differs from fiat *money* which has in itself no real value.

Commodity Space: The space bounded by axes representing the quantities of goods or services potentially available to the consumer. In two dimensions, commodity space is shown as a quadrant bounded by axes representing the amounts of two goods. As such it indicates the various combinations of those two goods over which consumers exercise choice.

Common Agricultural Policy: The common system of agricultural price supports and grants adopted by the *European* Economic Community. It attempts to encourage stable agricultural market conditions, ensure a fair return to farmers maintain reasonable prices for consumers and introduce policies designed to increase yields and labour productivity in the Community's agricultural sector. The policy has established a *common market* for most of the major agricultural commodities. Agricultural prices within-the community are based on common 'target' prices.The target prices are set in terms of fixed agricultural units of account officially defined as the value of 0.88867088 grams of fine gold, which in turn are converted into different national currencies using adjusted rates of exchange known as 'green' rates. *A* system of levies on non-EEC agricultural imports is used to protect target prices when they are set above the general level of world prices. In addition the community has established an internal price support system based upon a set of 'intervention' prices set slightly below target price. If, for example, the level of supply is in excess of that required to clear the market at the target price, the excess supply is bought by the community at the intervention price, thereby preventing over-production from depressing the common price level. The community also supports prices by means of export subsidies adjusted to influence the internal supply of agricultural commodities. 'The guarantee section of the European Agricultural Guidance and Guaranice Fund finances the price support programmes. The community also offers assistance to farmers in the form of grants designed to improve and rationalize methods of agricultural production.

Common Customs Tariff: The common external *turiff* of the EEC. There are no tariffs on trade between member countries of the EEC and a common tariff on imports from third countries This is essentially for protective purposes. There are many concessions. Thus most industrial products from EFIA enter duty free. Under the Generalized System of Preferences a wide range of goods from developing countries may be imported on a nonreciprocal tariff preference basis, Similarly, under the *Lome Conrention the* EEC members entered into a trade aid and co-operative agreement with 46 developing countries from Africa, the Caribbean and the Pacific. This agreement allowed the free entry of all industrial and many agricultural goods from these countries.

Common External Tariff: A *tariff* applied by members of a *customs union* common market or *economic community* at an agreed, similar rate on imports from non-members. While the rate for and given imported good is identical in all member countries, different rates of duty are applied to different goods.

Common Facility Co-operatives: A policy measure designed to facilitate the growth of progressive technology, by forming co-operatives which use common facilities or joint production workshops to raise productivity of local artisans and craft industries.

Common Market: In addition to the common *external tariff and* the concerted commercial policy of the customs *union,* a common market aims at a unified market area with the free movement of goods, services and factors of production.

Communism: In the strict sense a stage of economic development which is said to occur when all classes in society have been absorbed into the proletariat. In this ideal society the state would have withered away and each person would contribute according to ability and receive according to needs. This utopia envisaged by Marx is seen to be the stage of economic development which follows on from capitalism and socialism. The term is however often used to denote the planned economic system operated in the Comecon countries, China and elsewhere where the government hits centralized economic decisions and taken control of productive activity.

Community Indifference Curves: Each point along such a curve represents a bundle of commodities which can be distributed among individuals so as to yield a particular distribution of utility within the community. Community indifference curves can intersect. As many indifference curves will pass through any point in commodity space as there are different ways of distributing that commodity bundle.

Company: This normally signifies a joint stock company, which is a legal entity set up for the purpose of conducting commercial or industrial operations, and with a capital divided into *shares* that are held by its members. In principle the shareholders control the company through their right to vote at annual meetings and to elect the board of directors, whose function is to oversee the running of the company. The formation and conditions of operation of companies are regulated by the Companies Acts which confer rights as well as apply restrictions. The basic feature of a joint stock company is that it is a 'legal person', entirely separate from the individual shareholders, and able to act. e.g. make contracts, undertake legal proceedings in its own right.

Company Bargaining: *Collective bargaining* between the representatives of a single company, which may have one or more plants throughout the country, and employees representatives to establish rates of pay and conditions of work throughout the company. Where a company has a number of plants throughout the country in the same industry and the company is a monopolist this form of bargaining is equivalent to *national bargaining.*

Company Director: A person elected by *shareholders to* participate with the other directors in the running of a *company. A* director may be concerned solely with the shared responsibility for general policy or the person may have additional specialized responsibilities with respect to a particular branch of the firm's activities as, for example, with *marketing.*

Company Savings: That part of firms' *profits* which is

neither paid out in *taxes* nor distributed to shareholders as divi*dends.*

Comparability: Formal and informal comparisons drawn by work groups between their pay and the pay of other workers. Such comparisons influence the wage determination process. Formal comparisons are those embodied in the procedures for determining pay, for example the rates of pay of civil servants are established after detailed enquiries into the pay of individuals performing similar work in the private sector of the economy. Informal comparisons are those used as points of reference by either employers and employees but which are not recognized simultaneously by both parties as serving as a suitable frame of reference for establishing pay.

Comparability Argument: The belief that workers doing similar jobs and producing the same amounts should be paid the same wage.

Comparative Advantage: Credit for the discovery of the doctrine of comparative advantage, which is the basis of the case for *specialization* on the part of nations or individuals and for freedom of trade, is given to David *Ricardo* who explained the principle

Comparative Dynamics: A method employed in *dynamic economics* with a special feature that the rates of change in the values of the *parameters* and in the equilibrium values of the *variables* are constant. Comparative dynamics compares equilibrium values of the *endogenous variables* for different rates of change for one of the parameters. The economic models within which this method is employed are often referred to as steady state models.

Comparative Statics: The comparison of a new *equilibrium*

position with an old one after some change in the variables, without reference to the way in which the new position is reached, and usually without quantitative aspects. Simply, the determination of the direction in which variables will change consequent upon some disturbance to the original equilibrium.

Compensated Demand Curves: *A demand curve* in which the *income effect* of a price change has been netted out so that, along the demand curve real income is held constant. The demand curve then exhibits the shape it does because of the *substitution effect* only. The *Marshallian demand curve* includes both income and substitution effects. The method w mking the income effect out depends on how that effect is measured.

Compensation Tests: Such tests ask tile question whether the losers from some particular change can be compensated for their losses while still leaving the gainers better off than they were before the change. The compensation is hypothetical and not required to take place. The most famous one is the *Kaldor-Hicks test.*

Competition Act 1980: This legislation emphasized the importance in competition policy of business conditions and practices. It empowered the Director General of Fair Trading to undertake preliminary investigations into anti-competitive practices, defined as business conditions which may restrict, distort or prevent competition. The finding of these investigations must be published. In response to these findings the Director General of Fair Trading can accept an undertaking from the firm(s) involved to modify or drop the business practices in question. Alternatively, the Director General can make a reference to the Monopolies and Mergers Commission. These references are known as 'competition references'. The commission has six months to report on whether the practices, if confirmed, operate against the public interest. The Secretary of State can prohibit the practice in the event of an adverse finding.

Competition and Credit Control: The title of a consultative document issued by the *Bank of England* in mid-1971, outlining proposals for a major revision of the credit control arrangements applying to the banks and other financial institutions, and which were put into operation later that year. The essence of the changes was that they should permit an ending of quantitative controls over lending, especially that of the *clearing banks;* and that they should apply to the banks and *finance houses* in as wide and non discriminatory a fashion as possible.

The requirement of the London and *Scottish Clearing banks* to maintain certain mini *mum liquiditY ratios* was ended; instead all banks operating in the UK, as well as the larger finance houses, were required to observe a minimum *reserve assets ratio* in their sterling operations, and all were to be subject to the *special deposits* scheme on an equal footing. The object of these changes was to remove discriminatory restrictions on competition between banks, and for their part the London and Scottish clearing banks ended their respective agreements on deposit and lending rates. In further pursuit of flexibility, the old, administered *Bank Rate* was discontinued, to be replaced by *Minimum Lending Rate* which was intended to vary according to a formula relating it to the *Treasury bill* rate.

Competitive Markets: A market in which a very large number of small buyers and sellers trade independently, and as such no one trader can significantly influence price.

Complements: A good which tends to be purchased when another good is purchased since it 'complements' the first good. Favourite examples are cups and saucers, cars and petrol etc. Complementary goods have a negative *cross elasticity of demand. The indifference curve* for perfect complements is shown in the diagram.

Complex Number: Numbers which involve *imaginary* elements, i.e. which contain the square root of minus one.

Composite Commodity Theorem: Due to *J. R. Hicks* this theorem states that if there exists a set of goods whose relative prices do not change then those goods can be treated as if they were one commodity, the so-called 'composite commodity'.

Compound Interest: The procedure whereby future *interest* is paid on past interest earned. Thus if a sum of C1 is invested at a rate of interest *r*, its value after one year will be C *(I + r).* If the interest gained is now removed, the C1 will remain and will gather *r* per cent again in the following year. If however the C (I + *r)* is left to secure interest, then it will secure interest in the second year of C(l + *r) r,* and the original *k (I + r)* will remain.

Concave Function: A function which is concave towards the origin is one whose second *derivative* is negative. Such a function is also *convex* away from the origin.

Concentration: A term indicating the state of competitive conditions prevailing in an ridustry. Two extremes are *Perfect Competition and Monopoly* with market structures in between representing various degrees of imperfect competition. Conventionally, it is thought the higher seller concentration is, the less competitive the market.

A concept used either in connection with the *size distribution of firms* in an industry or economy, or with reference to the location of Industry. In its former use concentration refers to the extent to which a market's or an economy's total output is accounted for by the few largest member firms. When used in the context of industrial location, concentration means the degree to which an industry has become localized within a particular area.

Concentration, Coefficient of: A statistical measure of the degree to which an economic activity or feature is geographically concentrated within a nation, The coefficient of concentration of an industry may be calculated as the relation between the distribution of that industry across the regions of the nation and the distribution of some other characteristic. A value of zero would indicate a spread of the activity which corresponded exactly to that of population, while the greater the value of the co-efficient the greater the degree of geographical concentration of the activity.

Concentration Ratio: The percentage of total industry size accounted for by the few largest firms in the industry. The measure may be used as a proxy for one dimension of market structure, i.e. the degree to which an industry is centralized.

Concerted Action: The name given to the German variant of *incomes* policy in which the government, although not a party to the collective bargaining process, sets out criteria for relating pay increases to the aims of stability and growth. Since 1967, representatives of the German employers, trade unions, government and other official bodies have met several times a year to discuss the government's economic forecasts and analyses. The intention of such concerted action has been to provide an opportunity for the coordination of private decisions and official policy, and on occasions the government has quite explicitly given its view of the consequences of alternative actions.

Concertina Method of Tariff, Reduction: A procedure of *tariff* reduction, which involves cutting the higher tariff rates, while leaving lower rates unchanged, so that the gap between tariffs is diminished.

Conciliation: Intervention in an *industrial dispute* at the request of the parties to the dispute by an independent and impartial third party in an attempt to reconcile the views of the two parties.

Condorcet Criterion: A system of collective choice in which the chosen alternative is that which defeats all other alternatives in a series of pairwise contests using majority rule. The procedure is named after the Marquis de Condorcet who discussed it in 1785. While the Condorcet approach may be said to give a more complete reflection of voters alternatives than simple majority rule it can, like *majority rule,* fail to yield an unambiguous 'winner'.

Congestion Costs: When an increase in the use of a facility or service which is used by a number of people would impose a cost on the existing users, that facility is said to be congested. Thus. for example, it an increase in the number of vehicles using a road lengthens journey times then congestion occurs. If an increase in the number of economic activities located in a geographical area reduces the efficiency of those activities then the area gets congested. In the latter case congestion represents a agglomeration. Costs imposed by congestion are important in such areas as Cost Benefit Analysis the explanation of the actual pattern of economic activity and in the analysis of jointly consumed goods by the theory of clubs.

Conglomerate Merger: The consolidation of a previously independent firm with separate and distinct markets, as a new subsidiary of the holding company of a conglomerate.

Conglomerates: A firm comprising a *holding company* and a number of subsidiary companies, Such business organizations tend to expand by means of merger and take over rather than internal growth.

Conjectural Variation: Refers to firm behaviour in *oligopolistic markets* where, due to the small number of active firms, the decision-maker must before deciding upon appropriate strategies take into account rivals' potential responses. One of the applications of *game theory* in economics has been the analysis of firm behaviour under such conditions.

Consistency: A desirable property of econometric estimators. A consistent *estimator* is one whose mean tends to the true value of the *parameter,* and whose variance tends to zero as the sample size becomes very large. The *Ordinary Least Squares estimator* is a consistent estimator if there are no econometric problems.

Consortium Bank: A type of international bank formed by groupings of existing banks usually drawn from different countries. These banks appeared in the 1960s and are now established in several financial centres, including London. They engage to a considerable extent in medium-term lending, frequently to multinational companies; they obtain the greater part of their funds in the *euro-currency market;* but they also arrange 'syndicated' loans frequently bringing in lenders outside the consortium members.

Constant Amplitude: A characteristic of the *trade cycle,* where the *amplitude* does not change with time. This implies that the system being considered is on the verge of being an *explosive cycle* or of being a convergent cycle,

Constant Capital: In the Marxian scheme, that part of capital which is represented by the means of production, raw materials and instruments of labour. It is defined as constant since it can add no more to the value of output than its own value; value being defined as hours of embodied *socially necessary labour.*

Constant Clasticity of Substitution Production Function. The CES production function is a *linearly homogeneous production* function with a 'constant *elasticity of* input *substitution.* This elasticity can take on values other than unity.

Constant Market Share Demand Curve The relation between quantity sold and price which faces the firm if all its competitors exactly match any price change made by this firm. It is therefore more inelastic than the conventional *demand curve,* as each point will represent an equal share of the market. This concept has been used analytically in the kinked curve model of oligopoly and the theory of monopolistic competition.

Constrained Optimization: The maximization or minimization of an *objective function* where the *choice variables* are subject to some *constraint.* Examples include the maximization of *utility* subject to a *budget constraint.* Mathematical methods to deal with this sort of problem include *Lagrangean Techniques.*

Constraint: Usually, a mathematical relationship between the *choice variables of* an optimization problem, in which some function of the variable *is* not equal to a constant. An example is a budget constraint on the maximization of utility

Consumer: Any economic agent responsible for the act of consuming final goods and services. Typically, the consumer is thought of as an individual but in practice consumers will consist of institutions, individuals and groups of individuals. In the last respect, it is noteworthy that the consuming agent for many decisions is the household and not the individual. This matters in so far as households may well take 'group' decisions based on some compromise of individual wants within the household, or, even more likely, or paternalistic judgements by older members of the household. Consumer demand may therefore be partly considered in the context.of group decisions-reflecting some *social weltare* function which covers all members of the household.

Consumer Credit: This constitutes a loan to the consumer for a short period of time, for the purchase of a specific commodity. The term does not extend to credit accounts and hire-purchase as such schemes are not restricted to buying a specific commodity.

Consumer Demand Theory: That area of economics which defines testable theories of how consumers behave in response to changes in variables such as price, other prices, income changes and so on. The two main schools of thought are those based on *indifterence curve* analysis and *revealed preference* theory but considerable attention has also been given to the theories based on the *characteristics of* goods.

Consumer Durable: .Any consumer good which has a significant 'life' and which is not therefore immediately consumed. Consumer durables have some characteristics of capital goods in that they tend to yield a flow of services over their lifetime rather than one immediate 'service' in one act of consumption. Nonetheless the dividing line between consumer goods, consumer durables and capital goods is a hazy one in practice.

Consumer Equilibrium: The situation in which the consumer maximizes utility subject to a given *budget constraint.* In terms of an *indifference map* this situation is achieved when the consumer reaches the highest possible *indifference curve* given the limitations imposed by his *budget line.* This will be a situation where the indifference curve is tangential to the budget line-i.e. their slopes are equal. Formally, the *marginal rate of substitution* is equal to the price ratio of the two goods.

Consumer Goods: and Services. Tangible and intangible *commodities* which are consumed for their own sake to satisfy current wants.

Consumer's Surplus: Most commonly used to refer to the area under an individual's *Marshallian* demand curve between two prices. It is a monetar,, measure, although orginally represented in terms of surplus utility by Marshall, It is a measure of the benefit to a consumer, net of the sacrifice lie has to make, from being able to buy a commodity at a particular price. It is widely used in *cost-benefit analysis* and other areas of applied economics as an approximate measure of changes *in welfare,* in particular, of compensating variation and equivalent variation. Compensating variation is a measure of the change in an individual's welfare following, for example, a change in prices. The compensating variation is the maximum amount of income that could be taken from someone who gains from a particular change while still leaving him no worse off than before the change. The compensating variation of the loser from some change is the minimum amount lie would require following the change to leave him as well off as he was prior to the change.

Consumption: The act of using goods and services to satisfy current wants. While theoretically precise there are practical problems in measuring consumption. The main problem arises in the treatment of *consumer durables. If* they are included they overstate current consumption expenditure; if excluded they understate them. Ideally we wish to include only the value of the flow of the services of the consumer durable that are consumed in each period.

Consumption Expenditure: Aggregate expenditures on goods and services to satisfy current wants.

Consumption Function: The schedule detailing the relationship between aggregate consumption expenditures and income, that is C = C(Y). Consumption expenditure may be related to either *national income* or *disposable income.* This functional relationship is one of the cornerstones of *Keynes' general theory,* as consumption is the largest single component *of aggregate expenditure* in most developed countries. Keynes initial developments have come to be known as the *Absolute Income Hypothesis* but more recent developments have explained aggregate consumption expenditures in terms of relative income, the *Relative Income Hypothesis,* life-cycle income, the *Lift Cycle Hypothesis,* permanent income, the *Permanent Income Hypothesis* and related it specifically to wealth, the *Endogenous Income Hypothesis.* Considerable controversy surrounds the actual specification of the consumption function. Empirical studies have by and large revealed that the *short-run consumption function* and *crosssection consumption function* confirm Keynes' absolute income hypothesis. In contrast evidence on the long-run consumption *function* suggests a quite different form. Hence all of the above theories which post-date Keynes' pioneering work have sought to reconcile the conflicting evidence. Further problems abound with empirical work in this area and at present there exists no consensus for dealing with these. Principal among the problems are:

1 . in practice it is difficult to measure consumption accurately. *Consumer durables* provide a flow of services beyond the time of purchase and it is these services which should be included in consumption.

2. the variables C and Y can either be measured in current pounds or dollars or they can be *deflated by* the *consumer price index* to transform them into real terms.

3, aggregate, per capita, or even household values for C and Y can be chosen.

Contingency Reserve: The unallocated reserve for contingencies and other requirements which cannot be quantified when UK public expenditure plans are being considered. Formerly, only expenditure decisions increasing the volume of expenditure were charged against the reserve. However, in line with the move to cash planning, approved increases in cash limits have been charged to the contingency reserve since 1981–2.

Contingency Table: A device whereby the degree of association or dependence between two variables or characteristics can be assessed. Sample information is compared to a theoretical situation in which there is complete independence between the characteristics. *A statist ic* can be calculated from the table which is approximately *Chi-square* distributed under the *Null Hypothesis* of independence.

Continuous Variable: A variable which can take on any value between given limits

Contract Curve: In the context of two consumers the curve represents the locus of points where the *marginal rate of' substitution* between the pair of goods is the same for both individuals. These points of tangency between the individual's *indifference curves* are efficient or exchange optima in the sense that it is not possible by any reallocation to make one individual better off without the other becoming worse.

In the production case the contract curve represents the points of tangency between *isoquants* and thus is the locus of points for which the *marginal rate* of *technical substitution* is the same for the production of each good or in the one good for each firm.

Contractionary Phase: The phase of the *trade cycle* following a *peak* and lasting to the next lower turning point or trough. It marks a decline in the level of economic activity.

Convergence Thesis: The idea that socialist and capitalist economies are departing from their respective 'ideal' forms and are evolving increasingly similar modes of behaviour and thinking, institutions and methods. The hypothesis that the two systems are converging was originally put forward by *Jan Tinbergen* and has developed into a theory of inevitable convergence based on the necessity of similar patterns of technological development.

Conversion: The practice of issuing new stocks and shares in exchange for others. For example, the government may offer new stock to holders of existing stock at the time when it is due for redemption.

Convertibility: An attribute of a currency which is freely exchangeable for another currency, or for gold.

Convertible Security: A security, that is a claim or, the issuer, which is convertible into something else, including cash. The term is most commonly met in the form of 'convertible stock' or 'convertible debentures', which are fixed interest securities trial are convertible into another type of holding, *usually equities,* on specified dates and terms.

Convex Functions: A function which is convex to the origin is one whose second *derivative is* positive. Such a function is also concave away from the origin.

Cooling Off Period: A period of legally enforced delay before *strike* activity can commence so as to permit a de-escalation or cooling off of emotions and thus, it is assumed, a more rational evaluation of matters in dispute.

Corner Solution: In an optimization problem, a situation in which one or more of the *choice variables has* zero value at the *optimum. In* the *work-leisure model, for* example, the individual could choose to consume zero leisure or zero income.

Corporate Capitalism: A contemporary view of modern developed western economies in which the productive sector is dominated by large corporations characterized by a separation of ownership from control. A central contention here is that *economic power* has passed from the *capitalist* class to small groups of professional managers who, due to the increasingly ineffective constraints placed upon them by the *capital market,* pursue policies contrary to the raw ethic of *capitalism.*

Corporate Conscience: With the separation of ownership from control some analysts argue that managers in large *corporations* have broken away from the 'stock holderorientated conscience', and adopted instead a widespread sense of responsibility to the general public. Corporate conscience is a term used to represent this development in managerial behaviour.

Corporate Risk: The total risk involved in a business can be defined as corporate risk. This comprises two main types of risk. Financial risk which arises out of debt finance, and business risk which is the basic risk involved in the firm's day to day operations.

Corporate State: An economic and political system where the major sectors of the economy are organized into single large corporations and administered through the collaboration of government, workers' organizations and organized employers' associations. The corporation is an umbrella organization determining the running of individual firmsinput and output prices and quantities. The theory of the corporate state was an element of fascist economic theory, but the existence of large corporations, industrial democracy and government intervention in industry in many Western economies has led some people to suggest that these countries are moving towards the ideal of a corporate state.

Corporation Tax: This is a tax levied or the income of companies after the deduction of operating costs, *interest, allowances* and *stock relief* . Under this system a company pays corporation tax at 52 per cent irrespective of whether the profits are to be retained or distributed.

Correlation: The degree to which two variables are linearly related, whether through direct causation, indirect causality, or statistical chance. This is usually summarized by a correlation coefficient. This coefficient can take on values between plus and minus unity. A value of - 1 indicates a perfect negative relationship, +1 indicates a perfect positive relationship, and zero indicates no relationship. Values in between the extremes indicate the strength of relationship. Note that this will only reflect the degree to which variables are linearly related. For instance, two variables may be perfectly related in a non linear way and still result in a low value of r.

Correlogram: Normally, a graphical plot of the *correlation* coefficient between the current value of a variable and its own lagged values, against the length of the lag. The correlogram can give valuable information about, for instance, the characteristics of *serial correlation* characteristics of the *residuals* in *regression* analysis.

Correspondent banks: A bank which acts as agent for another bank in a place where the latter has no office, or for some reason is unable to conduct certain operations for itself. Examples of business conducted by a correspondent include paying cheques and bills drawn on the 'client bank', or obtaining payment of them for that bank. All banks with overseas business require correspondent banks abroad, and the arrangements are usually reciprocal with each party maintaining balances with the other.

Corset: The market colloquialism for the supplementary deposits requirement, introduced in 1973 to strengthen the Bank of England's control over the volume of bank deposits.

Cost: In general, a measure of what must be given up in order to obtain something whether by way of purchase, exchange or production. Economists usually employ the concept of opportunity cost which measures costs as the value of all of the things which must be foregone, lost or given up in obtaining something. The opportunity cost measure may, but will not always, coincide with the money outlays which an accountant would measure as cost. We should also note that economists sometimes distinguish between the private costs of a good or activity to the consumer or producer and the costs known as social costs imposed on the community as a whole.

Cost Push Inflation: It is different from demand pull inflation. The general price level may rise at times even when the aggregate demand remains practically same. It may be due to the increase in the cost of production specially of the labour in terms of wages. In these days of collective bargaining, trade unions exercise tremendous influence on the wage fixation. By means of a sketch it is shown below.

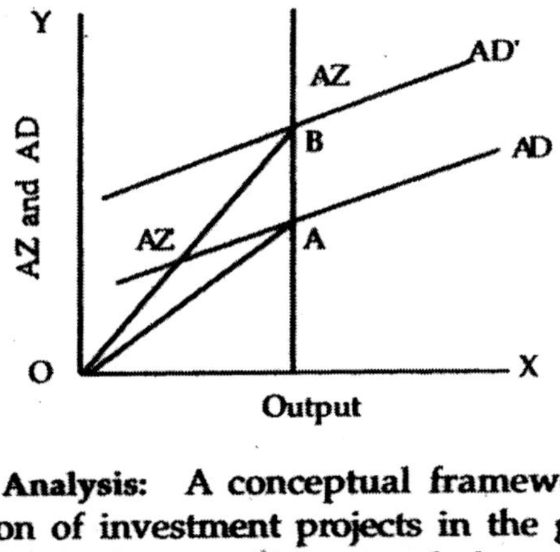

Cost-benefit Analysis: A conceptual framework for the evaluation of investment projects in the government sector, although it can be extended to any private sector project. It differs from a straight-forward financial appraisal in that considers all gains and losses regardless of to whom they accrue. A benefit is then any gain in utility and a cost is any loss of utility as measured by the *opportunity cost* of the project in question. In practice, many benefits will not be capable of quantification in money terms while the costs will be measured in terms of the actual money costs of the project.

Where money measures are secured, however, they should be corrected for any divergence between the *shadow* price and the market price it possible. Strictly pursued cost-benefit analysis would value all outputs and inputs at their shadow prices. Similarly, where inputs and outputs have no observable market, it is necessary to discover what the price would have been had a market existed. This involves the construction of models of 'surrogate markets' in which shadow prices may be derived.

An example would be the difference between the price of a house in a quiet area and the price in a noisy area. This differential can then be thought of as a first approximation of the 'price' of peace and quiet, although in practice there are formidable problems in making this translation. Cost-benefit analysis should also be 'timeless' in that all costs and benefits which occur and which are due to the project in question must be counted regardless of when they occur. In practice future costs and benefits may not get counted if the *discount* rate is relatively high. That is (i in 50 years'time will have a very low present value if the discount rate is positive and, say, 5 per cent or 10 per cent. Cost benefit practitioners therefore tend to ignore any costs and benefits which occur at far distant dates in the future. Others argue that the only 'just' discount rate for cost -benefit purposes is zero since this treats all generations as equals instead of downgrading the gains and losses to future generations.

Cost-effectiveness Analysis: Cost-effectiveness analysis is a technique closely related to *cost--benefit analysis.* It differs in that it asks a different question, namely, given a particular objective which is the least-cost way of achieving it? It thus aids choice between options but cannot answer the question whether or not any of the options are worth doing. It is utilized when there are difficulties in associating monetary values with the outcomes of projects but where the outcomes can be quantified along some non-monetary dimension.

Cost-inflation: A type of inflation, sometimes called costpush inflation, in which powerful unions are blamed for making large wage demands in the absence of excess demand in the labour market. The employers give in to these demands and the extra costs are passed on to consumers in the form of increased prices.

Cost of Capital: The cost measured as a percentage rate of the various sources of capital required to finance capital expenditure. All sources of capital have a cost which can be a direct one as, say, with a loan or an opportunity cost as, say, with retained earnings. At any time a company's cost of capital will be the weighted average of the cost of each type of capital. The weight is determined by the ratio of the value of each type to the total value of reserves and all securities issued by the company. These would include all ordinary shares, preference shares and long-term debt. The weighted costs are simply added together. The cost of raising new capital is the marginal cost of capital. The cost of–ordinary shares is related directly to the rate of return that the ordinary shareholders require before they will hold shares in the organization. This expected return must exceed the current market price. The cost of ordinary shares is often stated as growth rate of dividend.

The cost of preference shares is equal to the fixed dividend rate. Dividends on both ordinary shares and preference shares are generally paid out of earnings after tax and so the cost of these is on an after tax basis. The cost of retained earnings is an opportunity cost which is argued by some to equal the rate of return which shareholders could earn if the sources were distributed. Another view is that if the reserves were not there the company would have to raise new equity. Then the cost would be equal to the cost of ordinary shares.

The cost of debt capital is the effective interest charged. Interest is an allowable expense and so it is the after tax rate payable which is relevant here. Companies have a choice in the capital structure which they adopt and will generally try to minimize the overall cost of capital in making their choice. The cost of capital is used as the discount rate to find the net *present* value from new projects and is compared with the internal rate of return from projects.

Costs of Protection: The protection of domestic industry by tariff quota or other restriction normally imposes a cost on the protected economy in the two forms of misallocation of resources in production and of a distortion in the pattern of consumption. The former involves a reduced marginal revenue product from factors of production and the latter a loss of consumers' surplus.

Cost-plus Pricing: A pricing practice whereby firms add a margin on to average variable cost in order to cover fixed costs and some reasonable level of profits.

Cost-push Inflation: A sustained rise in the general price level arising from an autonomous rise in costs. This may result from either an autonomous decision by employees to demand higher real wages or by employers to raise their profit margins or it may result from an autonomous increase in import prices. Such events may be illustrated by an upward shift in the aggregate supply curve.

However a monetarist would argue that these events will result in inflation only if they are accompanied by an accommodating increase in the nominal money supply which shifts the aggregate demand curve out to the right. In the absence of such an increase in the money supply monetarists would argue that autonomous cost--push would result in deflation, Extreme Keynesians would deny that monetary policy could exert such a restraining influence on costpush pressures while moderate Keynesians would emphasize that the money supply plays a largely passive role and expands to accommodate these pressures.

Council of Economic Advisers (CEA): Executive agency of the US government, created in 1946, which acts as chief economic adviser to the US President. There are three members on the actual council, often highly respected academics. Council members arid staff personnel participate in inter-agency conferences, and often represent the nation as a whole against special interests represented within departments and agencies.

Council for Mutual Economic Assistance: An intergovernmental council, established by agreement in 1949 between Bulgaria, Czecho-slovakia, Hungary, Poland, Romania and the USSR, which seeks to improve and co- ordinate the planned economic development and integration of its member countries. Albania, Cuba, German Democratic Republic, Mongolia and Vietnam were later admitted as full members. Yugoslavia has participated since 1964 as an associate member whereas China and North Korea have enjoyed observer status. Osterisibly established in response to the *Marshall Plan* arid the emerging economic integration of Western Europe, the council contributed little to the integrated economic development of the socialist bloc until it approved a revised charter in 1959 which emphasized economic and technical cooperation among the member countries.

The council has promoted economic cooperation m foreign trade and ordination of national economic plans. A co-ordinated plan of' multilateral integration providing for the development of joint industrial projects was approved in 1975. However, as all decisions taken by the council must be unanimous, several plans and projects have been rejected by members, such as East Germany and Romania, who have attempted to pursue independent economic policies and,, or argued that most of the council's benefits accrue to the USSR. The EEC's refusal to enter into interbloc trade negotiations has also encouraged the council members to emulate Yugoslavia and develop individual economic ties with the West, Nonetheless, the council has established co-operative agreements with Finland , Iraq and Mexico.

Council of Arab Economic Unity: Established by the League of Arab States in 1957, the Council of Arab Economic Unity is an independent organization which provides a forum for achieving economic integration in Arab Countries. The council's efforts to encourage the free movement of capital, labour and goods between member countries led to the establishment of the Arab Common Market and the Arab Monetary Fund.

Countercyclical: Moving in the opposite direction to a

given phase in the *tradecycle.* Thus any deflationary policy aims to be countercyclical in the sense that it is applied during the latter part of the upswing of the trade cycle in order to prevent problems of inflation, bottlenecks etc. occurring.

Countervailing Power: Countervailing power is said to prevail when the market powers of firm(s) or economic agent(s) is counterbalanced by market powers possessed by trader (s) who buy from or sell to the former.

Coupon: Technically, a warrant to be presented for the payment of interest on a fixed interest security, such as a bond, and from which it may have to be detached. However, a common and derived meaning of the term is the nominal or facevalue' rate of interest on a bond or debenture, which defines the actual amount of interest payable per unit of the security it, each period. The coupon rate may differ from the true issue rate where bonds are issued at a price which shows a discount or premium on their nominal value.

Cournot, Antoine A: French mathematician, economist and philosopher. Although not the first to apply mathematical techniques to economic problems, Cournot is considered to be the founder of mathematical economics and because he was aware that his mathematical approach was capable of empirical quantification he can also be considered to have made the initial step in developing *econometrics.*

Cournot's Duopoly Model: Is based upon the behavioural assumption that each the two firms will maximize profits assuming that its competitor's output remain constant. Given a linear market demand curve, zero costs, an homogeneous product and two firms A and B, suppose firm A is the first to enter the market. The profit maximizing price is found by setting marginal revenue equal to zero, and this will correspond to an output which is exactly one-half of the market demand at a zero price, i,e. where X_0 equals market demand at *t* price of zero.

Covariance: A measure of the degree to which two variables are linearly related. The covariance can be either positive or negative, implying a direct or inverse relationship respectively, The lower the *absolute* value of the covariance, the lower is the strength of the relationship. The covariance between two variables is a determinant of the product moment correlation coefficient between them.

Craft Unions: Trade Unions which organize all workers possessing a particular skill, or group of related skills, regardless of the industry in which they work.

Crawling Peg: A method of controlling *exchange rates* this is a general term applying to any proposal with the characteristic that par values the official exchange rate as declared by the IMF can be adjusted over time, whereby the required change is split into much smaller parts which are spread over a certain period. Thus *a reualuation* of say 10 per cent might be achieved by successive changes of percent.

Credentialism: The problem of hiring standards that appear too severe for the limited skill requirements of the lower grade jobs in question. However, given the seniority principle and the presence of structured *internal labour markets,* job candidates may need to be of a sufficient calibre that will enable them ultimately to occupy positions on the highest rungs of the occupational ladder.

Credit: A wide term used in connection with operations

or states involving lending, generally at short-term. To 'give credit' is to finance, directly or indirectly, the expenditures of others against future repayment. Such lending or 'financing' is direct when, say, a bank extends an overdraft facility to a customer who then uses it. It is indirect when a trader or producer supplies goods' on credit', i.e. for payment at a later date. Again to 'have (a) credit' is to have a facility to acquire goods without immediate payment, or to be able to draw on finance from a lending institution in monetary economics 'credit' frequently connotes types of lending that are held to have monetary effects, either by causing increases in the money supply, as when increased banking lending leads to increases in bank deposits, or by increasing money substitutes such as, on some views, trade credit. This connection between credit and money is most direct at the macroeconomic level when changes *in* money supply are analysed in terms of domestic credit expansion.

Credit Card: A card issued to customers by a *bank* or group of bodies or other agency which gives the holder direct access to *credit,* e.g. from a retailer, hotel etc., or, in the case of some cards issued by banks, to cash from the banks operating the particular scheme. When goods or services are purchased with a credit card, the supplier secures rapid reimbursement from the issuing bank(s) or agency, which takes over the credit providing function. Cardholders may draw on such credit up to an individually defined limit; interest is payable on balances outstanding beyond a certain period; and repayment by instalments is normally provided for.

Credit Ceiling: In monetary policy an announced limit on the amount of *credit* which may be extended by specified in situtions, usually banks, during resiric tive policy phases, The limit may be fixed in relation to lending outstanding in a base period and allow for increase at specified rates, and it may discriminate between classes of borrowers.

Credit Control: General term denoting the set of measures used by the monetary authorities to control the volume of lending by certain groups of financial institutions.

Credit Creation: The process by which a group of deposit-taking and lending institutions which operate on fractional reserve ratios can, on the basis of an, increase in their reserve assets, produce an increase in the volume of their lending, and the associated deposit liabilities, of an amount greater than the increase in reserves. The term is normally applied to the effects of the operations of the banking system, but in principle it may apply to any group of deposit-taking financial intermediaries. Strictly, the term describes, the increase in lending but it is frequently used to denote the association of deposit liabilities. In all cas credit creation requires the presence o demand for loans by credit-worthy borrowers, and its extent is limited by of the reserve ratio and by induced leakages of reserve assets from the system of institutions concerned.

Credit Guarantee: A type of insurance hereby a credit guarantee association provides insurance against default. If a borrower lacks *collateral,* and although being otherwise 'sound' is unable to obtain a loan, the credit guarantee association or other institution will enable him to obtain credit from a bank.

Credit Multiplier: Strictly, the ratio of the change in the volume of lending by a group of deposit-taking financial intermediaries to the change in reserve assets which initiated the change. More commonly, in the traditional theory of *credit creation* by the banks, it denotes the ratio of change in bank deposit liabilities, caused by the increased extension of *credit*, to the initiating change in reserve assets. In this case it is sometimes called the 'bank deposit multiplier'.

Credit Rationing: The act of rationing loan finance by non-price means in situations of excess demand for credit, by *financial intermediaries*. The term implies that the institution concerned, e.g. banks or building societies, do not attempt to eliminate the excess demand by raising interest rates: they may be precluded from this by statutory or other rules, or for policy reasons of their own or of the monetary authorities.

Credit Restrictions: Measures taken or imposed by the monetary authorities, to limit or reduce the volume of credit extended by banks and other financial institutions. They may take the form of open market operations and movements of interest rates without any direct interference with the operations of financial institutions. Alternatively, banks and other institutions may be required to observe specified limits or criteria in their lending business.

Creditors: Are individuals or institutions who have lent money in return for promises made by the recipient, to pay a certain sum of money each year by way of interest, and to repay the principal at some date in the future.

Credit Transfer: The system by which funds can be transferred directly 'through the banking system to the account of a specified recipient. Such a transfer may be initiated simply by anybody, whether a customer or not, paying money into a bank office with the necessary credit slip. But a large number of credit transfers are made under regular 'standing orders', by payments from the transferors' accounts.

Creeping Inflation: A slow, but continuous inflation, which can result inter alia from increases in aggregate demand.

Critical Value: The a per cent critical value of a probability distribution is that value above which only a per cent of the probability ties. Thus there is only a 0.05 probability that a Standard Normal Variable will take on values above the 5 per cent critical value of the Standard Normal Distribution. This concept is usually used to define acceptance criteria for statistical tests, and in the calculation of confidence intervals,

Cross Elasticity of Demand: The responsiveness of quantity demanded of one good to a change in the price of another good.

Cross Elasticity of Demand: where Q, is the quantity of good *i*, and P_j is the price of another good *j*. The symbol D refers to a change in the variable in question. Where goods *i* and *j* are substituteN the cross elasticity will be positive i.e. a fall in the price of go will result in a fall in the demand for good *i* as *j* is substituted for *i*. If the goods are complements the cross elasticity will be negative, Where *i* and j are not related, the cross elasticity will be zero

Cross-entry: A category used with regard to new entrant firms who are already established firms in industries using similar technology to that in which entry is taking place.

Cross Partial Derivative: The derivative of a function first taken with respect to one independent variable, and then will-in respect to another.

Cross-section: A set of data involving observations taken Lit one point in time. Thus, for instance, cross section data on income would involve observations on say the incomes of different households in a country or the national incomes of a set of countries in a given year.

Cross-section Consumption Function: The functional relationship between consumption and income measured across different income groups at a point in time.

Cross-subsidization: With reference to multi-product firms, the funding of losses in one line of business from monopoly gains on other products sold by the firm.

Crowding Hypothesis: The argument that *entry barriers* and informational imperfections will tend to crowd certain groups, chiefly women and blacks, into a limited range of occupations and in the process lower the relative wage of these occupations

Crowding Out: A fall in either private *consumption* or *investment* as a result of a rise in government expenditure. In a fully employed economy a rise in government expenditure will cause an off seting fall in private investment in the following manner. The rise in prices that follows from the competition in the goods markets, as a result of increased government expenditure, reduces the real *money* supply which in turn reduces the amount of money available for speculative purposes, In consequence there is a fall in bond prices and a rise in the interest rate which leads to a fall in investment. If workers suffer from money illusion or for some other reason fail to adjust their wage demands in line with the rise in prices more Output may be forthcoming in the short run. In the long run however, it the economy was already at full employment increased government expenditure can only crowd out private expenditure.

Cubic: A cubic equation is one in which the highest power of an *independent variable* is three

Cultural change: One of the criticisms of certain types of economic development is that it destroys the indigenous culture but technological change and *economic development* can be achieved without profound cultural change.

Cumulative Causation Model: An approach to the analysis of regional economic growth, owing much to the work of G. Myrdal, which argues that market forces tend to increase economic Inequalities between regions of the same economy. It is argued that if one region experiences an initially higher rate of growth than other regions, the flow of factors of production from the slow growing regions to the fast growing regions will reinforce that initial advantage. The adverse effects on other regions are known as *backwash effects* and are said to more than offset the favourable effects on these regions from the creation of expanding markets and the 'generation of technical progress in the fast-growing region, The fast growing region is said to benefit from agglom*eration economies* which are production cost reductions resulting from the geographical concentration of economic activity.

The model predicts constantly widening divergences in regional growth rates, a prediction which is not borne out by empirical evidence. This result has led on the one hand to claims that regional growth rate divergences are only prevented by government *Regional Policy* and on the other to reformulations of the model which predicts divergences in regional per capita incomes but not widening divergences in growth rates.

Currency: Strictly, that component of a country's money

stock that literally circulates from hand to hand, i.e. coin and banknotes. But the term is also used in the broader sense of a country's money, e.g. sterling, the franc, the dollar etc., in which case it refers to the total money stock of that country.

Currency Appreciation: This is similar in essence to *revaluation* in that it refers to an increase in value of one currency wit reference to another hence an increase in the *exchange rate.* Revaluation refers to *fixed exchange rates* and currency appreciation to *floating exchange rates.*

Currency Control: Normally a *Central Bank* issues part or all of a country's currency and is subject to certain statutory rules in doing so.

Currency Depreciation: This is a fall in the value of one currency with reference to another, i.e. a fall in the exchange rate; it refers usually to falls infloating *exchange rates* whereas *devaluation* refers to a fall in a *fixed exchange rate.*

Currency Principle: The theory, prevalent in the middle decades of the nineteenth century and propounded by the *Currency School,* that monetary stability was best achieved by controlling the amount of currency, and most especially banknotes, in circulation, by means rules. In this context, monetary stability meant, first, the continuing convertibility of paper money into the metal of the country's chosen standard, but more fundamentally the avoidance of instability as manifested in periodic commercial and financial crises. Peel's Bank Acts of 1844 and 1845 embodied this philosophy, applying limits to the issue of paper money designed to make the banknote issue behave precisely as a wholly metallic currency would.

Currency Appreciation: This is similar in essence to *revaluation in* that it refers to an increase in value of one currency with reference to another, hence an increase in the *exchange rate.* Revaluation refers to *fixed exchange rates* and currency appreciation to *floating exchange rates.*

Currency Control: Normally a Central Bank issues part or all of a country's currency and is subject to certain statutory rules in doing so. The Issue Department of the *Bank* of *England* issues paper money under a statutory control imposed under the Currency and Banknotes Act, 1954, and which gives Parliament an ultimate sanction over the issue. However, under modern conditions there is no question of control over this money being exercised through currency control, and in fact the volume of notes in circulation is allowed to move to accommodate changes in the demand for currency.

Currency Depreciation: This is a fall in the value of one currency with reference to another, i.e., a fall in the exchange rate; it refers usually to falls in-floating exchange rates whereas devaluation refers to a fall in a fixed exchange rate.

Current Account: In banking, an account on which a customer may draw *cheques up* to the amounts of the credit balance in the account, or beyond it to an agreed *overdraft limit.* In some recent phases of high interest rates and consequent high profits some banks have remitted charges on accounts held continuously in credit.

Current Assets: There are three main components of current assets. The first is stocks, including finished goods, work-inprogress, and raw materials. 'The valuation of stocks is a difficult and sometimes contentious matter.

The second item is accounts receivable or short-term debtors. The main problem under this heading concerns the estimation of bad debts. The third element is cash and short-term investments.

Current Liabilities: This is a statement of a company's debts which have to be settled within the subsequent year. It is the measure of a company's total short-term debt. The debts may be for goods purchased, or for services received. They include credit obligations and interest payments. Their amount especially in relation to other financial indicators give a picture of the liquidity position of a company.

Current Profits: That excess of revenue over total opportunity costs which is earned during the current planning period of the firm.

Custom and Practice: Informal workplace rules which govern the allocation and performance of tasks and in many cases the criteria to be employed in deciding on the levels of pay for various tasks. In the *internal labour market* custom and practice may play a large part in determining the structure of pay *dijjerentials.*

Customer Markets: Product markets in which prices do not equate supply and demand. In such markets, firms offer their products with price lists or price tags rather than through an auctioneer or organized market clearing exchange.

Buyers and sellers are not trading anonymously but instead develop accustomed trading relations, even though on conventional standards the numbers in the market may be sufficient to ensure reasonably competitive behaviour at equilibrium.

Good customers, reliable suppliers, and a willingness to accommodate the exigencies of the other party are all valued trading attributes in customer markets.

The key to the argument is that 'shopping' is a costly process. Because of this buyers prefer doing business with customary suppliers, unless they have reason to shift their patronage.

Similarly, the supplier has an incentive to avoid actions that encourage his customers to go shopping. In particular, in response to a rise in demand, the supplier is likely to forego a price rise and instead seek to expand output.

However, if costs rise substantially, the supplier firm will raise prices, cost-based *mark-up* pricing becomes a convention, or a rule of fair play, that helps suppliers and customers to maintain the joint benefit of their interdependent relationship.

These relationships create a zone of indeterminacy for prices and a need for fair formulas for the sharing of *bilateral monopoly* surpluses. But by putting price making into a longer-term context, they lengthen the tags and weaken the causal connections between changes in demand and changes in prices.

Similar arrangements are likely to be found in labour markets, especially because of the non-standardized nature of the labour input. These have been termed obligational markets.

Customs Union: A grouping of countries within which trade restrictions are abolished but which has a concerted commercial policy towards nonmembers and a *common external* tariff on imports from them, though the tariff rate may vary between commodities.

D

Damage Cost: The money cost of damage done, usually confined to damage done by pollution. In economics, pollution is generally regarded as an instance of an externality. Placing money values on externalities is a complex and often dubious procedure as with valuing injuries, death, loss of recreational land, loss of wilderness, wildlife and so on.

Damped Cycle: One of a series of cyclical fluctuations which show a decreasing amplitude over time.

Data: Observations on the numerical magnitude of economic phenomena such as national income, unemployment or the retail price level. Data may be raw data where the observations are not processed in any way, or in a transformed state such as an index number.

Dated Securities: Any security, such as a bond, which has a stated redemption date. Such securities are conventionally divided into short-dated, medium-dated and long-dated securities depending on the length of time which has to elapse before they 'mature'.

Deadweight Debt: A debt which is not backed by a real asset in that it is only used to finance current expenditure. If a debt is incurred to purchase a physical or financial asset, then the debt is backed by the asset because if necessary the asset can be resold to repay the debt.

Deadweight-loss: Commonly used with reference to that loss of consumer surplus incurred by buyers and not captured by producers, which is consequent upon an initially competitive industry becoming monopolistic and therefore ceteris paribus, charging a higher price and selling a lower level of output.

Demand Curve: Graphic representation of the demand schedule makes it a demand curve as shwon below:—

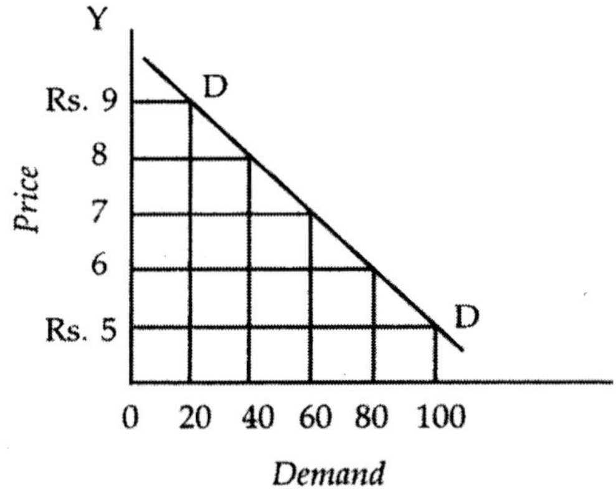

Dear Money: Term used to denote phases when interest rates are high compared with their historical average values.

Debentures: Debt securities carrying a fixed rate of interest, usually issued by a company and secured on its assets. They form one means., of raising finance for commercial or industrial operations. The debenture holder, is a creditor of the company entitled to be paid his interest regardless of whether or not the company makes profits, before any distribution of dividends.

Debt: An obligation or liability arising from the borrowing of finance or the taking of goods of services 'on credit', i.e. against an obligation to pay later. Depending on the terms of the transaction, interest is payable at specified periods on most forms of debt and the repayment on maturity date is also usually specified.

Debt Finance: This concept is used in two distinct senses, but in both cases it involves borrowing. It can refer to the use of loans by companies to finance their operations, particularly capital expenditure through long-term loans. The overall cost of capital may be reduced by the use of debt.

Debt Management Term used, generally in connection with public debt, to denote the action taken by the debt-issuing authority, or by the central bank acting for it, to regulate the size and structure of the outstanding debt, Such management includes deciding the types of debt to be issued, e.g. short-term or long-term, marketable or non-marketable, and the conditions of issue, e.g. coupon, issue price, maturity date.

Decile: A measure of location of sample data or a distribution. The *n*th decile is that value below which 10 *n* per cent of the observations on the variable concerned lie. Thus the 2nd decile is that value below which 20 per cent of the observations lie. The 5th decile is also the median.

Decimal Coinage: A system of currency which uses the base ten.

Decision Lag: The delay between the recognition of the need for action on an economic problem and a policy decision.

Decision Rule: A criterion employed in making choices,

such as whether or not to carry out a given project or how to price output. These rules emerge from economic analysis; for example, economic theory yields the decision rule that a firm which wishes to maximize profit should produce the output level at which marginal cost equals marginal revenue. Economists have also attempted to produce decision rules for, among other things, the evaluation of projects and the pricing policies of state industries. The precise nature of a decision rule will depend upon the objective pursued and the constraints on choice.

Decision Theory: The theory relating to the establishment of appropriate courses of action with the aim of achieving given objectives under specified circumstances, which may be subject to uncertainty.

Decreasing Cost Industry: An industry where the long-run supply curve is downward sloping. This could occur if there were important economies external to the firm and internal to the industry.

Deficit: A situation where outgoings exceed income, on an ongoing basis, or where liabilities exceed assets at a specific point in time.

Deficit Financing: A situation where expenditure exceeds income such that a deficit is operated deliberately. Keynes was the first to suggest that governments should deliberately run a planned deficit as part of monetary policy.

Deficit Units: Economic units who cannot meet their expenses in a given period from their incomes during that period, either from the sale of their labour, or their assets; such that they are dependent on borrowing money or obtaining credit.

Deflation: A sustained fall in the general price level. A proportionate rate of decrease of the general price level per unit of time.

Deflationary Gap Aggregate expenditure falls short of that required to produce a level of national income which would ensure full-employment.

Deflator: An implicit or explicit price index used to distinguish between those changes in the money value of gross national product which result from a change in prices and those which result from a change in physical output.

Degrees of Freedom The number of pieces of information which can vary independently of each other. Thus, a sample of *n* observations has *n* degrees of' freedom. However, the calculation of the sample mean involves the loss of one degree of freedom, since independent changes in n - I of the sample observations would require a specific offsetting change in the nth to maintain the value of the sample mean. Similarly, the calculation of *k* parameter estimates in an econometric exercise involves the loss of *k* degrees of freedom, leaving $(n - k)$. Degrees of freedom often enter as parameters of probability distributions, such as the 't' and Chi-square distributions, and can fundamentally affect their shapes.

Deindustrialization: A trend in a national economy towards a larger and larger share of the gross domestic product being taken up by services. For this to occur the rate of growth of the service sector must be greater than that of the manufacturing sector.

Demand: The quantity of a good or service which an individual or group desires at the ruling price. The total demand in an economy is referred to as aggregate demand. Aggregate demand backed by actual payment may be described as effective demand.

Demand-deficient Unemployment: Aggregate demand is too low to provide work for all those who wish to work at the current real wage no matter how they are trained or deployed. The unemployed outnumber the existing for vacancies at the current levels of money wages rates. On a classical view it is only the existence of rigid money wages that prevents a fall in the real wage and an elimination of this demand-deficient unemployment.

Demand for Inflation: The notion that there are potential gains for different groups flowing from inflationary policies. The resultant political (voting or lobbying) pressure from such groups is viewed as an implicit 'demand' for inflation. Although no group in society explicitly demands more inflation, pressures for the government to follow a more inflationary policy emanate from a variety of sources tax payers who resist tax increases made necessary by increases in expenditures, beneficiaries of government expenditure programmes who resist cuts, groups attempting to increase their share of the national income, and so on.

Demand Function: An algebraic expression of the demand schedule expressed either in general terms or with specific numerical values expressed for the various parameters, and usually including all factors affecting demand.

Demand Increase: Terminology varies widely, but an increase in demand tends to be reserved for a rise in demand at a giver price. That is, the demand curve itself has shifted outwards due to changes in income or some other variable besides the 'own price'. A rise in demand due to price change is simply referred to as a rise in demand, an 'extension' of demand and so on.

Demand Management: The control the aggregate level of demand in an economy through the use of monetary policy and/or fiscal policy.

Demand-pull Inflation: A sustained rise in aggregate demand beyond the full employment level of output which results in a sustained rise in the general pricelevel. Demand pull inflation may be illustrated by either upward shifts in aggregate expenditure beyond the full employment level in the simple income expenditure model, and thus result in an inflationary gap, or by rightward shifts in the economy's aggregate demand curve beyond the full employment level of output.

Demand Schedule: A table showing the of demand for a particular good at various levels of price of the good in question. The schedule relates to a specific period of time and is drawn up on the basis that other factors affecting the level of demand—income, tastes, the price of other goods—are held constant.

It is shown below:—

Price	*Demand*
Rs. 5/-	100
Rs. 6/-	80
Rs. 7/-	60
Rs. 8/-	40
Rs. 9/-	20

Demand schedule is of 2 types. (i) Individual and (ii) Market.

Demand-shift Inflation: A theory combining elements of demand-pull and cospush inflation which considers inflation to a result of a change in the structure of aggregate demand. If there are structural rigidities in the economy, while some industries will be expanding so me will be lining and factors of production will be able to move easily to the productive sectors. Hence higher prices will have to be paid to attract the means of production to the expanding industries.

Density Gradient: The rate at which the intensity of land use changes with radial distance from the centre of an urban area. Studies of a large number of cities in countries have indicated that population densities and the intensity of use of land for nonresidential purposes decline steadily from the centre of a town or city outwards.

Dependence Structure: The third world countries are part of a wide structure of economic, social and political dependence between power groups in advanced countries, especially multinational companies; and key interest groups in the poor countries.

Dependency Burden: This is when there is a very high proportion of children in a population dependent on a much smaller proportion of adults. As the result of high fertility rates the age distribution of a population becomes skewed in the direction of a high dependency burden.

Dependent Variable: The variable on the left hand side of the equality sign in art equation, so called because its value is 'dependent' or determined by those of the independent or explanatory variables on the right hand side.

Depletion Allowance: A tax advantage that allows the owner of natural resources to deduct against gross income the depletion in value of a nonrenewable asset, such as minerals, oil or gas. The deduction may be based on cost recovery or on a set percentage of related gross income. This can serve as an incentive to spur the discovery and extraction of resources essential to the national economy and defence; however, it can also prompt integrated producers to set high prices at the extraction stage, along with other devices, to shift reported earnings to this stage and thus reap the benefits of the tax preferences.

Deposit: Sums lent to certain financial institutions, e.g. banks, building societies and finance houses, on terms allowing withdrawal with or without notice, or providing for repayment after specified periods-such sums are usually described as 'on deposit'.

Deposit Account: A type of account designed to attract customers' less active balances, and also as a savings medium. Deposit account balances, which attract interest at a rate that varies with the banks' base rates, cannot be drawn on by cheque.

Deposit Money: Refers to that component of the money stock which is in the form of bank deposits. Whether or not both demand and time deposits are included depends on the money supply definition adopted. In turn this depends partly on the practices of the system considered, e.g. as to withdrawal notice required for time deposits.

Depreciation: This refers to the reduction the value of assets generally from wear and tear. The consumption of capital is recognized as a cost of production and an allowance for this is made before net profit is arrived at. Conventional accounting seeks to allocate the decline in value of the asset over its projected economic life. Annual provisions are conventionally calculated by one of two methods.

Depressed Area: A geographical area or region within a

nation which experiences significantly poorer economic performance than the nation as a whole. The index of 'depressed -ness' most frequently used is the rate of unemployment. However, other indices of economic performance used include economic growth rates and income per head, while persistent out-migration is also regarded as a characteristic of a depressed area.

Derivative: The change in the dependent variable of a function per unit change in the independent variable, calculated for an infinitesimally small interval for the latter. The process of calculating the derivative is called differentiation with respect to the independent variable. In nonlinear functions, the derivative will itself be a function of the independent variable. The derivative of the derivative is called the second derivative. The derivative of this is called the third derivative, and so on. The derivative has a graphical interpretation in the slope of the graph of the function, In economic terms, the first derivative of any total function can be interpreted as the marginal function. Thus, the first derivative of the total cost function with respect to quantity, is marginal cost.

Derived Demand: Demand for a factor of production is sometimes called a derived demand. This means that it is derived from the demand for the final good that the factor cooperates in producing. In some cases, however, a factor of production, say labour, is demanded for itself.

Desired Capital Stock: The optimal stock in the long run. The adjective 'desired' is often introduced in dynamic economic models to give substance to the concept of the long run optimal value of a particular variable, often the capital stock but also applied to other variables such as real money balances held by individuals.

Determinant: The determinant of an *n*th order matrix *A* is defined as

$$|A| = å_{ij} \pm a_{ij}\, c_{ij}$$

where a_{ij} is the element in the *i*th row and *j*th column, and c_{ij} is the cofactor of this element. The sign of the term is determined as

+if $i + j$ is even

–if $i + j$ is odd.

The determinant is often used in matrix inversion, and in the determination of the rank of the matrix.

Detrending: The process by which a time trend is removed from data, often by prior estimation of a time trend, and the calculation of residuals.

Devaluation: A fall in the fixed exchange rate between one currency and other. When the relative values of two currencies have been fixed at an officially agreed level, any reduction in the value of one currency against the agreed fixed level devaluation. Devaluation is used to correct a balance of payments deficit but only as a last resort as it has major repercussions on the domestic economy.

Developing Countries: This description of' the poorer nations of the world came into current usage in the 1960s and began to replace the less complimentary expressions 'underdeveloped' or 'back ward'.

Development Area: Regions of Britain within which various forms of government assistance are available to industry. This assistance, which represents part of Regional Policy, consists mainly of grants for industrial investment which are paid automatically', though selective or discretionary Support can also be given.

Development Planning: A plan is built up on the basis of a broad set of development aims, either referring to an economy a whole, specific areas or sectors.

Development Strategy: The approach taken to the problem of underdevelopment, which will depend on which particular growth model is being used.

Determination of the Market Period Price: Market period is a periodwhere no adjustment in the supply is possible. It refers to the period of a day or of an hour only. Supply in such a case being absolutely limited and fixed, it is the change in demand that bring the adjustment in the price and the final equilibrium between the forces of demand and supply. If there is a rise in demand due to some festival like Diwali, the price would keep on rising so far the fall in demand does not become equal to the fixed supply. Market period price determination is shown under:—

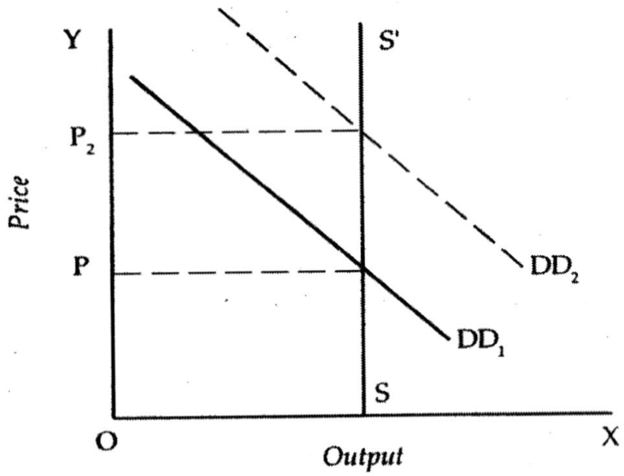

Supply curve SS' is shown verticel. It is fixed irrespective of the price in the market period. When

DD' is the demand curve, price in OP. When the demand curve rised to DD_2, the price also rised from OP to OP_2. Thus, the market period equilibrium is primarily determined by demand. It is very unstable price.

Determination of the Price of the Product: The price that the buyer is willing to pay depends up the utility from the article the he derives. Marginal utility of the article to the buyer constitutes the upper or the maximum limit of the price, while marginal cost of production to the seller consstitutes the lower limit for the price. In between, those two extremes, the price is determined at such a point, where the forces of demand and supply become equal. This is known as the point of equilibrium or equation. It is illustrated and represented as follows:—

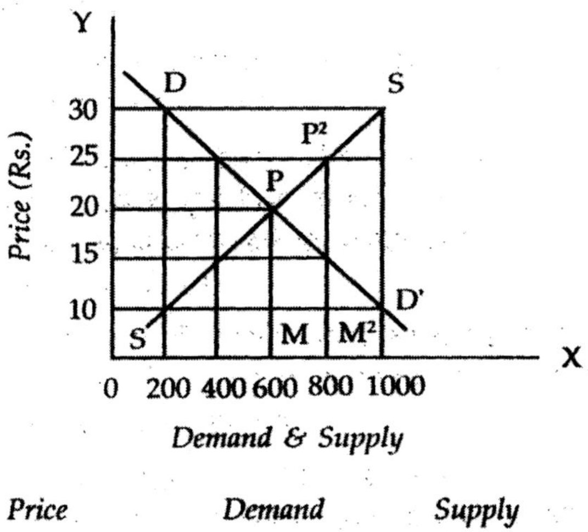

Price	*Demand*	*Supply*
Rs. 10	1000	200
Rs. 15	800	400
Rs. 20	600	600
Rs. 25	400	800
Rs. 30	200	1000

Deviation: The difference between the value of a variable and its mean.

Difference Equation: An equation in which the current value of the dependent variable is expressed as a function of its own previous values. An *n*th order difference equation is one in which the longest lag on the variable is n periods.

Differentiated Growth: An aspect of firm growth by diversfication, referring to that growth stimulated by the introduction of products which are sufficiently different from others as to be perceived as new by the consumers and the firm alike. The effects arising from the introduction of such a product are spread thinly over a large number of producers, in contrast to the impact produced by the introduction of imitative growth.

Differentiation: The process of calculating the derivative of a function.

Diffusion: In the context of technical diffusion, this term refers to the rate at which innovations spread amongst firms. With static demand and perfectly competitive markets the amount of new capital incorporating a recent innovation will depend upon the amount by which costs are reduced and by the elasticity of demand

Diminishing Marginal Utility: The phenomenon whereby it is assumed that the marginal utility attached to an extra unit of any good diminishes as more and more of that good is purchased. In the cardinal utility approach to demand theory, the existence of diminishing marginal utility is sufficient to explain the downward slope of the demand curve, other things being equal. The principle is also widely used to explain the convexity of indifference curves since more and more of one good will be required to compensate for the surrender of extra units of any other good the less there is of the latter good.

Direct Debit: A system of recent development for making payments through the banking system. Under this, the bank of a transactor who is due to receive a payment issues a direct claim on the bank of the party liable to make the payment, which in turn debits the payer's account. The direct debit is, like the credit transfer, much used for the making of regular payments, e.g. insurance premiums and mortgage loan repayments.

Direct Taxes: Traditionally direct taxes were defined as those levied directly on individuals or firms such as income tax, profits tax and capital gains tax. The original idea was that the bodies on whom these taxes were levied actually paid the tax. This is in contrast to indirect taxes.

Director's Law: A hypothesis, formulated by Aaron Director, that in a democratic system the government will tend to pursue policies which redistribute income from the relatively rich and poor towards the middle income groups.

Dirty Float: A type of floating exchange rate which is not completely freely floating because central banks interfere from time to time to alter the rate from its free market level. It is still a 'floating' rate because it has not been pegged at a predetermined par value which a government has committed itself to support, but it is not a pure 'floating' rate because it is influenced by central banks intervening on foreign exchange markets when and if they wish to alter it.

Disadvantaged Workers: There are defined as workers who

in terms of the skills they bring to the market or the 'signals' they transmit to would-be employers are at a relative disadvantage. They may alternatively be described as the working poor.

Discharges: The total number of people involuntarily leaving employment in any single period. Those may take the form of sackings, redundancies, temporary layoffs, or retirements.

Discounted Cash Flow: A technique of appraising projects which is based on the idea of discounting future costs and benefits to their present values. The essential idea is future cash flows-both inwards and outwards are worth less in today's terms. Income received now can be reinvested to produce additional income. The two best known techniques using the discounting procedure are net present value and internal rate of return. They both involve discounting all future net cash flows and finding their sum. Use of this method of project appraisal is considered superior to traditional accountants' methods where discounting is not employed.

Discount House: One of the eleven members of the London Discount Houses Association, a discount house is a financial intermediary which borrows money repayable at very short notice, mostly 'at call" or overnight, and most of it from banks. The borrowed funds are used to acquire a portfolio largely composed of hills and medium term bonds, though including certificates of deposit(CDs) and other short-term assets.

Discounting: The process of applying a rate of interest to a capital sum. It is widely employed to find the equivalent value today of sums receivable or payable the future.

Discount Market: Market in which treasury and commercial bills are traded.

Discount Rate: The rate at which future benefits and costs are discounted because of time preference or because of the existence of a positive interest rate.

Discouraged Worker Hypothesis: This concept deals with the responsiveness of labour force participation rates to cyclical changes in the economy. When the economy turns down it can be argued that there will be a fall in the real wage and family incomes. The discouraged worker hypothesis argues that the rise in the cost of market work relative to non-market work and leisure will, on balance, induce a shrinkage in the labour force as a result of the dominance of the substitution effect.

Discrete Variable: A variable which can take on only certain values. For instance, a variable which can only take on integer values is a discrete variable, since it cannot take on fractional values.

Discretionary Profits: Those profits in excess of the minimum necessary to ensure shareholder acquiescence. This is a concept used in the managerial discretion model of the firm where discretionary profits are posited as an argument within the managerial utility function.

Discretionary Stabilization: Direct intervention by the government usually in the form of monetary or fiscal policy to stabilize the growth or level of national income. As opposed to automatic, stabilizers.

Discrimination: There are three main types of discrimination, or unequal treatment, along the principal dimensions of race and sex. The first type is that which occurs even before those discriminated against enter the market. This pre- entry discrimination assumes its most tangible form in the inferior public provision of schooling and formal training for minority groups, particularly blacks. The second type is known as employment discrimination, and refers to the less favourable job slots occupied by women and blacks even after having standardized for their generally lower human capital endowments. The third type also occurs within the labour market and is termed wage discrimination.

Diseconomies of Growth: Refers to the dynamic constraints which set in beyond some high rate of growth and impair the efficiency of the firm's activities. On the supply side, organizational and financial constraints operate. The organizational constraint is the limit set by the existing management personnel of the firm who at successively higher rates of growth will find it increasingly difficult to impart the knowledge and experience to new personnel which is necessary for effective organization of the firm's activities.

Disembodied Technical Progress: Technical progress which appears costless like 'manna from Heaven', completely independent of capital accumulation or any other variable in the economic system.

Disequilibrium: A state of not being in equilibrium. In such cases forces may exist which will automatically bring the system back into equilibrium, or it may be the case that the system will diverge further from equilibrium.

Disinflation: The process of eliminating or reducing inflation.

Disintermediation: The process by which funds which had previously flowed from ultimate providers to ultimate users through a financial intermediary, especially the banks, for reasons connected with relative interest rates or control over the bank's ability to expand their deposit liabilities routed directly.

Disinvestment: The deliberate destruction of part of the capital stock or the intended or unintended failure of replacement investment to cover depreciation.

Displacement Effect: An observed tendency for Public Expenditure to rise during a war or other national crisis but not to fall to the original level after the crisis.

Dissaving: Consumption in excess of current income. Consumption financed out of wealth or out of anticipated future income by borrowing.

Distributed Lags The specification of econometric relationships often requires that an explanatory variable appears not only as a current value, but as a series of successively lagged values. A distributed tag formulation requires that the coefficients on these lagged values follow some mathematical relationship through time.

Distributed Profits: That portion of net profits released by firms in the form of dividend payments to the owners of equity capital.

Distribution, Theories Of: Theories relating to the mechanism by which the national income is distributed between individuals and groups in the economy. We may distinguish between the functional distribution of income which refers to the division of national product between the owners of' different factors of production—land, labour and capital, and the personal distribution of income which refers to the determinants of individuals incomes regardless of the factor from which income is derived.

Distributional Equity: Justice or fairness in the manner in which the economy's output is distributed between individuals. It is of interest to economists in that alternative economic arrangements, projects or policies generally have different effects on distribution, thus a concept of what is desirable in terms of distributional equity facilitates the evaluation of alternatives.

Distributional Weight: A numerical factor applied to changes in income of different individuals or groups of individuals and embodying some distributive judgement for the purpose of evaluating the distributional consequences of a policy or project.

Distribution Function: That part of government tax and expenditure policy which is concerned with altering the distribution of income or wealth within society. This function will be undertaken the distribution of income or wealth which emerges in the absence of government action is deemed to be undesirable.

Diversification: is used with reference to either the variety of industry within a region, or the range of products sold by a firm. In its former context diversification of a region's industrial structure increases the variety of industry from which employment opportunities arise.

Diversifier: A term describing an investor who holds part of his wealth in money and the rest in consols. If interest rates are rising then diversifiers will usually move more of their wealth into consols. Risk is likely to be the cause of portfolio diversification if risks increase then the diversifiers will move back to holding wealth in the form of money.

Dividend: A payment to shareholders in a company either in the form of cash or shares. A cash dividend is a payment made out of profits after corporation tax and after interest to debenture holders has been paid. Dividends to preference shareholders are also paid before payments to ordinary shareholders. Thus the risk borne by the latter is greater.

Dividend Cover: The ratio of earnings per ordinary share to gross dividend per share. The higher the figure the greater is the number of times that the most recent reported earnings exceeds the most recently paid dividend. The definition of earnings in calculating this ratio is made complicated by the imputation form of corporation tax where advance corporation tax (ACT) sometimes cannot be fully offset against corporation tax. The concept of 'maximum' earnings is employed, which, if there is no excess ACT, means earnings on a 'nil dividend' basis grossed up by the rate of imputation credit (which equals the standard rate of income tax).

Dividend Payout Ratio: That proportion of total profits accounted for by dividend payments.

Dividend Yield: This is the dividend per share as a percentage of the market price per share.

Division of Labour: The process whereby labour is allocated to the activity in which it is most productive.

Domestic Credit Expansion: Referred to DCE, it is an indicator of monetary change within an economy, developed strongly advocated by the IMF in the 1960s as a truer current measure of expansionary forces in the monetary system measured changes in the money stock. Broadly, it measures the total change within a given period in those of credit which lead directive to changes in the money supply, as conventionally defined.

Double-coincidence of Wants: If trade is to take place under a system of barter then it is necessary for there to be a double coincidence of wants between the two parties to the transaction, That is, the set of goods or commodities one Individual is willing to exchange must be exactly what is required by the other party.

Double Counting: The counting of a single element of benefit or cost more than once in a cost-benefit analysis. For example, if the construction of a new bridge makes a particular location More attractive to live in, due to its increased accessibility, property values will increase.

Double Taxation and Double Taxation Relief: An individual or organization may obtain income in a foreign country and may be liable for taxation on that income in both the foreign country and the country of origin. A system of reliefs for such double taxation has been developed by most countries in the world.

Dual Decision Hypothesis: In modern developments of Keynesian economics, the argument that conventional demand and supply functions do not provide the relevant signals for equilibrium to come about in markets.

Dual Labour Market Hypothesis: On this view, the labour market is dichotomized into primary and secondary sectors. 'Good' Jobs make up the primary sector of the dual economy, while 'bad' jobs and the workers frozen out of the primary sector comprise the secondary sectors.

Dummy Variable: A binary variable designed to take account of exogenous shifts or changes of slope in an econometric relationship.

Dumping: The practice of selling a good abroad at a price lower than that charged for the same good in the domestic market.

Duopoly: A market structure where there are only two firms. Models purporting to explain the determination of output and price base their analysis upon assumptions regarding decision making where there is perceived interdependence.

Duopsony: A particular market in which there are only two buyers of the product or service being traded.

Duration of Unemployment: The average period of time an individual spends on the unemployment register.

Dynamic Economics: The intertemporal analysis of the economic system. The economy may be passing from one equilibrium point to the other, or it may be continuing through time without reaching a state of static equilibrium.

E

Earned Income: Income of an individual is usually divided under two heads earne and unearned. Earned income is one which is person gets by his labour physical and mental like the wages. Pension is also regarded usually as earned income for it is related to the work and period of service of the past. In contrast, unearned income is one which is earned without any labour. It may be in the form of wind fall when due to several factors the value of land or building may appreciate considerably. Income from investment or interest is also a form of unearned income.

Elasticity: A measure of the percentage change in one *variable* in respect of a percentage change in another variable. Measures of elasticity tend to be carried out for very small changes in the variable causing the response—e.g. a percentage change in quantity due to a very small change in price.

Elasticity of Input Substitution: A measure of the responsiveness of the optimal labour/capital combination to a change in the relative prices of the two inputs.

Elasticity of Demand Curves: Perfectly elastic demand curve is absolutely horizontal. It runs parallel to axis of x as illustrated and drawn below:

DD' curve is perfectly elastic Rs. as represented below:

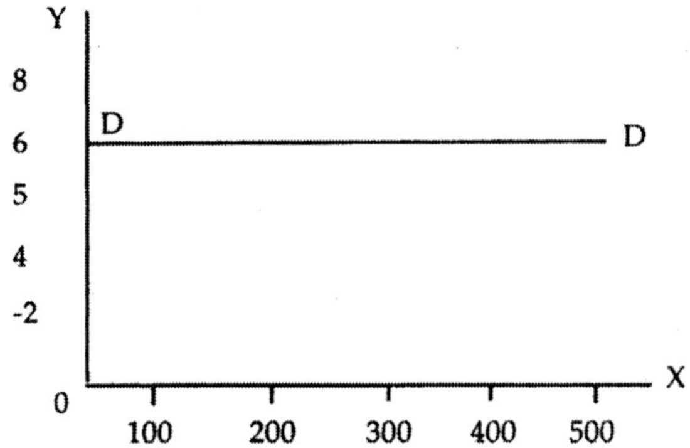

Eligible Paper: Financial *assets* which the *central bank* is prepared to buy (rediscount) or accept as security for loans, in particular circumstances and usually in dealings with defined institutions.

Embodied Technical Progress: Technical progress which cannot take place unless it is embodied in new capital. For example the silicon chip has rendered the capital of whole industries obsolete, requiring completely new physical capital to realise its potential.

Endogenous Income Hypothesis: A theory which suggests that utility is function of both *consumption* expenditure and of wealth. The implications are that once some optimum level of wealth ha been achieved, all income will be spent whereas normally one would expect some saving still to occur. The approach derived from a microeconomic approach to the consumption 'function which basically presents the household with a choice between commodities and wealth, both of which have positive marginal utility, but with a diminishing marginal rate of substitution of consumption for wealth.

Endogenous Money Supply: This is the situation where the level of the money supply is determined by forces within the economy itself, such as rates of interest, and the level of business activity. The is the average propensity to consume central bank does not impose any limit but merely provides what the market needs.

Endogenous Variable: A variable whose value is determined within the framework of an economic or econometric Model.

Engagements: The total number of people entering employment in any single period. These individuals may previously have been among the registered unemployed or hidden unemployed or they may be new entrants into the labour force. Engagements are one aspect of labour turnover.

Engel Curve: A line which plots the relationship between an individual's income and his consumption of a specified good. An Engel curve is illustrated in the diagram below. The slope of the curve at any point is the individual's marginal propensity to consume the good and indicates the ratio of change in consumption to change in income. The ratio of total consumption of the good to total income is the average propensity to consume the good --this is equal to the slope of a line such as O A. The ratio of the marginal propensity to consume the good to the average propensity to consume is the income elasticity of demand for the good.

Engineering Method: A method used in statistical cost analysis, where engineers estimates of the input output relation- ship form the basis upon which to calculate minimum production cost at different levels of output. The advantages of this method are that input prices and technology can be held constant and homogeneity of output and inputs can be satisfied.

Entitlement Principle: A principle of distributive justice which holds that individuals are to be regarded as entitled' to their possessions so long as these were obtained by 'legitimate' means such as voluntary exchange or gifts.

Entrepreneur: Refers to the organizing factor in production. Entrepreneurs are responsible for such economic decisions as what to produce, how much to produce and what method of production to adopt. Given that time elapses between the decision to produce and marketing of the product being produced, the entrepreneur must anticipate demand. It follows therefore that entrepreneurs bear the risks attendant upon fluctuations in demand which may take place during this interval.

Entrepreneurial Supply Price: In the context of the market for executives, neoclassical economic theory would formalize the entrepreneurial supply price as that return which is just sufficient to keep an executive of some given quality in his current employment. The supply price will then be that portion of an executive's salary and perquisites left after the deduction of emoluments.

Environmental Conditions: Although in level of world scientific and technical knowledge is increasing at an accelerating, rate, there are major gaps in this knowledge especially with relevance to the environmental conditions in developing countries. Machinery and techniques are often imported into an underdeveloped country with no prior knowledge of the long-run effects on climate or any of the environmental condition.

Environmental Determinism: if the underdeveloped countries of the world arc specified on a map, it can be seen that the., are either in tropical areas or very cold climatic zones; which raises the question as to whether the physical environment is a major determinant of the level of development however the differences in rate, and levels of development between, countries suggest that although important, environmental conditions are not the only cause of underdevelopment. Indigenous resources are nonetheless more significant "i countries which have limited supplies of capital, skilled tabour, technology and entrepreneurial experience; so their lack would be more keenly felt in the less developed areas.

Environmental Impact Analysis: An analysis which seeks to identify the effects on the whole environment of any investment project. This would include the forecasting of potential pollution emission, loss of visual amenity etc.

Equalization Grants: Funds made available by a national government to subnational or local governments with the objective of reducing the degree of inequality in the levels of income or revenue raised by the local governments.

Equal Pay: This term refers to equality between the sexes as regards the terms and conditions of employment: a concept of equal pay for equal work, although the precise definition of equal pay' and 'equal work' differs by country. In Britain, under the Equal Pay Act of 1970 which became fully operational in December 1975, employers are required to grant equal treatment to men and women where they are employed on the same or broadly similar work or where, with respect to different Jobs, a woman's Job has been rated as equivalent to that of a male employee by means of a job evaluation exercise.

Equal Sacrifice Theories: In the ability to-pay theory each taxpayer makes the same sacrifice of utility which he obtains from his income.

Equilibrium: A term borrowed from physics to describe a situation of economic agents or of aggregates of economic agents such as markets. Applied to an individual agent, such as a *consumer* or firm, it denotes a situation in which the agent is under no pressures or incentives to alter current levels or states of economic action, because given his aspirations and the constraints he faces he cannot improve his position in terms of any economic criteria. When applied to markets, equilibrium denotes a situation in which, in the aggregate, buyers and sellers are satisfied with the current combination of prices and quantities bought or sold, and so are under no incentive to change their present actions.

Equilibrium Level of National Income: That level of national income which exhibits no tendencies to change. In simple Keynesian income—expenditure model this would be where the level of injections equalled the level of withdrawals. In this model such an equilibrium could exist at full employment or at less than full employment: an unemployment equilibrium. Neoclassical economists would argue that equilibrium is possible at full employment only and that where involuntary unemployment exists we are off the labour supply curve. For neo-classical economists the equilibrium level of national income is the full employment level of national income; the level of in come consistent with tile natural rate of unemployment.

Equilibrium Rate of Inflation: The fully anticipated rate of inflation. That rate of price inflation at which expectations are fully realized. That rate at which the *expected inflation* rate equals the actual inflation rate.

Equities: Otherwise known as 'ordinary shares', these are shares in the issued capital of a *company* which are held on terms that make the holder a 'member' of company, entitled to vote at annual meetings and elect directors, and to participate through dividends in the profits of the company. The holders of the ordinary shares carry the residual risk of the business: they rank after debenture holders and preference shareholders for the payment of dividends and they are liable for losses, although in a limited liability company this liability is limited to the value of the shares themselves plus any uncalled liability on them. If the company is a public company and has a stock exchange listing, its shares may be traded on the exchange.

Equity Fairness or Justice: This concept is of importance to economists in a number of 'situations.

Equivalence Scale: A ratio or 'weighting' factor employed in evaluating levels of income or consumption required for households in different circumstances to reach a given 'standard of' living'. If we compare two households, one consisting of a childless couple and the other consisting of two adults and one child, it is clear that the larger household would require a higher income and higher consumption of certain commodities (for example, food) in order to achieve the same living standard as the smaller house-hold. Equivalence scales attempt to quantify these differences, for example it might be estimated that the addition of a child required household income to be multiplied by 1.25 in order to maintain living standards. Such scales can be used in studies of poverty and in setting levels of social security benefits. The scales rest on the assumption that one can validly compare levels of living standards or utility for different individuals and households, even although this assumption is generally rejected in theoretical welfare economics.

Equivalent Commodity Scale: A numerical factor applied to the level of consumption of certain commodities by households in different circumstances in order to indicate levels of consumption required for each type of household to reach a given standard of' living. Thus a couple with a child will require more total food consumption than a childless couple to achieve the same standard of living.

Equivalent Income Scale: A numerical factor applied to the incomes of households in different circumstances to give estimates of the income required for each household to reach a given standard of' living. Thus a large household will probably require a larger income than a small household if a given standard of living is to be reached. Equivalent income scales seek to quantify this difference in required income for different house-holds. The income scale represents an attempt to measure the income effect of different household circumstances.

Errors in Variables: (also known as Measurement Error). An econometric problem whereby particularly the ex*planatory* variables in a *regression* analysis are imperfectly measured, either because their actual values are unobservable, or through imprecision of recording.

Escalators: Cost of living clauses in collective bargaining agreements. Escalators provide a mechanism for periodic adjustments of wage rates based on movements in a specified *price index*. Escalators rarely fully compensate for price changes. This results from a number of factors. First, the relevant formula is generally insufficient to produce full compensation at other than relatively low wage earnings. Second, limits or caps may be placed on the maximum cost of living adjustment. Third, escalator adjustments typically lag behind price changes. Fourth, escalators may not be 'triggered" until a significant rise in the price index occurs. Finally, escalators are, of course, not the sole wage adjustment mechanism.

Estate Economy: This term refers to a sector or whole economy in an underdeveloped country which is used solely for large-scale production of export crops normally managed and owned by foreign powers; it was very prevalent during the colonial era. There is usually a marked difference between this sector and the subsistence agriculture of the local people and it was always very much in the interests of the estate owners it) maintain that differential; if the native people were very poor, they would be more ready to work hard for low wages.

Estimation: The quantitative determination of the parameters of economic models through statistical manipulation of' sample information. This is achieved through the use of estimators (i.e. formulae) which convert observations into parameter estimates. Examples of econometric estimators include Ordinary Least Squares and full information maximum likelihood

Estimator: A formula, or procedure by which estimates of' statistical quantities (such as the *mean* or *variance* of a variable), or the parameters of an equation are obtained from data. Examples of econometric estimators include Ordinary Least Squares and full information maximum likelihood.

Excess Capacity: Rigorously defined, a firm is said to be producing with excess capacity if its *output* level is below that at which average costs are at a minimum. The more common usage refers to firms operating plant at a rate of utilization below that considered normal, e.g. at some percentage level of output that could be achieved.

Excess Demand: A state in which *demand* exceeds supply at some given price. The excess demand curve will slope downwards from left to right and will cut the vertical (price) axis at the equilibrium price. To construct the excess demand curve, subtract supply from demand at each given price, In the diagram, for example, demand level D_1 is less than supply at that relevant price, P_1 Excess demand is therefore negative, as shown. At P_2 supply and demand are equal, so that excess demand is zero. At P_3, there is excess demand equal to D_3—S_3.

Excess Supply: A state in which supply exceeds *demand at* some given price. An excess supply curve can be constructed by subtracting the level of demand from the level of supply at each level of price. The resulting excess supply curve will, for normal demand and supply situations, slope upwards from left to right but will lie to the left of the vertical axis at first, cutting the axis at the equilibrium price.

Exchange Control: The system whereby the State exercises control over all or some transactions in foreign currencies and gold, undertaken by its nationals. Exchange control is applied for *balance of payment* reasons, and in the final analysis to avoid the depreciation of the *exchange rate,* which it is supposed, complete freedom in foreign transactions would produce.

Exchange Equalization Account: The system or arrangement, rather than simply an 'account', established in 1932 and operated by the Bank of England, for controlled undesired fluctuations in the sterling exchange rate following the UK's departure from the gold standard in 1931. Initially endowed with a quantity of treasury bills, with which to acquire sterling, and some foreign exchange transferred from the Treasury and the Bank the Account was, and continues to be operated essentially on buffer stock lines with purchases or sales of sterling according to whether the aim is to support the rate or to moderate its upward movement. In 1939, at the outbreak of war, the entire gold holdings of the Issue Department of the Bank were transferred to the Account. Since then it has effectively been the agency for holding and managing the country's external reserves, as well as the instrument for exercising control over the exchange rate.

Exchange Rate: The price of a currency in terms of another currency. Exchange rates are regularly quoted between all major currencies, but frequently one important currency, e.g. the dollar, is used as a standard in which to express and compare all rates. The exchange rate of all fully convertible currencies is determined, like any price,, by supply and demand conditions in the market in which it is traded, i.e. the foreign exchange market. More fundamentally, such supply and demand conditions are determined by whether the country's basic balance of payments position is in surplus or deficit., When there is no official intervention in the foreign exchange market, the rate is freely floating and will rise or fall to equilibrate the supply of and demand for that currency. 'Intervention' may take a number of forms, from *exchange control* to action which does not interfere with the operation of the market, but aims to stabilize or control the movement of the exchange rate. In the case of some groups of currencies, the exchange rates have been linked so as to limit the range of movement between them, as in the European 'Snake'. The situation of managed flexibility of exchange rates is sometimes referred to as 'dirty floating' implying that the influences exerted by countries over their own rates is dictated by self-interested motives.

Exclusion: The procedure whereby a consumer is 'excluded' from the purchase of a good by virtue of the fact that his willingness to pay for it is less than the market price. In some cases, as with Public *Goods,* exclusion may not be technically possible, whatever is supplied to one consumer being automatically supplied to all others.

Exclusion Principle: A criterion by which we may distinguish *public goods* from non-public goods. Where a producer or seller can prevent some individuals from consuming his product--generally speaking, those individuals who do not pay for the good—then the product can be supplied by means of a market. Where this principle does not hold, the provision of the good to one individual will automatically make it available to other individuals. Individuals will then have no incentive to pay tor the good but will be able to be 'free riders. The provision of goods such as National Defence or environmental protection, where the exclusion principle does not hold, generally requires some form of government action, Although exclusion by the supplier is used as a criterion to distinguish public and non- public goods, it does not suffice to define the case of a pure public good. In this case we must also consider (1) whether exclusion can be practised by the consumer-i.e., is the consumer 'forced' to consume the good and (2) whether the good is *rival* in consumption, that is whether one person's consumption reduces the quantity available to others.

Executives: An individual who has responsibility with respect to some branch or aspect of a firms activities. The term is often used to cover a fairly wide range of management levels from the executive *directors* to lower echelons where responsibilities are more limited.

Exhaustive Voting: A form of collective choice in which each voter indicates his least favoured alternative. The alternative ranked lowest by the greatest number of voters is then removed. The process is repeated with the remaining alternatives until only one is left. This is the chosen alternative. While complex, this system may be said to reveal more about individual preferences than simple majority rule voting and avoids the problem of inconsistent choice known as the paradox of vot*ing*.

Existence, Theorem of: Any theorem which seeks to establish, usually in a general equilibrium context, that there exists a set of equilibrium prices and quantities.

Exit-voice Model: A classification of the systems which individuals use to reveal their preferences which distinguishes those in which entry or exit is the mode of action from those which require some verbal communication. An example of the former would be a private market where individuals can increase (enter) or reduce (exit) demand.

Exogenous: A term which describes anything pre-determined or given in a piece of economic analysis.

Exogenous Variable: A variable whose value is not determined within an economic model, but which plays a role in the determination of the values of endogenous variables. Thus an exogenous various is an explanatory variable, but never appears as a dependent variable in the model. Exogenous variables can include lagged values of endogenous variables.

Expansion Path: With reference to the *firm*, this is the curve traced out by joining up the factor input choices at each output level as in the diagram below, i.e: the locus of the points of tangency between a set of isoquants and isocast lines. For given input prices, the curve indicates what the firm's chosen path of expansion will be in terms of factor input combinations. With a cost minimizing firm any point on this curve will satisfy the condition that the ratio of the marginal physical product of any two factor inputs will equal the ratio of their prices.

Expatriates: A general term referring to someone of foreign nationality which tends to be used very specifically for personnel from advanced countries working in underdeveloped countries. Many work under aid schemes but some are employed by governments of less developed countries at relatively high cost because of the high wage differential between the two countries.

Expectations: Beliefs or views on the future values of economic variables. Because of uncertainty about the future, individuals, firms and governments form expectations on the future values of economic variables. It has become an important topic since its introduction in the 1930s through the ex ante and ex post concepts applied to saving and investment. Expectations relate to the ex ante concept, i.e. they refer to some view of a future event or set of events which, ex post, may turn out to be realized or not. The correctness or otherwise of expectations is crucial to the notion of equilibrium; as a state of economic affairs arrived at through decisions taken on the basis of expectations which turn out to be incorrect cannot be considered an equilibrium one. There is currently no universally accepted theory about expectations. For the three main areas of theoretical work, see Adaptive Expectations, Rational Expectations, and Behavioural Expectations.

Expectations, Augmented: Modifications to an economic model to allow for an expectations effect. Probably the most widely known example is the expectations *augmented Phillips curve,* where the expected price inflation rate is included as an explanatory variable augmenting the basic model.

Expectations Lag: The lag in the revision of the expected value of a variable as a result of changes in its current value. This is often dealt with by the *adaptive expectations* hypothesis.

Expected Inflation: Anticipated *inflation:* the rate of inflation that is expected to occur over some specified time in the future. Expectations about just what the rate may be are hypothesized to be formed by a number of mechanisms.

Expected Net Returns: The flow of expected gross revenue minus expected costs, i.e. the flow of expected profits, from an investment project.

Expenditure-switching Policies: This is one of the policy alternatives necessary to remove an international trade imbalance, Examples are *devaluation,* and import restrictions which are intended to encourage domestic expenditure on domestic output and also foreign expenditure on domestic output. These will raise *national income* and *national product* via the mul*tiplier* process.

Expenditure Tax: A comprehensive tax on consumer expenditure. It has been suggested as an alternative to an income tax, and could be levied on a progressive basis. Advocates such as Lord Kaldor and more recently Professor Meade have argued that expenditure may be a superior tax base from both equity and efficiency viewpoints. The critics of income tax have argued there are great difficulties in finding a definition of income for tax purposes which is both conceptually sound from an equity viewpoint and readily operational. For example, there are problems in dealing with miscellaneous windfall gains, irregular income flows and capital gains in an inflationary situation. Advocates of the expenditure tax argue that these problems disappear if expenditure is used as the tax base. Critics of the tax argue that there will be corresponding conceptual problems and that there will be greater difficulties in operating an expenditure tax system than an income tax. Under an expenditure tax there may be problems of the definition of taxable expenditure. For example, the border line between consumption and investment may not be clear in practice. There would be problems from large, irregular items of expenditure and special provisions would be necessary for family size. A fairly large amount of additional information would also be necessary to effectively administer the tax.

Advocates of the expenditure tax also argue that it is superior from an incentive viewpoint to an income tax. The argument that investment will be higher under this tax compared to an income tax because incremental earnings are not taxed is not foolproof' when the effect of lossoffsetting arrangements under an income tax is considered. There is certainly a greater incentive to save under an expenditure tax than an income tax. Whether work effort would be higher under an expenditure tax than an income tax is arguable faking all aspects into account it is difficult to give convincing evidence that the radical change would be worthwhile.

Expenditure-variation Controls: By varying the level and composition of the budget and by controlling the extent of, and cost of, credit a trade in balance can be corrected. The *absorption approach* concentrates on the relationship of real *expenditure* to real *income* as affected by changes in price levels between countries through changes in the value of *exchange rate.* The foreign balance, B, is the difference between the total output of' goods and services in the economy, Y, and the absorption. Although consumption or investment, of goods in the economy, B = Y— A. To improve the foreign balance, Y must rise relative to .4 in response to a change in the exchange rate.

Expense Preference: A concept which refers to the satisfaction managers derive from certain expenses of the firm such as *marketing* outlay and *staff outlay* Positive values are attached to them because of the way in which they facilitate the achievement of such managerial objectives as salary, prestige and power

Explanatory Variable: A variable which plays a part in explaining the variation in a *dependent variable in* a regression analysis, appearing on the right hand side of the equation.

Explicit Function: The most usual form of a function in which the *dependent* variable is written on the left hand side of' the equality sign, and related to a set of' *independent variables* on the right hand side, usually to express a causal or definitive connection. The name is used to distinguish this way of writing an equation from *implicit functions.*

Exploitation: The term has two meanings in economics. First, the use of a resource, natural or human. Second, a worker is said to be exploited if payment for work done is less than the value of that work. The latter meaning of exploitation was used by *Karl Marx.*

Explosive Cycle: A cycle characterized by an amplitude which grows exponentially overtime.

Exponential: An exponential function is a)unction, usually relating the dependent variable to the number e, raised to some power containing the independent variable where e = 2.7 18, and is the base of the natural logarithm.

Exponential relations are useful in describing time paths of economic variables. For instance, a constant growth rate implies an exponentially increasing level of income through time.

Export: A good or service which is produced in one country and sold to and consumed in another. A visible export is a 'good which is physically tangible and an invisible export is the provision of a service, which is consumed by someone from another country.

Export-Import Bank: A US public agency, created in 1937, which encourages US foreign trade by providing capital in the form of direct loans and loan guarantees to overseas countries, The bank also extends export credit insurance facilities to cover risks undertaken by US exporters.

Export-led Growth: The expansion of an economy, which

is stimulated by a rising volume of exports. Such a source of growth not only has real linkage effects and multiplier effects on the rest of the economy but also ensures that growth will not be constrained or halted by balance of payment difficulties, since it makes available any foreign exchange necessary to pay for additional imports required for expansion.

Exports Credits Guarantee Department: The principal risks covered include insolvency of the buyer, political restrictions delaying payment, cancellation of a British *export* license and imposition of new *import* licensing restrictions and *exchange controls* in the buyers country. The department also provides subsidized credit facilities to exporting firms in order to finance the production and delivery of export goods prior to receipt of payment. In 1978 it introduced a foreign currency bank guarantee scheme to encourage exporters to sell fixed rate finance for export contracts in foreign currencies rather than sterling so as to take advantage of overseas *interest rates which* are usually lower than British rates. Limited cover against cost escalation associated with exports on overseas projects executed by British exporting industries is also provided by the department.

Extensive Margin: The situation of *diminishing returns* to land as a whole. The *Classical School,* following *David Ricardo,* talks of the extensive margin where, as the population increases, additional land of lower fertility must be. brought into cultivation. At such a stage equal amounts of other productive resources applied to these areas produce less and less output.

External Balance: Usually defined as a situation where the balance of payments of a country is in equilibrium in the sense that autonomous monetary inflows match autonomous outflows, without the need for accommodating monetary flows into or from the foreign exchange or gold reserves.

External Economies and Diseconomies of Scale: The beneficial or adverse effects which the production activities of firm have on those of another firm.

External Finance: The funds raised firms either by issuing *shares* (equity capital) or borrowing (debt finance of bonds) to aid the financing of their activities.

External Growth: That part oft he expansion of a firm which is brought about by acquisition and merger activity.

Externalities: Externalities are variously known as external effects, external economies and diseconomies, spillovers and *neighbourhood* effects. The term 'technological external effects' is also sometimes used, the adjective 'technological' being introduced in order to differentiate it from *pecuniary external economies.* Externalities involve an interdependence of *utility* and/or *production functions.* For example, the upstream pulp mill which discharges effluent in the river thus reducing the scope for fishing downstream is said to impose an externality on the fishermen.

Some economists add the qualification that the interdependency must not have been taken account of through trade.

A beneficial externality, that is, where an externality-generating activity raises the production or utility of the externally—affected party is known as an external economy.

For example, a beekeeper may benefit neighbouring farmers by incidentally supplying pollination services.

An external diseconomy is where the externality-generating activity lowers the production or utility of the externally—affected party. Examples of these are the numerous forms of environmental pollution.

A Pareto-relevant externality occurs when the extent of the activity may be modified in such a way that the externally—affected party can be made better off without the acting party being made "worse off, that is, where there exists the possibility of gains from trade,

Externalities arise because of the failure of markets to exist, i.e., there are no markets in clean air, peace and quiet and, so on.

A major although not the only source of such market failures is the inability to define and enforce property rights.

External Labour Market: This may be said to comprise clusters of workers that ire either immediately available or potentially available for new jobs.

Within the external labour market, pricing and a locating decisions are controlled directly by economic variables-there is a competitive market for the jobs in question.

External Reserve: This normally refers to he officially held reserves of internationally acceptable means of payment which a country holds, for the purpose of covering short to medium-term deficits on external *balance of payments,* and the elated purpose of exerting control over the movement of the *exchange rate* of its currency.

F

Factors of production: Primary factors of production are two—lan and labour. Land in economics is not only the land or surface of the earth on which we walk it includes the surface under the mines as well as the surface covered by the rivers lakes and oceans. Land also includes free gifts of nature like air and sun-shine.

Factor Endowment The levels of availability of factors of production in an area, or country: these are usually defined as land, labour, capital and entrepreneurial skills. The high-level technology of the western world uses a very different factor mix to that which is available in under-developed countries which causes many problems with transfer of technology. 2. The quantities factors of production in a country. The different relative abundance of factors of production is made the basis for explaining comparative cost differences in the HeckScher-Ohlin approach to international trade.

Factor Incomes: Incomes derived directly from the current production of goods and services. The reward to the factors of production for services to current production of goods and services. It is usual to distinguish four main categories: rent; wages and salaries; interest; profits.

Factoring: A method of disposing of trade debts where a company 'sells' these debts to a financial institution.

Factor-price Differentials: The situation where a factor of production can have two separate prices; for example the price of labour between capitalistic wage-based production and family based production activities.

Factor Proportions: The ratio in which factors of production are combined.

Factor Reversals: The production functions for commodities differ in the ratios in which they use factors of production and that a commodity which uses a higher ratio of, say, labour to capital than another will do so at all possible relative factor prices.

Factors of Production: The resources of society used in the process of production. These are usually divided into three main groups land, labour, capital, but may also include entrepreneurship.

Factor Utilization: The amount of the available factors of production which are actually being utilised; full utilisation is dependent on the implementation of an appropriate technology, such that, highly capital intensive techniques should not be used in areas with little capital endowment a rid surplus labour.

Fair Comparisons: The belief that workers doing roughly similar jobs should be paid the same wage. Frequently such beliefs form the basis of coercive comparisons but take no account of the differing levels of productivity in the two jobs. As a result they can serve as a basis for inflationary wage claims.

Fair Trading act 1973: This legislation extended competition policy to cover oligopolistic markets, and centralized responsibility for the implementation of monopoly and restrictive practices legislation with the new office of the Director General of Fair Trading.

Fair Trading, Office Of: This office is responsible for the collection of information relevant to the structure of industries and business conduct

Fair Wages: Fair wages are those fixed under national minimum wage legislation.

Family-unit Agriculture: An agricultural system prevalent in less-developed areas, which is based on the family unit. Production is usually for subsistence purposes with some produce being sold or traded locally to provide other needs. Agricultural methods are often primitive and inefficient and are usually on a very small scale and very labour-intensive.

Featherbedding: Make-work practices that encompass over-manning and/or rejection of technologically advanced machinery. Feather-bedding often has its origin in technical change and can thus be viewed as the carrying forward of a set of practices appropriate for one technology to another where it is alien-more a 'protective' than a restrictive' practice. Feather-bedding tends to be more of a problem with craft than industrial unions.

Feudalism: A type of political and economic system dominant in Europe in the Middle Ages. It was characterized by a social pyramid extending from the dependent peasant through the 'fief' endowed fords and knights to the monarch. A rigid class or status structure linked to the land was the basis of the society. The lord who was granted an estate in return for a military obligation to the monarch rented this land to serfs in return for a rent in kind or money, and having his estate cultivated by these serfs. This decentralized economic system relied on the legal immobility of the serf and went into demise with the growth of the urban population and a system of wage labour.

Fiat Money: The status of which derives from legal enactment. Normally, this decrees that the money concerned shall be 'legal tender' i.e. the law will recognize the offer of it as evidencing intention to settle a debt. That money may be distinguished from commodity-based moneys, e.g. gold and silver coin, or paper money convertible into such coin; or from money based on the credit of—in the sense of trust in—the creating authority.

Filter: A name given to any formula or procedure which removes unwanted variation from data. A low pass filter will remove high frequency variation, such as seasonal or random variation, leaving low frequency components such as business cycles or the trend. A high pass filter has the opposite effect, removing trends etc., leaving short-run cycles and random variation.

Filtering: A term used in urban economics to describe a process by which housing changes in quality, generally passing from occupation by higher income groups to occupation by lower income groups. Thus if a house is divided into units for multiple occupancy, or merely loses value by a process of decay, it will become available to lower income groups. In this way, it is argued that construction of new housing for high income groups can benefit those on lower incomes as the former residences of the rich 'titter down' to the poor. Filtering also provides an explanation of the process by which slums are formed; in many cities areas of low-quality housing are in fact the converted former residences of middle-class households.

Final Goods: Those goods used for the purposes of consumption and not utilized as inputs by firms in the process of production. As such they should be distinguished from intermediate products. It is of course possible for a good to be used in both functions.

Final Product: All those goods and services which are purchased by their ultimate users. The total output of the economy after eliminating intermediate products.

Finance: Narrowly interpreted it signifies capital in monetary form, that is in the form of funds tent or borrowed, normally for capital purposes, through financial markets or institutions. But in common parlance the term is applied to funds from almost any source, used to undertake any kind of expenditure.

Finance House: A financial intermediary, not a bank, which may obtain funds from its own capital resources, by accepting deposits or even by borrowing from other institutions and which it on-lends for a variety of purposes, especially to finance hire purchase contracts, but also leasing.

Financial Capital: Companies can have a variety of types of capital. The principal distribution is between share capital and loan or debenture capital. Share capital is split between ordinary and preference capital with the holders of ordinary shares being the owners of the company. They accept more risk than the owners of other classes as their dividends are paid last. It is possible to have classes of ordinary shares with preferred shares being allowed priority to dividends up to a specified amount before the owners of' deferred shares receive payment. Ordinary shares may also be split between voting and nonvoting or 'A' shares, Preference shares rank just before ordinary shares regarding dividend payments, which in their case is usually fixed.

Financial Instrument: Any document which is an evidence of debt, and the sale or transfer of which enables the seller to acquire finance.

Financial Intermediary: In the wide sense, any operator engaged in bringing together ultimate providers and ultimate users of finance. An important distinction is between intermediaries engaged as brokers in bringing together borrowers and lenders, or buyers and sellers of securities, without entering into the transaction as principals; and intermediaries who themselves borrow or take up funds in order to on-lend them. Prominent among the latter are institutions like Banks, Building Societies, and Insurance Companies, which in taking up funds create claims on themselves, these being matched by the assets, largely claims on others, which they acquire.

Financial Ratios: Ratios between particular groups of the assets or liabilities of an enterprise and corresponding totals of assets or liabilities; or between assets of liabilities and flows like turnover or re venue.

Financial Times Industrial Ordinary Index: The most commonly quoted index of share prices used as a general indicator of the state of the stock market.

Financial Times Stock Indices: There are four different stock indices published by the Financial Times newspaper. They include: government securities, fixed interest securities, gold-mine shares, and industrial ordinary shares. In its daily financial reports, the newspaper also publishes averages of earnings, yield, and price-earnings ratios for ordinary shares, and an index of the level of activity on the stock-exchange based on the number of daily dealings.

Financial Year: Different bodies use different financial years for financial accounting and this need not be coincident with the standard calendar year.

Fine Tuning: A term used to refer to government policies which aim to make small changes in taxation or expenditures which in turn are designed to influence employment levels, national income and price levels.

Firm: In standard neoclassical economics an analytical device which transforms inputs into output. Thus the firm is viewed as an abstract entity which fulfils a mainly technical role.

Firm, Theory of the: The theory of the firm is an important topic in microeconomics which is concerned with explaining and predicting the behaviour of firm particularly with respect to pricing and output decisions.

First Difference: The difference between a variable and its own value lagged by one time period.

First Order Conditions: Generally the condition which states that the first derivative(s) of the objective function with respect to the choice variable(s) should be equal to zero for the determination of an extreme value.

Fiscal Drag: This refers to the effect of inflation on average or effective tax rates. Thus under a progressive income tax system the effective tax rate is increased when money incomes increase even though real incomes may not be increasing. This is because income earners are pushed into income brackets where high marginal rates apply. The result of this is to cause a dampening effect on the volume of economic activity. Its prevalence led to a campaign for indexation of tax allowances.

Fiscal Dederalism: A system of taxation and public expenditure in which revenue raising powers and control over expenditure are vested in various levels of government within a nation, ranging from the national government to the smallest unit of local government.

Fiscal Illusion: A situation in which the benefits of particular government expenditure are clearly identified by recipients but the costs are not, being widely dispersed over time and population. That is to say, the direct fiscal costs are spread over the entire taxpaying community and individual costs are hidden amongst a large number of other government spending programmes which the taxpayer is called to finance by general taxation.

Fiscal Multiplier: A coefficient that indicates by how much an increase in fiscal expenditure affects the equilibrium level of income.

Fiscal Policy: Generally refers to the use of taxation and government expenditure to regulate the aggregate level of economic activity. Thus if unemployment is regarded as excessive taxes will be reduced. Income and expenditure taxes may be varied for this purpose. The overall effect on economic activity will depend on the size of the tax cut and the multiplier. Increasing government expenditure will also raise the level of activity by an amount equal to the change in expenditure times the multiplier. It is argued by some economists that changes in taxation and transfer payments proportional to the existing distribution of income are the appropriate weapons to regulate aggregate activity. Changes in government expenditure should only be made if there is a shift in demand for public goods. The use of fiscal policy entails changes in the government's budget including the possibility of deficits. The conventional view is that the use of deficit finance in this situation is perfectly proper though attention has to be given to the impact of this as well.

Fixed Asset: Any non-financial capital asset of a company which is relatively long-lived and specific to particular productive processes, and the cost of which is normally recoverable only over an operating period of some duration, e.g. plant and buildings. Such assets are illiquid compared with current assets such as stocks of materials or semifinished or finished goods.

Fixed Coefficients Production Function: A production function in which inputs must be combined in fixed proportions.

Fixed Cost: For a firm the short run is defined as the period of time over which some factors of production cannot be varied. The latter are known as fixed factors and the costs associated with them as fixed costs. Fixed cost does not therefore vary with output.

Fixed Exchange Rate: This is when the value of one national currency has been fixed in relation to another. It is not free to fluctuate on the international money market because there has been a prior agreement to hold it at a par value.

Fixed Factors: Those factors of production which cannot be changed in quantity. Usually this will apply to some factors, such as capital, in the short run.

Fixed Investment: All final goods purchased by firms other than those additions to inventories which are not intended for eventual resale. Additions to the capital stock.

Fixed Labour Costs: These comprise costs of employment

that vary less than proportionately with hours worked. There are two main forms of fixed cost. First, there are turnover costs associated with the hiring, layoff or dismissal of employees. These include the costs of recruitment, screening and initial training, in addition to termination costs in the form of severance pay. Second, there are those costs which, although continuing throughout the period of employment, are not related or fully related to hours of work.

Fixed Proportions in Production: This refers to production processes in which the capital/labour ratio is fixed i.e. they can only be used in fixed proportions. The resulting iso- product curve is 'L' shaped. Since fixed proportions characterize input-output analysis this type of isoproduct curve is sometimes called an input-output isoquant, or Leontief isoquant.

Flat Yield: The annual amount paid in interest on a security expressed as a percentage of the purchase price.

Flexitime: The name given to flexible working hours. Economic theory indicates that there are gains to be made by following flexitime because of the divergent tastes and preferences of different workers. Flexitime has its attendant costs in the form of monitoring, supervision, communication and coordination expenses. Recent increases in the use of flexitime would indicate that the benefits are outweighing the costs in many employment situations.

Flight From Cash: This refers to moving wealth from cash into interest-bearing assets; either because of expectations of price increases or a fall in the interest rate.

Floating Capital: A term with the same meaning as

working capital; it refers to money invested in work in progress, wages paid or any other type of investment which is not a fixed asset. It is still considered an investment as it is part of productive capacity being utilized.

Floating Charge: A form of security given by a borrower for loans, or other debt, e.g. debentures. The security is not attached to specific items of the borrower's assets but constitutes a floating charge on stocks or other assets which individually are turning over in the course of trading.

Floating Debt: That part of the national debt borrowed on very short-term securities, and frequently denoting the part represented by Treasury Bills. It is 'floating' in that it is continuously failing due for repayment. Unless met from a fiscal surplus or the proceeds of selling longerterm debt, such repayment requires the issue of new short-term debt or the creation of money.

Floating Exchange Rate: When the relative value of two currencies is allowed to fluctuate with international market forces the rate is said to 'float'.

Floor: The limit to downward movements in output in trade cycle theory. The fundamental element in the lower limit to movements in output is autonomous investment but in certain theories the interaction of the multiplier and accelerator will ensure that the floor is never actually reached, in contrast to the ceiling along which income 'crawls' in the same theory.

Flotation: The practice of issuing shares to the public in order to raise new capital.

Flow: The quantity of an economic variable measured over a period of time. Thus, the flow of investment may be measured as the amount of investment expenditure per year. The term is used to distinguish such measurements from stocks, which measure the physical quantity as an economic variable existing at any moment in time

FOB: (Free On Board) A term which describes a price for or valuation of a good which is calculated on the basis of the process of manufacture, and does not include the cost of transporting the good to the consumer.

Food and Agricultural Organization: Established in 1945 the FAO has its head-quarters in Rome. With a view to improving the production and distribution of agricultural commodities and food, the organization is entrusted with the task of collecting and studying relevant data and of promoting international commodity agreements and technical assistance.

Footloose Industries: Industries which are not bound to particular locations by specific locational requirements and thus can effectively locate anywhere.

Forced Riders: The mirror image of the free rider. Forced riders are those who value the pecuniary and non-pecuniary benefits of belonging to an organization which enforces membership at less than the pecuniary and non-pecuniary costs. When coercion is used to eliminate the free rider problem, the forced rider emerges. The issue of forced- ride has traditionally taken second place to free-rider problems associated with the characteristics of public goods.

Forced Saving: A form of saving which occurs because consumers are unable to spend their money on desired consumption goods simply because those goods are unavailable. In the markets such a situation is likely to be temporary—suppliers of goods will observe the unmet demand through such 'signals' as decreases in inventories and will react by increasing supply. In planned economies such a response may not occur if increases in the supply of such goods are deemed inconsistent with the overall planning of the economy.

Foreign Aid: This is any capital inflow or other assistance given to a country which would not generally have been provided by natural market forces. There are four main types of aid. First, long-term loans which have to be repaid in foreign currency but are usually repayable over ten or twenty years. The advantage to the recipient is that the annual repayments are far less burdensome than those of short and medium-term loans. Secondly, there are 'soft loans' which can be repaid in local currency.

Foreign Exchange: Currency or interest-bearing bonds of another country.

Foreign Exchange Market: The international market in which currencies are transferred between countries. The transactions, mainly carried out by telephone or cable are between financial institutions buying and selling foreign currencies thus making profits when the exchange rates and interest rates differ between financial centres. The 'market' operates 24 hours a day as each centre throughout the world begins trading during 'office hours' or when their respective stock markets and banks are open.

Foreign Investment: This usually refers to any investment in another country which is carried out by private companies or individuals as opposed to government aid. There are arguments for and against foreign investment in underdeveloped countries: those against, say that it constitutes economic colonialism and is an attempt to retain control of ex-colonies.

Foreign Payments: Any payment that has to be made to a foreign country whether in return for goods and services or repayment of debt: these usually have be made in hard currency.

Foreign Trade Multiplier: The ratio which a change in income bears to the change in exports responsible for this change in income.

Forward Exchange Market: A market in which currencies are bought and sold at rates of exchange fixed now, for delivery at specified dates in the future, A transactor expecting to acquire a currency, or to have to make a payment in it, at a future time, may sell or buy the currency forward, thus covering himself against any changes in its exchange value in the intervening period. Others may operate in the market as pure speculators; this is facilitated by the fact that no payment is due on a forward contract until it matures.

Forward Linkage: The relationship between an industry or firm and other, industries or firms which use its output as an input. A change in output or price will be transmitted forwards to users of its product.

Forward Market: Any transaction which involves a contract to buy or sell commodities, or securities at a fixed future date at a price agreed in the contract, is part of a forward market.

Forward Rate: The rate of exchange at which a currency may be bought or sold for future delivery, on the forward market. Different rates apply to different forward dates; and depending on expectations the forward rate of a currency may be at a discount or a premium on the spot rate. With completely neutral expectations the forward rate between two currencies will theoretically reflect the difference between short-term interest rates in the respective countries, the currency of the country with the higher interest rate being traded at a forward discount on the spot rate.

Fractional Reserve Banking: The practice by which commercial banks maintain a reserve of highly liquid assets equal to some fraction, normally a small one, of their total asset portfolios. The purpose of the reserve is to meet unforeseen variations in the Outflow of deposits by withdrawals or transfers to other banks, and when calculated as a proportion of total deposits, as it usually is, the fraction is termed the 'reserve ratio'.

Franked Investment Income: This generally refers to income which has already borne corporation tax and is thus not subject to further corporation tax in the hands of a company which receives it.

Freedom of Entry: The ability of a new firm to enter a market for a good or service. In the complete absence of barriers to entry then entry is free.

Free Good: A good, the supply of which is at least equal to the demand at zero price. Price in this context refers not simply to money price but rather to whatever has to be foregone in providing the good opportunity cost.

Free Rider: A phenomenon arising from the characteristics of public goods. Basically, the fact that public goods are non-rival means that the provision of the another person. If potential consumers are therefore faced with the issue of financing the provision of the good, each one has an incentive not to state his true willingness to pay since he can gamble on the good being provided to others who will express some willingness to pay.

Free Trade: A policy of nonintervention by the state in trade between nations, where trade takes place according to the international division of labour and the theory of comparative advantage. Such a policy would lead to the most efficient allocation of resources on a world scale and to the maximization of world income.

Free Trade Area: A loose grouping of countries within which tariff and other barriers to trade are removed, while each member country retains its own commercial policy to countries outside the area.

Frequency Distribution: A summary, usually in the form of a table of numbers or a histogram, of the number of times a random variable takes on certain values, or ranges of values in a sample of observations. If each of the frequencies is divided by the number of observations in the sample, the resulting figures constitute a relative frequency distribution, which approximates to the probability distribution of the variable as the sample size becomes very large.

Frictional Unemployment: Traditionally thought of as search unemployment that is, the amount of unemployment that corresponds to job vacancies in the same local labour market and occupation. It takes time to match workers and jobs and as a result unemployment and unfilled vacancies can exist side by side.

Fringe Benefits: All those non-wage and salary elements in the total pecuniary rewards an employee receives from his employment. Example would be employers' pension contributions on behalf of the employee, the free use of a car, employers' payments of subscriptions to clubs and associations or discounts on purchases of certain goods and subsidized meals.

F-Statistic: A statistic which follows the F-distribution. Often used to test the overall significance of a set of explanatory variables in regression analysis.

Full Cost: Is defined for any given level of output as the sum of average variable cost, average fixed cost and the net profit margin. It is a concept used with reference to firm pricing rules.

Full Cost Pricing: A pricing rule where firms add a net profit margin onto unit costs where the calculation for the latter, includes all costs.

Full-employment Budget Surplus: A measure of the thrust of fiscal policy, which does not rely solely on the magnitude of the budget surplus. The budget surplus alone can be misleading as to the direction of fiscal policy for it can change passively as a result of autonomous changes in private expenditure. As the economy moves into recession tax revenues decline and expenditures may rise and therefore the budget moves into deficit. Conversely an increase in economic activity will cause the budget to move into surplus. The budget deficit alone therefore provides no guide as to whether fiscal policy is expansionary or contractionary.

Full-employment National Income: A measure of the real value of the goods and services that can be produced when the country's factors of production are fully employed; when the economy is at the natural rate of unemployment.

Full Information Maximum Likelihood (FIML): A technique for estimating systems of simultaneous equations, which may be linear or nonlinear. It is an estimator which takes account of the fact that errors may be correlated between equations.

Function: A mathematical formalisation of the relationship whereby the values of a set of independent variables determine the value of the dependent variable.

Funds: Business houses as apart of their business and accounting practice, usually set aside a part of their profits into separately duly constituted funds like the depreciation fund. It is so created for the eventual replacement of the concerned fixed asset like a plant or a machinery when it has to be written off.

Future Markets: In contrast to the spot markets, future markets are the one where products, shares and bonds are bought and sold for delivery at some future date.

G

Gains from International Trade: Comparative difference in cost is the major factor accounting for the international trade. Each nation specialises in the production of such products in which it has greater efficiency. The gain resulting from the trade is apportioned between the trading nations in accordance with the rate of exchange settled mutually. The exchange rate depends upon the mutual elasticities of demand and supply of the two nations for the two products.

Game Theory: A theory of individual rational decisions taken under conditions of less than full information concerning the outcomes of those decisions. The theory examines the interaction of individual decisions given certain assumptions concerning decisions made under risk the general environment and the cooperative or noncooperative behaviour of other individuals.

Gauss-Markov Theorem: This states that under certain conditions that the ordinary least squares estimator is the best linear unbiased estimator. The latter is a desirable property of econometric estimators.

Gearing: The indicator of relative proportion of debt capital and equity capital. The higher the proportion of debt the more highly geared is the company. The degree of gearing affects the overall cost of capital. The concept is difficult to measure in practice. The most elementary measure is nominal value of fixed interest capital/nominal value of equity capital.

Gearing Ratio: The ratio of debt finance to the sum of debt and ordinary share capital finance.

General Agreement on Tariffs and Trade (GATT): The General Agreement on Tariffs and Trade, commonly known as GATT, was signed at the Geneva Conference in 1947. It is a multilateral trade agreement which both sets out rules of conduct for international trade relations and provides a forum for multilateral negotiations regarding the solution of trade problems and the gradual elimination of tariffs and other barriers to trade.

General Equilibrium: A situation where all markets in an economy are simultaneously in equilibrium, i.e. where prices and quantities do not change.

Geometric Lag: A distributed lag formulation in which the weights on successive values of the lagged variable decrease according to some multiplicative scheme. An example is

$$Y_1 = l\, X_t + l^2 X_{t-1} + l^3 X_{t-2} + \ldots$$

$$\text{with } 0 < l < 1$$

This type of formulation is usually estimated after a Koyck transformation in econometric work.

Geometric Progression: A series of numbers, or algebraic terms, in which each element bears some multiplicative relationship to its predecessor and successor. For instance, the series

$$1, a, a^2, a^3, a^4 \ldots$$

is a geometric progression, since each term is equal to its predecessor multiplied by *a*. The Keynesian multiplier can be thought of as the sum of a geometric progression.

Gibrat's Law of Proportionate Growth: Due to R. Gibrat this is a formulation describing how a process of random growth can produce a lognormal distribution of firm sizes. Specifically the law assumes that the number of firms is fixed, the distribution of growth rates confronting each firm is identical, and is therefore independent of both firms absolute size and past growth history. Thus whether the firm is large, medium or small it has the same average proportionate growth rate, and the dispersion around this common average will also be invariant across all firms. Such a law of growth can be shown to produce a lognormal size distribution of firms whose relative dispersion increases overtime. The significance of such a distribution is that it conforms with that most typically found in real world industries, that is, positively skewed with a few large firms and many small firms. Thus some economists argue that the parameters of the log-normal distribution can be used as indices of market concentration.

Gold Exchange Standard A variant form of the gold standard under which a country pegged the value of its currency to the value of' the currency of a centre country, e.g. sterling, which was itself on gold. The pegging was effected by the monetary authorities holding all or part of the country's external reserves in reserve currency assets, and by exchanging the domestic currency for the reserve currency at determined and stable rates.

Gold Standard: The system of monetary organizations under which the value of a country's money is legally defined as a fixed quantity of gold, and domestic currency takes the form of gold coin and/or notes convertible on demand into gold at legally determined rates. For a full gold standard to exist requires two basic conditions: the obligation of the monetary authority to exchange domestic currency for gold to any amount at the specified rates and the freedom of individuals to import and export gold.

Goodwill: A term used in accounting for intangible assets usually measured by the difference between the price paid for a going concern and its book value.

Green Revolution: A term applied to the major increase in agricultural productivity obtained in developing countries by the introduction of high-yielding, disease resistant seeds. It has applied to rice and wheat in particular. Adequate water supplies and the use of artificial fertilizers are necessary requirements for the success of this policy.

Gresham's Law: A 'law' formulated by Sir Thomas Gresham. Although usually expressed in the phrase 'bad money drives out good' and applied to episodes of currency debasement or depreciation, the 'law' actually embodies a more general principle. It predicts that where two monetary media circulate together, then if their intrinsic relative values as determined by market forces diverge from their legally determined values, the money of higher intrinsic value will be withdrawn from circulation and hoarded. Such a situation can arise without any currency debasement; for example, historically, where gold and silver coin have circulated together at legally established values which have come to differ from the relative commodity values of the two metals.

Gross National Product Deflator: A price index used to

correct the money value to all the goods and services entering gross national product for price changes. This enables the changes in the real output of the goods and services in the economy to be isolated.

Growth Path: This is the pattern of change of a variable overtime; the variable is a measure of development, usually per capita income or consumption and the growth path represents its actual, or predicted pattern of change overtime. Development strategies will result in different paths; if large amounts of capital are being invested in the capital-goods industry, the growth path will rise slowly until such time as these industries are well established enough for further industrial development in consumer goods to take place when the growth path may rise sharply.

Growth Pole: A group or cluster of industries centred on and linked with one or more propulsive industries which form a centre of growth and dynamism in an economy. However, the theory has been widely applied in Regional Economics both as an explanation of the geographical clustering of particular industries and as a policy model for stimulating economic growth in depressed areas or underdeveloped regions of an economy.

Government Outlays for the Restoration of Economic Stability: In free unregulated economics with profit motive being the underlying inspiration quite often the enterpreneurs indulge in such economic activities that de-stabilise the economy. At times they expand their production level to an extent which can not be sustained and at times they unduly become pessinist and adopt contraction policy of utmost the last about sixty years, reliance is placed on the fiscal policy. In case of Depression huge investment projects, are undertaken with a view to raise employment and production and income. Role of fiscal policy occupies to day a prime place and has replaced the monetary policy.

Government Sector: Role of the government has immensely increased these days. Areas of much larger dimensions, the governments are called upon to administer. The Government is mainly subdivided under three heads—central state and local. Economic activities of the Government are called as the govt. sector.

Government Securities: Among the stock exchange securities these are considered to be the safest for they have the government backing. The commercial banks consider these as ideal for giving advances and loans giving advance and loans. The banks readily accept these as securities. The banks can easily as certain of the person and likewise can get a good and safe title over these without much of the procedural formalities.

H

Hard Currency: After the second world war. U.S.A. emerged as the first rate power of the world with commanding heights in the trading, commercial and industrial spheres. Her products were demanded every where and so U.S.A.'s dollar currency shot up in demand. As compared to the high demand for U.S.($) dollar, its supply and availability with the different nationals became very restricted for their proucts did not find ready acceptability in U.S.A. So demand far dollar went for ahead of its supply. It came to be called as hard currency while the other currencies by comparison came to be called as soft currencies.

Hard-core Unemployed: Those amongst the registered unemployed who find it extremely difficult to obtain a job because of their mental and physical condition their attitude toward work or their age. It has been argued that these may form an irreducible minimum number of unemployed but this ignores both the fact that devoting greater resources to these groups might reduce the undesirable characteristics and the fact that attitudes towards work are themselves likely to be a function of the level of unemployment.

Heterogeneous Capital: Physical *capital* of different types highly specific to certain production processes and not transferable to alternative processes. This concept is at variance with the idea of a single malleable capital good which can be used for the production of many different goods by different processes. If capital is considered to be heterogeneous then, as noted by the Cambridge School, it raises serious problems for the use of an aggregate production function such as is commonly the case in neoclassical growth models. However some critics of aggregate production functions are willing to concede the usefulness of some measure of aggregate capital provided this does not include incorporating such a measure into an aggregate production function.

Heterogeneous Product: When commodities or services supplied by economic agents in a given market have attribute combinations which are not identical in the eyes of buyers, the product is said to be heterogeneous.

High Powered Money: In the traditional theory of the credit multiplier, the reserve assets which form the base on which the banking system creates bank deposits, and which constrain the lending activities of the banks which lead to deposit creation, are collectively termed 'high-powered money' since, according to the theory, a change m the quantity of these assets will produce a multiplied change in the bank deposit component of' the money stock. The term also refers to the fact that the clearest constituents of high- powered money are the monetary liabilities of the public sector, i.e. circulating currency and bankers' balances at the central bank. However, short-term assets, e.g. certain bills which can readily be converted into public sector monetary liabilities at the central bank should arguably be included if they are treated as reserve assets by the commercial banks, it' bank lending is influenced by the banks' holding of them, and if their supply is an object of central bank control.

Hire Purchase: The consumer obtains credit for the purchase of a specific good by putting down a deposit and paying the balance, with interest, in a fixed number of instalments. However the consumer does not own' the goods until he has completed the payments, and they can be repossessed in event of default. The level of HP and other consumer credit in the UK was in excess of 9,820 million at the end of 1981. Governments control HP terms directly in an effort to limit consumer credit spending. Such controls although limiting expenditure have a repressive effect on some industries which rely heavily on HP sales i.e. the motor industry and other consumer durable producers.

Consumer credit expanded a great deal during the 1970s, with the increased usage of credit card schemes owned by banks, i.e. Barclaycard and Access and with many large retail stores beginning their own credit schemes; Marks and Spencer Ltd. has instigated one supported by Citibank Trust in England, and Bank of Scotland in Scotland, and Boots the Chemist, have a scheme which is run by Access. These differ from HP in that goods once purchased belong to the consumer and he has an outstanding debt to the bank or finance company; they are however included in the figure mentioned above.

Holding Company: A company that has control over a number of other companies, through ownership of a sufficient proportion of the latters' common stock. A sufficient proportion is 51 per cent or over, however, where there is a dispersed and inert group of stockholders *minority control* can be exercised with a proportion of the common stock which is below 51 per cent. This enables holding companies to acquire subsidiaries at a cost which is less than could have been the case if it had purchased their physical assets. This pyramiding of control, as it is called, is subject to limitations imposed by company legislation.

A holding company tends to concern itself' with control over the financial, managerial or marketing functions of its subsidiaries, and thus performs more of a monitoring role. The subsidiaries are then given an element of independence, which facilitates the retention of the individual subsidiary's image and control over its production and investment plans.

Homogeneity The quality of goods, services or factors which ensures that they cannot be differentiated in the minds of suppliers and consumers, A range of commodities is said to be homogeneous if all commodities in that range are perfect substitutes for each other. The commodities may be physically distinct but economically homogeneous. Individual workers are physically distinct, but may be almost identical in their ability to work and may therefore be treated as a homogeneous group by firms.

Homogeneous Functions A function is said to be homogeneous of degree n if the multiplication of all of the independent variables by the same constant, say A, results in the multiplication of the dependent variable by . Thus the function

$$Y = X^2 + Z^2$$

is homogeneous of degree 2 since

$$(X)^2 + (Z)^2 = 2\ (X^2 + Z^2) = 2y.$$

A function which is homogeneous of degree one is said to be linearly homogenous, or to display linear homogeneity. A *production function* which is homogeneous of degree one displays constant returns to scale since a, say, doubling of all inputs will lead to a doubling of output.

Horizontal Equity: Fairness or justice in the treatment of' individuals in similar circumstances. In general, the principle that like-individuals should be treated in a like manner where economic arrangements are concerned. The concept is most frequently used with regard to tax and income, thus horizontal equity is held to be attained if individuals with the same income face the same *tax burden*. However, it may be applied in other areas, for example with regard to the benefits of public expenditure horizontal equity may be said to require that individuals with similar income or *need* should receive the same benefit. In using the concept we must be clear which characteristics are employed in defining 'similar' generally income is the relevant variable but other characteristics might be thought relevant-such as health.

Human Capital: The essence of human capital is that investments are made in human resources so as to improve their productivity. Costs are incurred in the expectation of future benefits; hence, the term 'investment in human resources' Like all investments, the key question becomes: are they economically worthwhile? The answer to this question depends on whether or not benefits exceed costs by a sufficient amount, and the standard *investment criteria* apply. There Is thus a direct analogy between investment in human capital and investment in physical capital, although there are differences.

In particular, human capital is not collateral because it cannot be sold. Moreover, an individual cannot spread or diversify his risk in the manner that owners of physical capital can. These factors apart, the parallel between human and physical capital is a close one,- for example, human capital like physical capital is subject to *depreciation.*

The concept of man investing in himself has a very wide application. It Covers not only investments in formal schooling and post-school training, but also home investments in the form of family care in the pre-school years, the acquisition of improved health, and investments in labour market information via job search.

Human capital theory underpins many of the important developments in modern economics and provides one of the in explanations for wage and salary differentials by age and occupation, the uneven incidence of' unemployment by skill, the job regulatory practices of trade unions and so on as well as contributing to Policy decisions on, say, the allocation of resources to schooling and training vis-a-vis other claims on resources.

Hyper-inflation: A position of rapidly accelerating inflation. Under conditions of hyperinflation prices rise ten or even a hundred-fold in a single month.

I

Idle Money: Is the other term used for the inactive money idle or inactive money does not render any help in the productive process. One keep a certain portion of the funds into liquid form—mainly for three motives—transaction, precautionary, or speculative.

Implicit Contracts: The notion of implicit contracts seeks to provide it rationale for the existence of sticky wages (and prices), and is based upon the differential *risk aversion* characteristic of employees and employers (entrepreneurs). Employees are assumed, to be relatively more averse to risk than their employers partly because owners of human capital (employees) cannot diversify risk in the way that owners of physical *capital* can; and partly because employers are considered to be self-selected individuals who are relatively indifferent toward (or actually lovers of) risk. As a result, it becomes optimal (long-run cost minimizing) for employers to offer employees a joint product consisting of employment and insurance against income instability. Implicit contracts emerge which cause firms, and in some models, workers to act as if they are legally constrained-contracts that fix the employees' incomes, or at least wage rates, and transfer risk to the employers. With such contracts in effect, wages do not move to clear the labour market in response to changes in aggregate demand; rather employment changes via reduced working time, or, more, importantly via layoffs.

Income Consumption Curve: The tangency of the consumer's indifference curve and his budget line defines the consumer's equilibrium. If income is varied such that the budget line moves outwards in a parallel fashion, new equilibrium will be established. The locus of all such equilibrium is the income consumption curve. If the curve slopes upwards in commodity *space it* indicates that both goods (measured on the axes) are *normal goods.* If it slopes backwards or downwards one of the goods is an *inferior good.* (See diagram.) The income consumption curve is widely referred to as an *Engel curve,* although some writers distinguish the two.

Income Differentials: The difference in income levels between different people; these can be due to types of job, i.e. skill differentials or geographical location in that some areas have higher wage levels than others, or there may be differences between urban and rural wage levels. This is a particularly marked phenomenon in less developed countries, because in general, development plans, introduction of new techniques and high-wage type occupations are situated in urban areas, while the agricultural sector is often left behind, using primitive methods for subsistence farming it) addition payment may be made in kind, in foodstuffs, seeds, clothing which is difficult to quantify in money terms and will give the rural sector an appearance of 'earning' less than it actually does.

Income Effect: A change in the price of a good will reduce or increase the consumer's real income. In response to this change in real income we can expect the consumer to buy less (more) of all goods including the one which has changed in price. This is the income effect of a price change.

Income Elasticity of Demand: A measure of the responsiveness of the quantity demanded of any *good* to a change in the level of income of the persons demanding the good. To avoid the measure being sensitive to the units used, the measure is expressed as

Income —expenditure Model: A simple Keynesian one sector model which shows the determination of the *equilibrium level of national income.* Under the assumptions of a fixed *capital stock, labour force* and technology and rigid wages and prices and, therefore, expectations, it details the static equilibrium in which the supply of *real national output* equals the quantity of national output people wish to buy. In the model the volume of *aggregate expenditure* determines the volume of output and the associated level of employment the model concentrates exclusively on the demand side of the macro- economy. There is no reason why the equilibrium that is eventually established will be associated with full employment, on the contrary this simple representation of the Keynesian system seeks to demonstrate the possibility of an *unemployment equilibrium.* The equilibrium level of national income is established where *withdrawals* equal *injections* and this may occur at less than full employment. Under these circumstances the Keynesian prescription is for a rise *in government expenditure* which when magnified by the actions of the *multiplier* will result in a level of national income and output just sufficient to ensure full-employment. Graphically equilibrium is shown as the point at which the *aggregate expenditure* function cuts the 45° line as below.

This simple approach can however, be criticized on a number of counts. First, it concentrates on the demand side of the economy assuming that the appropriate supply will be forthcoming at any level of expenditure. Second, money plays no role in the model; prices are determined exogenously. The model in fact concentrates exclusively on the goods market and it is the ISLM *diagram which* integrates this with the money market.

Indicative Planning: The use of centrally determined targets to co-ordinate private *and public sector investment* and output plans. Decision-making remains decentralized but sectors of the economy are encouraged to meet agreed targets. There are two approaches to indicative planing. The first is to ask firms in all sectors of the economy to submit output and investment intentions for the forthcoming planning period; these plans are scrutinized for possible bottlenecks and if identified, attempts to resolve the inconsistencies are made by persuading the relevant sectors to raise targets, The second takes as its starting point a target national growth rate which is then used as the basis for detailed sector targets which are compatible with this growth rate. If the resources are available and the sector targets are believed then the plan can be expected to induce the investment necessary to satisfy the plan. A major rationale of indicative planning is improvement in the flow of information within a *market economy,* and reduction in the uncertainty surrounding decision-making. By doing so business confidence is improved and stability and cohesion within the national economy promoted. The French have been major proponents of indicative planning, while Britain experimented during the 1960s with the Labour Government's National Plan.

Indifference: A statement that one good event or project is neither preferred nor not preferred to any other good, etc. If an individual is indifferent between goods X and Y then his utility from X is the same as his utility from Y.

Indirect Least Squares (ILS): A procedure for estimating the parameters of simultaneous equations, which avoids simultaneous equation bias. ILS involves the Ordinary Least Squares estimation of the parameters of the reduced form of the equations, and the calculation of the values of the structural form parameters from these. The procedure can only be used if the equations are just identified, since, otherwise, there will be no unique values of the structural form parameters which are consistent with (or can be calculated from) the reduced form.

Indirect Taxes: Traditionally these were defined as taxes levied on goods and services and thus payment was only indirect. *Excise* and customs *duties, value-added tax* and rates are examples of indirect taxes. The distinction between *direct taxes* and indirect ones is traditional in public finance. The distinction is not, how-ever, a particularly watertight one, nor is it especially useful from an analytical point of view. There are several examples of taxes whose classification is not obvious and the distinction is not very helpful from the viewpoint of *incidence.*

Indirect Utility Function: A utility function that expresses the utility obtained from a set of goods as being determined by the prices of the goods and the level of income. Reference to the consumer's *equilibrium will* show that the equilibrium is given when maximum utility is achieved for a given income and set of relative prices. However instead of expressing utility as a simple function of the goods consumed, the indirect utility function indicates the fact that income level and price levels themselves determine the utility level.

Indivisibilities: The characteristic of a factor *of production or* commodity which prevents its use below a certain minimum level. This may arise out of the specialist nature of many commodities and cause a discontinuity in the production junction or utility *function*. If for example a machine input cannot be reduced in proportion to output, *economics* of scale may arise and marginal costs of production may fall as the scale of operations increases. In general where the size of an indivisible unit of production is large relative to output, plants or firms will also tend to be large.

Industrial and Commercial Finance Corporation: A development finance company formed in 1946 by the Bank of England and the London and Scottish clearing banks at the instance of the government, to fill one of the gaps' in the capital market identified by the Macmillan Committee. The ICFC advances capital on *equity* and *debt terms* to small companies, in amounts too large or too long-term for bank lending but too small to be raised by a public issue of securities, and it also assists with management advice.

Industrial Bank: An alternative name for a finance house, for example an organization which gives hire purchase credit. This name is usually given to the smaller organizations of this nature and not the big finance houses in London.

Industrial Democracy: An extension of the decision-making process within an enterprise away from a single body and towards the whole workforce. It represents a recognition of the 'rights' of workers, as suppliers of labour, to participate in decisions, and take part of the responsibility that these necessarily imply, alongside the nominated management derived from the body of shareholders as owners of capital. One may distinguish between direct and indirect forms of industrial democracy. Direct, or participate, democracy is said to be that in which the worker has an immediate effect on decisions. Indirect, or representative, democracy refers to situations in which workers are given decision-making power through the placing of representatives on high-level boards within companies, Included in the latter category are the Yugoslav workers councils, which consist almost entirely of worker members and have full power; boards of directors in state-owned companies in various countries; the German Mitbestimmung or Co-Determination system; and the relatively few private companies that have voluntarily given workers seats. The aim of both direct and indirect forms of industrial democracy is to diffuse decision-making power throughout the organization.

Industrial Inertia: A term used to describe the observed phenomenon on whereby firms fail to change location when the existing location ceases to be the most profitable location. Industrial Inertia, or 'inertia in location, appears to be inconsistent with standard location theory which assumes firms seek the most profitable location. Such inertia may be explained by costs of relocation which outweigh the extra profits to be obtained in a new location. Alternatively, we may the maximization analysis and argue that firms aim at 'satisfactory' rather than , maximum profits, that is their behaviour is 'satisficing'.

Industrial Organization: Traditionally, the field of applied price theory. It is concerned with the working of the market economy and generally organizes its approach in terms of market structure, conduct and performance. Market structure encompasses the questions of seller and buyer concentration in the market, product differentiation, barriers to entry, cost structures, vertical integration and merger. Market conduct treats firms' pricing behaviour, product strategy, advertising, research, innovation, plant investment and legal strategy. Market performance is the evaluation of the results of firms' conduct in their markets in terms of production and allocative efficiency, economic growth and progress and equity. With the advent of concepts such as satisficing behaviour and bounded rationality and with advanced applications of game theory, the field has broadened to deal with non-profit maximizing and strategic behaviours and their roles in market structure, conduct and performance.

Industrialization (in developing countries): The development of industries as a general development strategy. In the early postwar period and indeed up to the early 1960s many economists considered that industrialization constituted by far the most promising means by which a poor country could develop. Governments of many developing countries accepted this judgment and proceeded to draw up strategies and plans giving priority to industrial development. The import substitution approach was adopted by most countries but some did favour export- promotion. In fact many have in recent years reversed their policies and given priority to developing agriculture. In some cases the difficulties experienced were the result of devoting too many investable resources into industry and neglecting agriculture which is, of course, the dominant sector in developing countries. Other countries found that the costs of industrializing were very high in the sense that effective rates of protection had to be very large before new domestic industry became competitive with imports. Small, very poor countries found that they had great difficulty in establishing viable industries because their markets were so small in relation to the minimum efficient size of plant. Some countries found that their balance of payments situation was not significantly improved.

Industrial Relations: The study and practice of the rules that govern employment. These rules are of three main kinds. Substantive rules that regulate pay and employment, procedural rules that govern the making and challenging substantive rules and finally disciplinary rules that deal with a breach of both the above sets of rules.

Industrial Wage Differentials: Differences in the average levels of pay of groups of workers classified according to the industry in which they are employed. In the long run in which workers are free to move between different employments the levels of pay for any single occupation within different industries should differ only to the extent that industries provide more or less agreeable working conditions, differing pecuniary rewards, which are not included in the pay under analysis, or exhibit differing variability in the pattern of employment, Where industries exhibit differing degrees of competition in product markets this may result in some division of monopoly profits between entrepreneurs and workers which could result in substantial differences in the short run.

Industrial Wage Structure: The ranking of the average pay levels of different groups of workers classified according to the industry in which they are employed.

Industry: An industry within the framework of a perfectly competitive market structure can be defined as a large number of firms competing with each other in the production of a homogeneous product. Under such conditions the individual firm demand and supply schedules can be summed to form the industry demand and supply schedules. In contrast, with monopoly the firm and the industry are one and the same.

Conceptual and operational difficulties arise in the analytical treatment of the industry when the assumption of product homogeneity is relaxed. The monopolistic competition model redefines the concept of an industry using 'product groups' as the criteria for identification. Product groups are a category of closely related products in the sense that they are close technological and economic substitutes. It is then theoretically plausible to use 'product groups' as a basis for the demarcation of industries. There are a number of difficulties with this definition. Firstly, there is the operational one of how closely related products should be before they constitute a product group for instance, are motor cars and motorcycles part of' the same 'product group"? Secondly, heterogeneous goods cannot be summed to form industry demand and supply schedules unless some common denominator is used. Price would be appropriate here but unless highly restrictive assumptions are utilized, there will be no one unique equilibrium price in monopolistic competition, but rather a cluster of prices reflecting consumer preferences for the products of the various firms within 'the group'. Lastly, multi-product firms raise the problem of overlap across product groups and the use of some criterion for establishing when a firm should or should not be included in 'the group'.

Inflation Accounting: Refers to techniques for dealing with the impact of inflation on accounts and accounting procedures. Traditionally, historic cost methods have been employed whereby accounts were built up from actual records of transactions. In periods of rapid inflation the replacement cost of fixed assets would greatly exceed historic costs. Consequently in real terms depreciation will be understated when historic cost accounting is employed and profits overstated. The system of capital allowances may then not permit the recovery of capital costs in real terms. Similarly, rapid inflation can give an artificial boost to profits from stock appreciation. If such profits are taxes a company which has to replace its stock at the higher price level is penalized. Several different approaches to a solution to the problem have been suggested.

The current purchasing power method retains historic cost notions but expresses accounts in terms of purchasing units' employing a retail price index. The Sandilands Committee which examined the whole subject in the UK recommended the use of value accounting whereby assets were to be measured by reference to their value and not cost. The use of replacement cost accounting whereby assets are revalued from historic to current costs was recommended. There has been much controversy about the detailed procedures that should be adopted, Eventually a consensus was reached with the publication of Statement of Standard Accounting Practice 16 entitled 'Current Cost Accounting' in 1980. Three adjustments to trading profits calculated on a historic basis are required to arrive at current cost operating profit. The first is the *depreciation* adjustment which allows for the impact of price changes when determining the charge against revenue for the part of fixed assets consumed in the period. The second is the cost of sales adjustment which allows for the impact of price changes when determining the change against revenue for stock consumed in the period. The third is the monetary working capital adjustment which represents the amount of additional (or reduced) finance needed for monetary working capital as a result of changes in the input prices of goods and services employed in the business.

Inflationary Gap: Aggregate expenditure exceeds the maximum attainable level output with the result that there is upward pressure on prices. In the simple income *expenditure* model this is shown by an aggregate expenditure function which cuts the 45', where E = Y, beyond the full employment level Yf . At Yf the sources of capital and labour are full employed with the result that this represents the maximum attainable level of output. As a result there exists an inflationary gap of magnitude AB with the associated upward pressure on prices.

This was initially advanced to explain the inflation of the 1940s and 1950s the first real inflation since the publication of the general theory of employment, interest and money. However the treatment neglects the role of money either, in bringing inflation under control in exacerbating an upward spiral of' wages and prices. The model may be considered a *demand-pull* explanation of inflation.

Inflation Subsidy: Due to institutional inflexibilities interest rates and debt repayments may fail to rise in line with inflation and as a result real interest rates and the real value of debt will fall; indeed real interest rates may even become zero. In this case there is an inflation subsidy to those borrowing although of course there is a corresponding tax on those who made the loans.

Inflation Tax: The situation where a government adopts a policy of promoting inflation in place of an increase in taxation to pay for its expenditures. If the government finances its purchases by means of an increase in the money supply when the *aggregate supply curve* in the economy is *inelastic,* prices will rise so that all holders of money balances will find their real purchasing power diminished in a manner analogous to an increase in e.g. income taxes.

Informal Sector: This refers to the large volume of self-employed in a developing country who are engaged in small-scale labour-intensive work such as tailoring, food preparation, trading, shoe- repairing, etc. These people are often regarded as unemployed or underemployed as they cannot be included in national employment statistics, but they are often highly productive and make a significant contribution to national income. Their work in general is characterized by a low *capital output ratio, that is* the ratio of the level of equipment, or capital relative to output, and a low capital -labour ratio; that is the ratio of the levels of factor inputs of capital equipment to labour.

Instalment Credit: The general term for finance lent on conditions which provide for repayment of the principal, together with the *interest, by* regular instalments. The greater part of' instalment credit is advanced to finance the purchase of consumer goods under *hire purchase* contracts, where the finance is linked to a particular transaction with the lender and purchaser having certain legal rights in the object purchased. Such credit may be financed by the retailer concerned, although in the case of hire purchase the contract may be between the buyer and a *finance company.* Other forms of instalment credit include *personal loans* by banks, and credit extended through *credit card* and budget account facilities. As normally used the term does not embrace mortgage finance for house purchase. It should be noted that, increasingly, producer goods are purchased under various instalment credit arrangements.

Institutional Economics: A type of economic analysis which emphasizes the role of social, political and economic organizations in determining economic events. This movement flourished in the early twentieth century particularly in the US under the influence of T. B. *Veblen* and W. C. Mitchell. The emphasis on the role of institutions in economic affairs is a criticism of conventional economics which may be said to ignore the non-economic environment in which individuals make decisions. Many economists such as G. K. *Myrdal* have emphasized the importance of the social and political structure within which the economy operates and attempted to use a broader method of economic analysis encompassing the disciplines of politics and sociology.

Institutional Training: Usually used to describe job training that is provided directly by the government, Its rationale, at a micro-level, is that the private market does not provide a socially optimal amount of training. Thus, trainees may be unable to 'purchase' training by accepting a lower wage during training or otherwise be unable to borrow because of an inability to use their *human capital* (future earnings) as collateral for a loan. Also, to the extent that training generates external (third party) benefits that are not paid for in the market, there will be a socially sub-optimal amount of training. Note that shortages of skilled workers may result from the actions of unions and/ or government in restricting the supply of and demand for training places.

Instrumental Variables: (I.V.). Variables which are used to replace actual expla*natory variables* as weights in *regression an*alysis. The I.V. technique is often used where one or more of' the explanatory variables are correlated with the error term of the equation. Under these circumstances, the use of the explanatory variables themselves will result in biased Ordinary Least Squares estimates. The ideal instrumental variable is one which is highly correlated with that explanatory variable it is to replace, but which is uncorrelated with the error term. The technique results in *consistent* estimates.

Instruments: The term comes from the classification of variables in economic *stabilization* into policy instruments, policy *targets* and *exogenous* variables, Instruments are those variables which are assumed to be under the control of the decision making agent (i.e. the government), to attain certain values of the policy targets or to *optimize* the *welfare function* or loss *junction.*

If the classification of variables into instruments and targets is used then economic policy may be seen as the solution of a system of equations to achieve the target values, provided the number of instruments is at least as great as the number of targets, If the number of instruments is less than the number of targets then some targets will be unattainable.

Insurance: Insurance permits individuals to exchange the risk of a large loss for the certainty of a small loss. The losses most commonly insured against are loss of property, life and income. The purchase of insurance, by payment of an insurance premium, spreads the risk associated with any specified contingency over a large number of individuals. Insurance is said to be fair if the mathematical expectation of gain from purchasing the insurance is zero. The existence of administrative costs and any departures from perfect competition in the insurance market tend to make insurance less than fair, although this is frequently balanced by the tax treatment of insurance premia and in practice insurance may be more than fair, i.e. the mathematical expectation of gain is positive.

Integrated Economy: A term referring to a situation when different sectors of an economy, usually the agricultural and industrial sectors, work together efficiently, and are mutually interdependent. As part of the development -process, this situation is usually coincident with the achievement of *sustained growth.*

Integration: The reverse process to differentiation. *By* integrating a *marginal* function we can obtain the corresponding total function.

Intended Inventory Investment: The deliberate buildup of stocks. 'The deliberate run- down of stocks is intended inventory disinvestment.

Intensive Margin: The case of decreasing physical returns to capital or labour applied to a fixed quantity of land. Often accredited to *David Ricardo,* this theory states that if to a given piece of land equal increments of]about (or capital) are applied the increment in the output of the crop produced will at some point reach a maximum and thereafter continuously decline.

Inter-Bank Market: One of a group of interrelated *money markets* in London. It developed in the 1960s actually as a market in which the non-clearing banks lent to one another, but it has since become a general money market used by the whole range of financial institutions both for lending and borrowing. The funds dealt in are in large sums—generally not less than a quarter million pounds—and they are lent, unsecured, at terms which may be 'overnight' or 'at call', or for fixed periods. The market, which is served by a number of firms of money *brokers,* is used by the banks and other institutions to adjust their short-run *liquidity* positions, or to obtain funds for on-lending.

Intercept: In a linear function the constant term, i.e. that term which does not contain any independent variables. For instance, in the function

$$Y = a + bX$$

a is the intercept, so called because the graph of the function crosses (or intercepts) the Yaxis when Y is equal to *a* (i.e. when X = 0). In a simple linear *consumption function,* the intercept can be interpreted as autonomous consumption, i.e. consumption which would take place even if income were zero.

Internal Drain: A movement of cash, i.e. circulating media, from the banks into domestic circulation. Under the pre- 1914 *Gold Standard,* seasonal movements apart, this might take the form of an increased demand for gold coin by the public, arising from a mistrust of paper money or of the banking system generally.

Internal' Labour Market: An arrangement whereby labour is supplied and demanded within the firm without direct access to the *external labour market.* Different treatment is accorded to the 'ins" (i.e. those already employed in the firm) and the 'outs'. Most jobs within the firm are filled by the promotion or transfer of workers who have already gained entry. The internal labour market thus consists of a set of structured employment relationships, embodying a set of formal/ informal rules that govern each job and the interrelationships between jobs. This complex employment relation ship is said to that developed partly because of the elaboration of tasks that are specific to a job and thus require *specific training*, often Acquired on the job.

International Bank for Reconstruction and Development: An international development bank established in 1945, along with the IMF, by Articles of Agreement signed at the United Nations Monetary and Financial Conference held at Bretton Woods, New Hampshire in July 1944. The Bank, commonly referred to as the World Bank, became a specialized agency of the United Nations in 1947. Initially the Bank was concerned with raising and allocating capital resources for postwar reconstruction in Europe. However, following the establishment of the *European Recovery Programme* in 1948, the main objective of the Bank has been to assist the economic development of member countries by providing loans where private capital is not available on reasonable terms to help finance investment projects. Loans are generally long term (for periods up to 30 years) and are made directly to governments or to private firms with their government as guarantor.

The Bank finances its activities by members' contributions, calculated according to their quotas in the IMF, borrowing in world capital markets and selling portions of its loans. Approximately 80 per cent of the Bank's debt, mostly in the form of bonds and notes, was collectively held by the Federal Republic of Germany, Japan, Saudi Arabia, Switzerland and the US at the end of 1978. The Bank's lending rate is reviewed at quarterly intervals and is based upon the average weighted cost, by amount and maturity, of capital funds borrowed by the Bank in the proceeding year. The Bank also provides and coordinates a wide range of technical assistance for member countries. It conducts project feasibility and evaluation studies and acts as executing agency for a number of development projects financed by the United Nations Development Programme. In addition, the Bank collaborates with numerous international and regional development agencies, including the African Development Bank, the Arab Fund for Economic and Social Development, the European Development Fund and the Inter-American Development Bank. The Bank also administers the Economic Development Institute, a staff college which provides training for government officials of member countries,; who are directly involved with the evaluation and implementation of development programmes. The Bank's lending and technical assistance activities are complemented by two affiliated organizations; the International Finance Corporation and the International Development Association, established in 1956 and 1960, respectively.

International Commodity Agreements: Agreements made between producer and consumer countries, but occasionally only on the part of producers, in an attempt to secure price stability for primary commodities. Consumers and producers may agree to purchase and supply respectively certain quantities at set prices, while in those involving only producers the schemes usually involve quotas, and occasionally buffer stocks, to control the level of supply. There have, for example, been agreements for wheat, sugar, coffee, tin and olive oil.

International Division of Labour: Specialization in production on a national basis. While division of tabour within an economy may include concentration upon a particular part or process in the production of a good, specialization in the international sphere tends to be concentrated more on products.

International Economics: That part of economics which

deals with transactions between countries in the fields of goods and services, financial flows and factor movements. It is conventionally divided into two subject areas, pure theory and monetary theory. In the former, attentions focused on real magnitudes such as gains from trade terms of trade patterns of trade, etc., while the latter is preoccupied with the determination of the exchange rate between currencies and adjustment mechanisms for attaining equilibrium in the balance of payments.

International Finance Corporation: An international development agency established in 1956 and later made specialized agency of the United Nations 1957. Although affiliated with the international Bank for Reconstruction and Development, it is a separate legal entity with its own share capital and equity holdings in development projects. It seeks to encourage economic growth and the development of local capital markets in member countries by-providing loans and equity capital, without government guarantees, to finance projects where sufficient private capital is not available on reasonable terms. The Corporation also carries out underwriting operations, provides financial support for pre-investment evaluation studies and co-ordinates industrial, technical and financial" aspects of development projects, activities are financed by subscriptions from its 107 member countries and periodic sales of its investments

International Labour Office: An intergovernmental organisation established in 1919 by the Treaty of Versailles which became a specialised agency of the United Nations in 1946.

International Liquidity: In the final analysis, debts between nationals of different countries are settled by the transfer of some internationally accepted means of payment i.e. gold, one or other of the major reserve currencies, or-to a more limited extent--Special Drawing Rights (SDRs). International liquidity'is used to denote either the total stock of these various means of payment, or the stock of them relative to the potential demands on that stock. So far as such demands arise from imbalance in payments between countries, they may be held to be related to the level and growth of world trade. However the availability of international lending facilities, either through bodies such as the IMF or through the Eurocurrency it markets, greatly affects the international liquidity situation since such facilities are a means of redistributing the available stock of international means of payment. When the demands arise be cause of a loss of confidence in a particular currency, liquidity may have to be mobilized on an international scale, and provided in a way analogous to that given by a central bank acting as lender of last resort.

International Monetarism: A school of thought which holds that changes in the world money supply are the principal source of inflationary and deflationary pressure in the international economy. Thus rapid monetary expansion by either a large country relative to the rest of the world or simultaneously by a number of small countries will result in inflationary pressure throughout the world under a fixed exchange rate regime. In a world of fixed exchange rates, flows of international reserves add to and reduce the domestic money supply of surplus and deficit countries respectively, and thus there is a tendency for a uniform rate of price inflation to emerge throughout the world. It follows that in a world of fixed exchange rates the rate of price inflation in a small open economy cannot be independent of the world rate of inflation.

In a world of fixed exchange rates the following mechanism is postulated excess growth in the money supply of a particular country results in excess cash balances and the subsequent attempt to bring this back into the desired ratio within the country's portfolio, leads to the purchase of both domestically and foreign produced commodities and securities. Thus a deficit on either or both current and capital account will emerge which will have to be financed by borrowing abroad and running down foreign exchange reserves. The magnitude of tile reserves and the borrowing facilities places a limit to the extent to which the country can continue to increase the money supply, and thus the domestic price level. Conversely a country with a balance of payments surplus on either capital or current account will experience a new inflow of foreign exchange and thus an addition to the domestic money supply. It may attempt to neutralize or sterilize the impact of such inflows by the sale of bonds to the public to reduce their cash balances, but again there are limits to this process. The continued sale of bonds will push down the price and raise the interest rate which in turn will increase the net inflows on capital account. Thus in the deficit country there will tend to be a net outflow of money reducing the inflationary pressure while the surplus country will experience a net inflow and hence inflation. In this manner inflation rates will tend to equality and equilibrium of the balance of payments be restored.

In the case of floating exchange rates, a rapid expansion of the domestic money supply will lead directly to depreciation *of* the currency. Domestic residents will seek to reduce their holdings *of* cash and restore the value of cash balances within their portfolios by purchasing foreign commodities and securities. Conversely the countries with a rate of growth of the money supply less than the rate of growth *of* income will seek to increase their cash balances to enable them to finance their increased volume of transactions. The country will thus experience a net inflow of funds as the residents of this country increase their exports or their sales of foreign securities in an attempt to increase their cash balances. Thus a country with a rapid growth *of* real income and a slow growth of domestic money supply will experience an appreciation of its currency due to the tendencies toward a surplus on either capital or current account.

International Monetary Fund: The International Monetary Fund was established in December 1945 following ratification of the Articles of Agreement of the Fund, formulated at the United Nations Monetary and Financial Conference held at Bretton Woods, New Hampshire in 1944. The fund became a specialized agency *of* the United Nations in 1947. The purposes *of* the fund are to encourage international monetary co-operation, facilitate the expansion and balanced growth of international trade, assist member countries in correcting balance of payments deficits and promote foreign exchange stability. The 'Bretton Woods System', or international monetary system established by the fund, was based upon a policy of fixed exchange rates, the elimination of exchange restrictions, currency convertibility and the development of a multilateral system of international payments. Exchange rates were based upon a par value system which required member countries to constrain fluctuations in their exchange rates within a margin of + 1 per cent around a par value expressed in terms of US dollars, which in turn were directly convertible into goal at a fixed rate. However, following the 1971 decision of the US to suspend the convertibility of dollars into gold, the ministers and central bank governors of the Group of Ten met in December 1971 at the Smithsonian Institute in Washington DC and ratified, the 'Smithsonian Agreement' which—resulted in a 10 per cent devaluation of the dollar and a realignment of exchange rates, including wider margins of fluctuation in lieu of par values. This adjusted par value system was largely abandoned when, following another dollar devaluation in 1973, the European Economic Community member countries introduced a joint system of floating their currencies against the dollar. In 1972, following the initial collapse of the Bretton Woods System of exchange rates, the fund established a Committee on Reform of International Monetary System Related Issues which issued a set of commendations eventually adopted 1976 by the Jamaica Agreement.

International Payments System: A general term referring to the way in which international financial transactions are carried out, that is payments between residents of different countries who hold different domestic currencies. The term covers the different systems of *exchange rates, exchange contrd* and questions concerned with international liquidity.

International Trade: Trade between nations in goods and services. The essential difference between internal trade and international or foreign trade is that the latter involves the use of different currencies and is subject to additional regulations such as tariffs, quotas and exchange controls.

International trade is held to take place because of cost differences between nations or because of the absolute non-availability of goods or services in countries,

International trade leads to gains from trade. The theory of comparative advantage shows that the difference required in costs between nations is not an absolute advantage but a comparative advantage, based on a difference in cost structure among countries.

International Trade Organization: In 1947 the United Nations Economic and Social Council convened in Havana, Cuba, an International Conference on Trade and Development 'for the purpose of promoting the production, exchange and consumption of goods'. The Conference drew up the Havana Charter which proposed both the establishment of an International Trade Organization under the aegis of the United Nations, and a 'code of conduct' for member countries regarding commodity agreements, customs unions, export subsidies, free trade areas, quotas, tariffs and other topics related to the development of international trade. Although 50 countries signed the charter, it failed to receive—the necessary number of ratifications and the idea of a permanent international trade body was temporarily abandoned until 1964 when the United Nations Conference on Trade and Development (UNCTAD) considered the establishment of a universal trade organization. The proposed trade organization would represent all countries, irrespective of United Nation membership, provide a forum for discussing all aspects of international trade, an implement corresponding policy decisions and recommendation. However once again the proposed international Trade Organization was not, set up as to conference established itself as an organ of the United Nations General Assembly which together with the General Agreement on Tariffs and Trade has cried out most of the functions outlined the proposed organization.

Interquartile Range: A measure of dispersion of sample data or distributions, defined as the difference between the upper and lower *quartiles,* and therefore containing the central 50 per cent of the observations on the variables concerned.

Inventory Cycle: Fluctuations in the level of output caused by changes in *inventor v* holdings. Demand for output arises from sales of output and from inventory holding by firms. Sales can be (partly) met from a rundown of inventories such that output is depressed; likewise output is boosted if *inventory investment is* in progress. Many firms try to maintain a constant inventory to sales ratio which implies that changes in sales lead to greater changes in output as the constant ratio is maintained.

Inventory Investment: The accumulation of inventories when production exceeds actual sales. If production is less than sales inventory *disinvestment* takes place. Often such investment is unanticipated and acts as a buffer between output and uncertain sales.

Investment Criteria (for developing countries): Criteria proposed on which to base the allocation of investable resources. Capital is in very scarce supply in developing countries and so it is important that the available supply be allocated in the most efficient manner to obtain development objectives. Many criteria have been proposed by economists, These are often contradictory. Sometimes the contradictions arise because different development goals are assumed by different authors. Different assumptions are made about the priorities which should be reflected in the pattern of investment undertaken. Thus one objective may be to maximize the total output per head at the end of a specified time period (say 10 years). This objective would require a different ordering of investment from the situation where the goals were to maximize output and consumption over a much shorter period. The first objective would require an allocation of investable resources which gave a low priority to consumption in the short term compared to the second.

Investment Grants: Funds made available by government or other agencies B the purpose of encouraging firm to make expenditures on the acquisition of physical capital. These grants are generally provided in the form of a fixed percentage of approved expenditures.

Investment Function: According to Keynes, investment in a country depends on two factorys i) rate of interest ii) Marginal efficiency of capital. A higher interests rate, other things being equal, lowers the investment while or lower rate raises the investment. Marginal efficiency of capital however, is a determinant of far greater importance than interest. HEC in other words is expected rate of returns. M.E.C. exhibits two characteristics i) it is highly uncertain ii) it slopes downward from the right to the left as shown below:

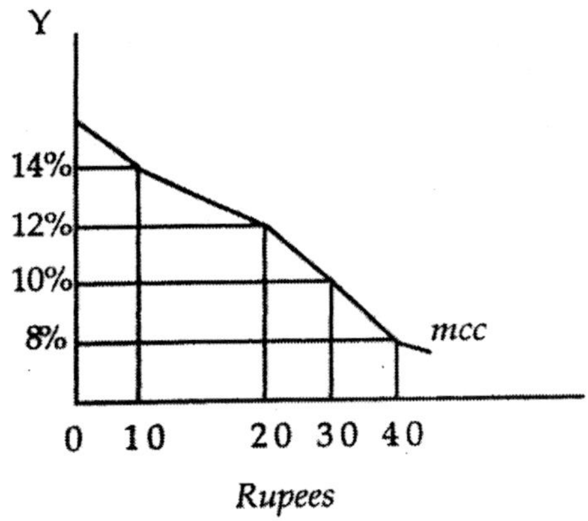

M.E.C. showing investment function is also known as the investment demand curve.

J

Job Evaluation: When the requisite staff is to the appointed, it is essential that the prospective job seeker should exactly know the nature of work and skill that it involves, academic and professional qualification it needs and the relative pay that it carries. Job evaluation is made with a view to have a complete insight on all these related matters.

Job Creation: In its widest sense, job creation aims to reduce the stock of unemployment in recession, either by reducing the flow of redundancies or by increasing the rate of outflow from the ranks of the unemployed. Job creation may be either direct or indirect in form. By direct job creation is meant the provision of jobs in the public sector. This method is favoured by those of dual labour market persuasion and by those who see in the very directness of the measures the prospect of a 'bigger bang' per fiscal pound. Indirect job creation, on the other hand, operates via the subsidization of the private sector. Private sector employers may be given subsidies to preserve employment. Employment subsidies are a relatively recent addition to the array of economic policy measures, and the analytical technique necessary to appraise them are as relatively underdeveloped. It has be claimed that job subsidies can reduce budget deficit and dampen the rate inflation-m the same time as they promote or maintain employment. However, each of these claims has been strongly countered and there is no consensus on the efficacy of the measures in question.

Job Duplication: This occurs when individual has more than one for employment at the same time and t fore is not dependent on only ones of income. It is particularly prevalent underdeveloped countries especial the informal sector.

Job Search: Even in a world of homogeneous commodities there will normally exist some dispersion of prices. Only if perfect information is costlessly provided to market participants will there be a single price in the absence of perfect information, there will be some dispersion in prices because it costs more to learn about alternative prices than this information yields at the margin. The labour market is characterized neither by job/ worker homogeneity nor by perfect information. Thus there will be wage dispersion and because of this it will pay workers to search the market for a better offer.

The more an individual searches the greater the probability that he will locate the highest paying job offer obtainable, although the search process will yield marginally diminishing potential basically because there are fewer options to examine. Clearly, the search for job information is costly--the chief cost being that of time. It is often assumed that the search process is most efficient when the worker is unemployed. There is, therefore, a concept of search unemployment. Here, the cost of search is the income foregone from employment less any unemployment benefits received.

The costs represent an investment on which a return in the form of a higher wage offer is expected. Not all wage offers will be identified: the worker will stop searching when it seems that the benefits to additional search are probably not worth the costs of additional search. An actual or perceived change in the costs and benefits of search will thus have an effect on the optimal duration of search and hence upon search unemployment and wage dispersion.

Job Search Channels: The methods through which jobs are identified and/or obtained. They are classified as either 'formal' or 'informal'. Formal methods include the public employment service, private employment agencies and trade union networks. Informal methods comprise employee referrals and gate applications. Informal search activities are not only the most common they are also the most effective job search methods for *blue-collar workers* - effectiveness here being defined as the change in the probability of finding a job when the particular search activity is used, rather than cost-effective.

Joint Profit Maximization: The maximization of the combined profits of an existing group of firms. This is a feature which can characterize oligopolistic market structures, where firms mutually recognize their interdependence and are thus motivated to overcome rivalry and adopt goals such as joint profit maximization.

Joint profit maximization requires the group of firms to find that industry output level at which industry marginal cost and marginal revenue are equal. Each individual firm's output level is found by equating industry marginal revenue with the firm's marginal cost. If there is variance in the cost conditions facing each individual firm, then this requires each firm adopting an output level which they would not have adopted if acting independently. To induce allegiance to the goal of joint profit maximization side payments between the firms in the oligopoly will be necessary.

Joint Stock Company: Joint stock companies developed out of the requirement by many undertakings for large amounts of financial capital. A distinctive feature of these business units is their issue of financial capital in the form of shares which are of small denomination, thus allowing investors to purchase small or large sums as they please. Dividend payments are made out of profits and are distributed in proportion to the number of shares held.

Regulation over the establishment of stock companies is the responsibility the Registrar of Companies, who em that all legal formalities are carried joint stock companies are often referred to simply as limited companies.

Joint Supply: Same as joint Products: When two or more than two articles are produced together, it is known as joint supply. With sheep breeding, wool and mutton are produced simultaneously. The producer of such joint products has the objective of converting his total expenses by the sale proceeds of the joint articles. An article for which the demand is inelastic he keeps a higher price. Joint supply may be compared to joint demand under which two or more than two articles are demanded together like car and petrol.

K

Keynes Plan: It refers to the proposals made primarily for the establishment of an international Clearing Union at the Bretton Woods Conference in 1944. The functions of this clearing Union was to be on the lines of domestic. Bank and Clearning House. Between the member nations, their debts were to be cleared on the multilateral basis. The members running an adverse balance of payment of a temporary nature were to be given overdraft facility. The plan could not be approved at the aforesaid conference at Brettan Woods. But these proposals all the same remained of historic and academic interest.

This indirect change in the demand for commodities for investment should be distinguished from the direct effects of a change in the general price level on the demand for commodities for consumption as described by the direct real balance effect.

Keynesian economics: A term used to describe macro-economic theories of the level of economic activity using the techniques developed by J. M. Keynes. The methodology of Keynesian economics may be distinguished from neoclassical economics by its concern with aggregate behaviour, especially the income generating effect of total expenditure and the emphasis placed on the investment component in determining the level of activity. The development of Keynesian theory has centred around three related topics: (1) the stability of a market system and particularly its ability to maintain full employment, (2) the role of money in such a system and (3) the long term dynamics of the market economy.

The standard exposition of the Keynesian system attributes the possible instability of the system to rigidity in wages and the existence of a liquidity trap. The latter phenomenon and an interest inelasticity of investment were sufficient to recommend the adoption of fiscal policy as opposed to monetary policy.

Kinked Demand Curve: Based on the presumption that in markets characterised by oligopoly perceived interdependence leads businessmen to believe that reduction of price below that which prevails will be imitated by rivals, but not so with a price rise. This introduces a kink into the demand curve at the prevailing price and a corresponding discontinuity in the marginal revenue curve, both of which result from different perceived elasticities of demand above and below the prevailing price.

Kinky Demand Curve: It is a particular shape of a demand curve that has become very popular under monopoly price determination. This curve is drawn on the assumption that the kink in the demand curve is always at the ruling price. Price above the kink makes the demand curve elastic while for the price below the kink, the demand curve is in-elastic. It can be briefly and clearly explained thus. If a particular dealer raises the price beyond the kink, the other dealers who are his rivals in all probability would not follow suit; with the result that a dealer raising the price would lose a considerable number of his customers. SO the demand curve becomes elastic as the higher price. In case he is to lower the price below the kink and resort to a price cut, the other dealers knowing that they would be directly affected, would also likewise lower the price or their products. Such a situation where each rival has by the some margin reduced the price, there would be no increase in anybody's demand or turnover. Thus demand remains the same even at a lower price so the demand is inelastic below the kink. The upper portion beyond the kink is elastic while the lower portion of DD is below the kink is elastic.

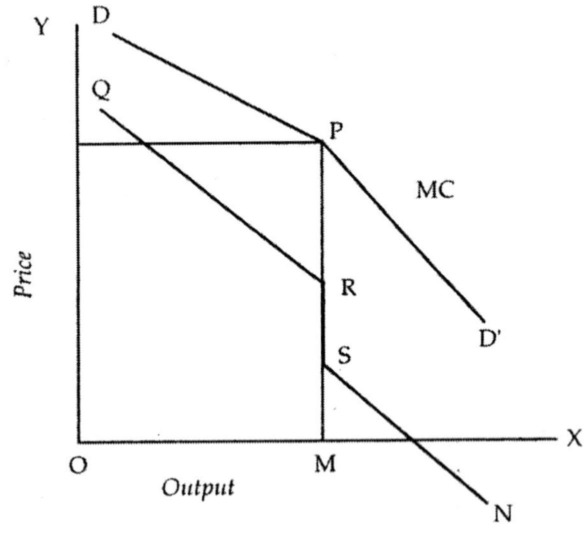

Kondratier Cycle: It is of quite a different and of a much longer duration than the normal business cycle. This cycle is named after the reputed Russian economist N.D. Kondratier who in the twenties of the present century advanced its study. Such a cyclical fluctuation is of a much longer duration of about half a century. A revolutionary change in the technique of production and technological innovation such as mass generation of motive power and mass production of steel coupled with extension of markets and of transport system results into Kondratier cycle.

L

Labour: Any physical or mental exertion that takes place with a view to earn money is called labour. Labour is both a means to an end as well as end.

Labour Force: The labour force basically consists of persons who are either working or looking for work: it comprises the employed plus the unemployed. Those who are not in the labour force are usually students, retired people, housewives, female heads of families and some 'discouraged workers' who are usually not considered as unemployed because they are not actively seeking work.

Labour Force Participation Rate: For the population as a whole, or for any section of it by age, sex, or race, the participation rate is defined as the ratio of he economically active population failing within that category to the total population of that category.

Labour Hoarding: When firms have invested heavily in the hiring and training of a worker they will be reluctant to dismiss that worker during an economic downturn.

As a defensive mechanism, the firm will thus attempt to retain or hoard workers in whom firm-specific investments have been made. Thus at the onset of a recession, labour input is not simultaneously cut back with output and the labour utilization rate falls accordingly.

Labour Intensive: A process or technique of production A is said to be more tabour intensive than an equivalent process or technique B if the ratio of tabour to capital used is greater in A than in B.

Labour Market: A tabour market concerns the activities of hiring and supplying certain tabour to perform certain jobs, and the process of determining how much shall be paid to whom in performing what tasks. In addition, the way in which wages move and the mobility of workers between different jobs and employers falls within the definition. Note that to use the term 'market' is not to imply that tabour is exactly the same as any other commodity; rather, the tábour market is to be seen as a 'place' in economic theory where tabour demand and supply interact.

Law of constant cost: When marginal returns are constant the marginal cost also remains the same. In the above illustration, if a dose cost Rs. 500/- each unit of output would cost Rs. 5/-. It is represented by means of a diagram as below:—

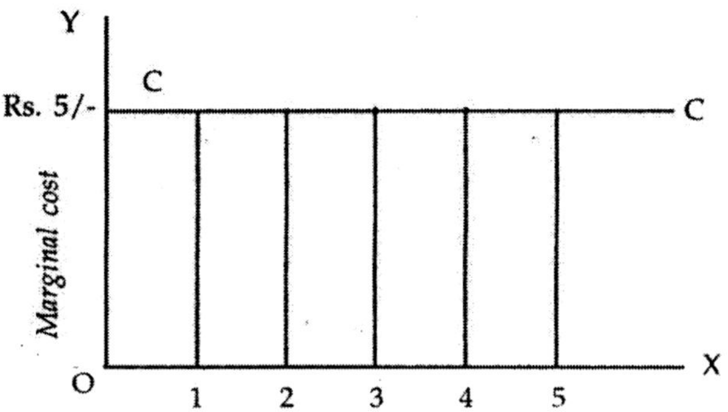

Doses of Capital and labour

Labour Power: A term used by Karl Marx to describe the commodity which workers sell to capitalists. The distinction which Marx makes between tabour and tabour power stems from his development of the labour theory of value. The price of all commodities is related to the tabour time embodied in their production. The wage rate is the price of the commodity tabour power, and is determined by the tabour embodied in the production of the workers' means of subsistence, though the level of subsistence was not fixed e.g. at the physiological minimum but was subject to an upward drift with the development of society.

Labour-saving Techniques: A technological process or production method which is biased towards mechanization and sparing use of manpower. If manpower is scarce then these are the ideal processes to implement, and are more common in industrialized nations than less developed countries.

Labour's Share: The share of wages in the national income. There are two competing theories of tabour's share: the marginal productivity theory with its emphasis on relative factor prices, factor quantities and technology, and the neo-Keynesian theory stressing aggregate demand and differences in savings propensities between the classes of workers and capitalists. The share of wages in national income has increased considerably over the course of the present century, to about three-quarters. In part, this increasing share is explicable in terms of structural changes within the economy, namely a shift towards high tabour share industries, and measurement biases in the form of the undervaluation of government capital income and farm tabour income.

Labour Standard: A term coined by J. R. Hicks to express his particular interpretation of the manner in which wages were determined. According to Hicks, it is no longer useful to regard wage determination/inflation as simply determined by the interaction of supply and demand, Rather, wages are best understood as the product of an interplay between social and economic forces, and the money wage level as determining the money supply.

Labour Theory of Value: A theory employed by the classical economists, e.g. Ricardo and especially Marx, to explain the determination of relative prices on the basis of quantities of tabour, immediate and accumulated, embodied in goods. By immediate labour is meant the current effort of a worker and by accumulated tabour is meant the services of capital which represent the past input of labour. It was argued that prices would be proportional to quantities of embodied tabour in goods.

Land: A term used in economics to cover not only that part of the earth's surface not covered by sea, but also all those natural resources such as forests, minerals, resources of the sea, soil fertility, etc. which can be used in the process of production.

Land Intensive: A process or technique of production A is said to be more land intensive than an equivalent process or technique B, if the ratio of land to other factors of production used is greater in A than in B.

Land Reform and Tenure: A broad term generally referring to the possibilities of obtaining increases in prosperity in the rural areas usually in developing countries through changes in the institutional arrangements in the agricultural sector there is a wide variety of such arrangements and several are inimical to progress. Sometimes ownership of land is extremely fragmented with each family having only a tiny plot of land. New equipment and machinery may not be economic propositions on such small farms. Output per acre may be lower than on larger farms simply because the farmer cannot afford the inputs necessary to increase productivity.

Land Tax: A tax based on land values or size of land holdings. It has been proposed by some economists as a device for mobilizing any surplus from agriculture and for encouraging productivity growth. The experience of Japan in the nineteenth century is cited as an example in favour of this tax. The tax could be formulated in such a way that it encouraged farmers to cultivate land more intensively. Administration of a land tax could be very expensive in most developing countries. Considerable information on land-holdings would be required. On balance the arguments in favour of such a tax appear stronger than those against it. What is frequently lacking is the political will to introduce it because of the influence of the landowning classes on government.

Least Squares: A general term descriptive of the basis of a family of econometric estimation techniques. The objective of the estimators based on the principle is to minimize the sum of the squares of the vertical distances between the observed data points, and the regression line. Examples of this type of estimator include ordinary least squares; two stage least squares and generalized least squares.

Letter of Credit: A document issued by a bank on behalf of a customer which guarantees payment by the batik of cheques drawn by the customer, or more commonly today of bills drawn on that customer by parties from whom he has bought goods. Letters of credit are used largely in association with bills of exchange, to which they give added security in the financing of foreign trade.

Level of Significance: A concept used in hypothesis testing to determine the critical value against which to compare the test statistic. A test at, say, the 5 per cent significance level involves choosing the critical values such that under the null hypothesis there is 5 per cent probability of the test statistic failing outside them.

Leverage: An indicator of the relationship between long-term debt and capital employed. It is measured by the ratio, long-term debt total capital employed. The denominator includes all fixed interest securities. This measure considers that the more relevant issue concerning capital structure is the proportion of capital employed represented by long-term debt. All capital is invested in a company's activities and it is not meaningful to say that any one operation was financed by any particular class of funds.

Linear Programming: A technique for the formalization and analysis of constrained optimization problems in which the objective function is a linear function, and is to be maximized or minimized subject to a number of linear inequality constraints. The method is very useful in such problems as the determination of the optimal allocation of scarce resources.

Liquidity: The quality in assets of 'nearness' to free spending power. Money is by definition completely liquid. Other assets vary in degree of liquidity, depending on whether they meet two, not wholly consistent, criteria. An asset is the more liquid the more readily-in terms of time and other transactions costs involved-it may be converted into money. The second characteristic of liquidity, emphasized more strongly in recent times, is degree of freedom from the risk of fluctuation in capital value. By the convertibility criterion a deposit withdrawable at short notice may be only fractionally more liquid than a 5-year giltedged stock which is readily saleable in a highly organized market. But by the criterion of capital risk, the stock is decidedly less liquid than a deposit, or for that matter, than a short-term bill.

Locational Interdependence: An interrelationship between firms where one firm's decision concerning a choice of location for its plant is affected by the locational choices of its competitors. Thus locational interdependence can be seen as one facet of the problems dealt with in the theory of oligopoly, since in oligopoly there is an identifiable effect of any firm's actions on the experiences of its rivals.

Various attempts have been made to analyse the patterns of location which will emerge when interdependence exists. For example, in an early, classic, contribution H. Hotelling demonstrated that, under certain assumptions, two rivals serving a market which was spread out in a straight line would both locate at the midpoint of the line. However, as with oligopoly theory in general, no single solution has been developed to the problem of location patterns when locational interdependence exists; both the particular circumstances of the case analysed and the assumptions made exert a strong influence on the results obtained.

Location Quotient: A statistical measure of the extent to which a particular economic activity is comparatively over or under-represented in the economy of a region, compared to its representation in the economy as a whole.

Location Theory: That body of economic theory which analyse, the forces which determine the location of economic activity, and seeks to explain, and predict the spatial pattern of the location of economic agents.

Long Cycle Theory: A prolonged period of relatively prosperous times followed by a period of hard times of similar duration, often called the Kondratieff cycle. It extends much beyond the periodicity of the trade cycle. A full cycle being considered of about 50 years in length. Some economists considered that price and interest rate movements alone were involved, with the Kondratieff a price and not an output phenomenon.

Long-dated Securities: Securities in the form of debt rather than equities—e.g. gilt-edged stock or debentures—which have a long term to their maturity dates, usually more than 10 years. Long-dated securities and the dealings in them are frequently referred to, collectively, as the 'long end of the market'.

Long-haul Economies: The tendency for transport costs to rise less than in proportion to distance travelled. Thus where long-haul economies are present the average cost per unit distance travelled is a decreasing function of distance. These economies arise principally because any mode of transport will involve certain costs which are fixed and uninfluenced by the distance of the journey. The fixed costs consist of the terminal costs of movement—i.e. those involved at each end of the journey, such as loading and unloading a cargo.

Long Rate: The rate of interest, or rather set of interest rates, obtainable on long-dated securities, and therefore payable on new long-term borrowings.

Long-run: A time period relating to the process of

production during which there is time to vary all factors of production, but not sufficient time to change the basic technological processes being used. In the very long run it is possible totally to change the type of technology being used.

Long-run Consumption Function: The functional relationship between consumption and income over periods of over 50 years. In these studies 10-year averages of income and consumption are usually considered to remove the effects of the business cycle.

Long-run Marginal Cost: The extra cost of producing an extra unit of output in the *long run*. Since all costs are variable in the long run there is no 'law' governing the shape of the long-run marginal cost curve-it may increase, decrease or be constant with the level of output. It nonetheless obeys the same geometric rules as the short-run marginal cost curve in that it must cut the long-run average cost curve (LRAC) at its minimum point, must lie below it when LRAC is declining and must lie above it when LRAC is rising.

Long-term Capital: Capital in financial (i.e. monetary) form which if borrowed on *debt* terms, has a long term to maturity, usually over 10 years; or which alternatively is raised by an equity issue and hence is not repayable at all, other than on the winding up of the company.

Loss Leader Pricing: The practice of diversified firms who offer some portion of their product range at prices below cost, in the belief that this will encourage sales of other higher profit margin products. This is common amongst retailers who use 'loss leaders' to attract customers, who then may buy high profit margin goods as a matter of convenience or impulse.

Loss-offsetting: Provisions Generally refers to the

arrangement whereby losses from a project can be offset against income from other sources. It is very significant when analysing the effects of income taxation on investment. Such taxation by itself reduces the return from a project but if loss offsetting arrangements exist the government shares in the gains as well as in the losses and the mean expected return from a new project may not be reduced.

Loss Leader: Is a different type of strategy in accordance with which certain products may be sold either at no profit or even at a nominal loss. This is with a view to induce buyers to visit their retail stores, so that certain other articles with higher margin profit may also be sold. It would more than neutralise the loss incurred in the sale of certain specific products.

Lump: It pertains to a system prevailing in the construction industry where self employed persons offer their services at a sub-standard basis. Such a practice is discouraged by the government for apart from its other defects, it leads to tax evasion as well.

Lump Sum Tax: As the words indicate it does not mean that the person pays all his tax dues in one go. Lump sum tax means its imperative nature irrespective of what are his circumstance or his income for the imposition of taxation, it is of an usual occurrence; for example a tax of Rs. 1,000 or persons of over weight by 50kg or more. Such a tax as said above is considered impractical and is not equitable either.

Luxury Goods: Luxury is defind as a superfluous good. Luxury goods are non-essential. They are consumed for the pleasure that they import such as costly carpets or five star hotel living and entertainment.

M

Macro-Economics: Study of the origin of Macro-Economics is traced to the Mercantalist school of thought as early as the 16th century. Its influence lasted till the 18th century. It discussed the ways by which a nation could grow rich and become prosperous. It advocated a favourable balance of payment approach for a nation in the sphere of foreign trade; which would result into inflow of gold.

Malthus, Rev. Thomas Robert: Malthus was a clergyman and a professor of Modern History and Political Economy at the East India College at Hail-eybury. Though he made contributions to monetary analysis and the 'theory of gluts' and engaged in a celebrated controversy with his friend Ricardo, he is best remembered as the author of an essay on the priciple onthe population.

In this he challenged the conventional view of economists that a numerous and increasing population was synonymous with wealth and argued that numbers would increase until they met the constraint of limited food supplies. He stated that population tended to grow in a geometric progression and food supply in arithmetic progression.

Population growth could be checked either positively by e.g. wars, pestilence etc. or negativelyby e.g. moral restraint, later marriages etc. This Malthusian theory of wages implied a constant level of wages at the subsistence level. Both population and wages have tended to increase in developed countries despite the prediction of Malthus; this is due to technical progress, whose role Malthus undervalued, to a decline in the birthrate as income rises and to the opening of new lands.

The spectre of the Malthusian problem is still raised today in underdeveloped countries as they import the medicine that gives developed country deathrates along with developing country birthrates. It is also raised on a global scale by the eco-doomsters who predict that growth in population and industrial production will cause the world to run out of resources.

Management: Those staff within the firm who exert control over its activities on behalf of owners. Of interest to economists is the influence which the pursuit by management of their objectives can have on firm behaviour. The management class has in the post World War two period become increasingly professional. The benefits which management science can provide for management training are increasingly accepted.

Management Science: In he context or the study of firms, this discipline applies scientific principles to aid pursuit of operational efficiency with regard to business objectives. Importance is therefore attached to deducing the principles underlying rational co-ordination of the units which comprise firms.

Manager-Controlled Firm: A company which has no individual shareholder or group of share-holders owning a sufficiently high. proportion of the voting stock to exert control over company policy The execution and design of policy is thereby placed in the hands of the company's managers.

Managerial Capitalism: The organization of the economy into large corporations with the power over resources located within a definable managerial class separated from the property owning class and largely independent of their control. It differs from corporate capitalism that the managerial class pursues goals which may be independent of those of workers, the state and society.

Managerial Discretion: Refers to the ability of a corporation's manager to pursue objectives which they themselves deem beneficial. The extent to which this discretionary behaviour can be sustained will be determined by how competitive product and capital markets are.

Managerial Revolution: A label associated with the Galbraithian idea that economic power has passed from capital to the owners of technical expertise.

Managerial Theories of the Firm: Have developed from a belief that contemporary capitalism is characterized by the dominance within the production sector of large corporations, where ownership and control is separated between shareholders and managers respectively.

It can then be argued that given imperfect capital markets and uncompetitive product markets, managers will have the scope to pursue objectives other than profit maximization.

Managerial Theories of the Firm: Have generally made use of managerial utility functions to formalize the objectives pursued. When maximized subject to given specified constraints, predictions on firm behaviour can be derived. Thus for example, a specification representative of growth theories of the firm is one in which managers are assumed to maximize a utility function whose arguments are growth and the firm's valuation ratio.

This is maximized subject to a constraint imposed exogeneously by the capital market, which states that the firm's valuation ratio must achieve a value greater than or equal to the valuation ratio set by the most dangerous raiderfirm, this being based on the policy it would pursue if successful.

Managerial Utility Function: This relationship specified the arguments upon which the preference ordering of firms' managers depends. Variables commonly used are growth, stair outlay, valuation ratio and managerial involvements.

Manpower Policy: An attempt to improve the functioning of the labour market, and, if possible, the tride-offbetween unemployment and inflation. Two main forms of manpower policy may be distinguished.

The first accepts the existing characteristics of supply and demand and aims for bettermatches between workers and jobs by improving placement efforts and by counselling workers looking for jobs and employers looking for workers.

Programmes of this kind may also include schemes for increasing the mobility of workers. The second form attempts to influence the pattern of the supply of labour by upgrading skills and abilities.

Manual Workers: Employees engaged in physical work and who are paid a wage. Frequently used interchangeably with blue-collar worker. The opposite of nonmanual worker.

Margin: In economics, at the margin' means at the point where the last unit is produced or consumed.

Marginal: A marginal unit is the extra unit of something, as with marginal cost, marginal utility etc.

Marginal Cost: The extra cost of producing an extra unit of output. In the short run the marginal cost curve slopes upwards due to the operation of the law of diminis*hing returns.* Note also that marginal cost cannot be affected by the level *of fixed costs.* Quite simply, if an extra unit of output is produced fixed costs do not change and hence extra fixed costs must be zero.

Marginal Cost of Funds Schedule: The schedule detailing the true cost of financial capital to the enterprise. In an imperfect capital market the true cost will exceed the *interest rate.*

Firms can raise money to finance investment from many sources and the cost of finance will vary with the source. The least expensive source of finance may be the firms retained profits or its depreciation fund. More expensive will be a *rights issue* or new issue of *equities* or borrowing on fixed interest.

Marginal Cost Pricing: A pricing practice pursued by private firms or public corporations in which price is made equal to *marginal cost.* Given continuous revenue and cost curves, this implies setting price at the point at which the demand curve cuts the marginal cost curve. The market conditions prevailing in perfect competition ensure marginal cost pricing since average and marginal revenue are the same. Hence the requirement for profit maximization, that marginal cost be equal to the marginal revenue, means that price equals marginal cost.

Under *imperfect competition,* however, profits will not be maximized with price equal to marginal cost since average revenue will exceed marginal revenue. Hence marginal cost pricing under imperfect competition will only come about through some form of regulation or taxation. In the public *sector, nationalized industries* are recommended to use marginal cost pricing, the rationale being that it maximizes economic welfare.

Marginal Efficiency of Capital: That unique *rate of discount* which would make the *present value* of the expecied net returns from a *capital asset just* equal to its supply price when there is no rlse in the supply price *of* the asset. The term originates with *Keynes* and is som, enmes known incorrectly as the *internal rate of return.*

Marginal Efficiency of Capital Schedule: The schedule detailing the long-run equilibrium relationship between the desired *capital stock* and the *interest rate.* At all points along this schedule the *marginal efficiency of capital* is just equal to the *interest rate.*

The schedule is downward sloping reflecting *diminishing returns* to the capital stock. At the firm level this schedule is sometimes considered to represent the demand curve for capital. However, it cannot do so for the concept of the marginal efficiency of capital takes no account of the rising supply price of capital assets the firm will encounter in the short run.

Marginal Efficiency of Investment: That *rate of discount* which would make the present value of the expected net returns from the *capital asset* just equal to its supply price where it is recognized that this price will rise in the short-run

Marginal Efficiency of Investment Schedule: The demand curve for investment. The schedule detailing the relationship between the *marginal efficiency of investment* and the interest rate. Investment will be carried on until this point in the short run while in the long run the equilibrium of the capital stock is given by the point of equality of the *marginal efficiency of capital* and the interest rate. In contrast to the *marginal efficiency of capital schedule* this schedule describes a flow and not a *stock* relationship.

Marginal Per Capita Reinvestment Quotient Criterion: An investment criterion with the objective of maximizing income per head at a future date. It states that the best allocation of resources will be achieved by equating the marginal per capita reinvestment quotient of capital in each of its uses. It is assumed that profits are reinvested and wages consumed.

Marginal Physical Product: This is defined as the addition to total output resulting from the employment of an additional unit of labour, and may be derived from the *production junction* holding other factors fixed.

The marginal physical product schedule may be regarded as the demand curve for labour. Labour is employed up to the point at which the payment to the last unit equal to the output produced by the last unit. It is more conventional by means of a simple change in scale to convert marginal physical product into value of marginal physical product namely by multiplying the former by product price. A wage rise, for example, will have a negative *substitution effect* as the firm substitutes cheaper capital for the more expensive labour, thereby reducing the quantity of labour demanded.

There will also be a negative scale effect as a wage increasc lcads to a higher *marginal cost* of production which in turn reduces the firm's optimal output and hence *derived demand* for labour. The two effects reinforce each other to lead to an unambiguously inverse relationship between wages and the firm's demand for labour. This demand curve is more elastic than the short-run demand,

Marginal Product: The extra *output* obtained by employing one extra unit of a given *input* . Thus the term should be qualified with respect to which input is in question--e.g. the marginal product of tabour, the marginal product of capital, etc.

Marginal Rate of Tax: Usually refers to the rate of tax on an incremental unit of income but also applies to increments of expenditure, wealth or gifts. The higher the marginal rate of tax the greater is the substitution *effect likely* to be. Thus very high marginal rates of income tax could encourage people to take more leisure or possibly to undertake less risky investments.

Marginal Rate of Technical Substitution: The marginal rate of technical substitution of two inputs, for example, of labour for capital is the difference in the amount of capital that needs to be substituted for a very small reduction in the amount of tabour employed in order to maintain the level of output. Its value is equal to the ratio of the marginal product of tabour to the marginal product of capital and is equal to the slope of the production *isoquant.*

Marginal Rate of Transformation: The numerical value of' the slope of the production possibility frontier. The marginal rate of transforming good A into good B is the fall in the rate of output of I good A which permits an additional unit of good B to be produced. It is equal to the ratio of the marginal cost of good B to the marginal cost of good A.

Marginal Revenue: Is the addition to the total revenue by the sale of an additional unit. Under conditions of perfect competition, marginal revenue is equal to the price of the product; for a delaer can produce and sell more at the same prevalent price. If he sells 10 units of an article at 10/ each the told revenue is Rs. 100/- sale of an additional (11th) units at the same price of Rs. 10/- raises to total revenue to Rs. 110/- (11 units X Rs. 10/-). Marginal revenue thus is Rs. 10 (Rs. 110-Rs.100) and is equal to the price.

The difference between the two curves of marginal revenue is graphically shown below.

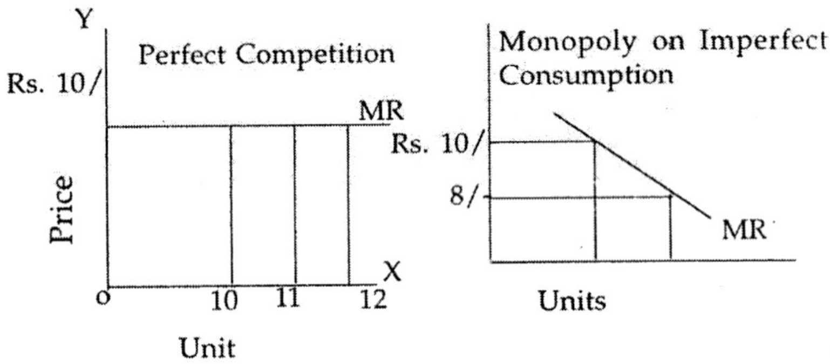

Marginal Revenue Product: The marginal physical product multiplied by the marginal revenue from the sale of the extra unit of output from the employment of the extra unit of input. Under perfect competition price equals marginal revenue, so that we can write

$MRP = MPP. P$

where MPP is marginal physical product and P is price.

Marginal Utility of Money: The rate at which an individual's *utility* increases as his personal budget (income) is expanded by one unit . When consumers maximize utility it will be the case that the marginal utility of each good purchased will equal its price multiplied by the marginal utility of money.

Strictly speaking, the term is better defined as the *marginal utility of income* since money as money has particular attributes which affect the utility it may provide to someone holding it. *Marshall* assumed the marginal utility of money was constained did not change as the prices of goods in an individual's shopping basket changed. This was held to be reasonable as long as the items in question formed a small proportion of the consumer's budget.

Market: Generally, any context in which the sale and purchase of goods and services takes place. There need be no physical entity corresponding to a market-it may, for example, consist of the network of telecommunications across the world such that, say, shares are traded. Various classifications of markets have been suggested.

Market Classification: Various ways of classifying markets exist. The market for something could be defined according to the *substitutes* available for a good in question. That is, the size of the market is determined bytherange of goods thatcan be held to be substitutes for the good.

Another suggestion is that the market for a good is

determined by the extent to which producers of the good express concern about the reactions of other producers to any change in the price, output or quality of their own product. Finally, it has been suggested that the type of market should be classified by the extent to which new producers can secure entry into a given market.

This seems reasonable where the *barriers to entry* are based on product differences between existing and new firms, but less reasonable if the barriers are based on deliberate policies by existing firms to prevent entry-e.g. by engaging m price reductions below new firms' average costs of production, legal manoeuvres etc.

Market Demand Curve for Labour: With a constant product price, the market or industry demand curve is simply the horizontal summation of constituent firms' *marginal revenue product* curves. However, increased output resulting from a fall in the price of labour can only be marketed at a reduced price.

This reduced price will feedback into labour demand at the level of the firm by reducing the value of labour's marginal revenue product; i.e. the curve will shift leftwards. Consequently, the market demand curve will have a steeper slope than that of the constituent firms. The implication is that unions will seek to organize an entire industry and thus reduce the *elasticity of derived demand.*

Market Economy: An economic system in which decisions about the allocation of resources and production are made on the basis of prices generated by voluntary exchanges between producers, consumers, workers and owners of *factors of production.* Decision making in such an economy is decentralized.

Market Failure: The inability of a system of private *markets* to provide certain goods either at all or at the most desirable or 'optimal' level. In general, market failure arises because of (1) *nonexcludability* and/,or (2) *non-rival consumption* of a good. Non-excludability means that individuals who have not paid for a good cannot be prevented from enjoying its benefits. For example, everyone benefits from clean air whether they have contributed to an anti-pollution programme or not.

In this case individuals will not pay for a good which they can obtain at no cost. The market system of exchange cannot operate. If a good is nonrival, its consumption by one person does not preclude its enjoyment by anyone else. Units which prevents people from using the good is undesirable since the good could be made available at no cost to someone who would benefit from it.

For example, it' I am inoculated against disease I obtain a purely personal benefit but I also provide a benefit to everyone else in the community by reducing the risk of infection. This is a case of a beneficial *externality* being produced by my consumption. In the presence of externalities markets may fail to produce the optimal level of output—though some economists argue that the problem may be overcome by private bargaining.

The existence of market failure is usually held to provide a case for collective or government action to improve *allocative efficiency.*

Market Forces: Pressures produced by the free play of market supply and demand, which induce adjustment in prices and/or quantities traded.

Market Imperfection: Any deviation from the conditions necessary for *perfect competition.* This should be distinguished from *market failure,* whichis in the inability of a private market to prwide certain goods in sufficient quantities.

Marketing: A term used to cover those activities of firms associated with the sales and distribution of product(s). Broadly speaking it covers such activities as sales promotion, advertising and market research: i.e. all activities which promote and organize the sale of products to the purchaser.

Marketing Boards: These have been set up in a number of African countries, for example, Nigeria and Ghana and they serve various purposes. They give small farmers a stable and secure market for their produce and because the goods are then marketed on a large scale on international markets, the authorities have a better basis for bargaining for a fair price. Sometimes the marketing boards will pay farmers a price greater than the current world price in order to subsidize their activities.

However this system is also used to provide revenue for the government as a form of forced savings on the part of the growers as they are often paid below the market price. This is usually done as an attempt to raise capital where the level of voluntary savings and investment is very low.

The disadvantages are that it does not create much incentive for small farmers unless they are sure that they will receive the benefits from this revenue. As an example, one of the marketing boards in Ghana provided funds to build a hall of residence for the University of Ghana, near Accra.

A further problem with the system is the high incidence of smuggling; in central Ghana a great deal of cocoa is smuggled across the borders by small farmers who can receive nearly double the price in Togo or Ivory Coast.

Market Orientation: In Location Theory a market orientation is generally explained on the grounds that production is 'weight gaining'—i.e. weight per unit of output is greater than the weight per unit of raw materials which have to be moved to the factory—because of the addition of some local or generally available input consequently costs of movement will be minimized by locating production near the market thus minimizing the transportation of the relatively heavy output.

An alternative explanation of market orientation would be the advantage., in terms of information. of close contact with the market.

Market Power: Is the ability of a single, or group of buyers or seller(s) to influence the price of the product or service in which it is trading. A *perfectly* competitive market in equilibrium, ensures the complete absence of market power.

Market Share: The proportion of total market sales accounted for by one firm. It has been argued that the maintenance of market share is an important objective of firms in oligopolistic market structures.

Market Socialism: Sociolist economic system which leaves the day-to-day running of the econoymy to the market me chanism. Oskar Lange originally put forward the notation in 1930's that the means of production can be socially owned and basic decision and directions of development may be ceatrally planned but otherwise the operation of the economy may be left to market forces.

Marshall, Alfred: An English economist, Marshall spent most of his academic life as Professor of Economics at Cambridge. A mathematician by training, Marshall limited the use of mathematics in his published works. Although a pioneer of marginal analysis Marshall never totally abandoned his link with English Classical economic thought. In contrast with *Stanley Jevons* and the *Austrian School,* he emphasized the costs of production as much as the utility of consumption in his theory of value.

To the extent that Marshall used a 'real cost' theory of value based on the disutility of labour together with the waiting required for saving, he emphasized, like the *Classical School,* the ultimate importance of accumulation, rather than the efficiency aspect of resource allocation stressed by Leon Walras, Jevons, and the Austrians. Marshall's analysis of allocation, although static, was not as restrictive as the *general equilibrium,* stationary, and perfectly competitive models of the *Lausanne School,* Instead he favoured partial analysis of markets with particular emphasis on the long-run development of industries in a less than perfectly competitive setting.

The fundamental idea of Marshall's work is the power *of demand* and supply to generate equilibrium prices in markets. Marshall was as critical of' the classical school as he was *of* the Austrians, claiming that both had a one-sided view of price determination. He stressed that demand and costs of production each play an important role in the determination of equilibrium values. Marshall envisaged price determination as the outcome of the interaction of market demand and market supply.

Marshall derived the law of a downward sloping demand curve from the hypothesis (a) that individuals obtain utility from commodities at a declining rate *(falling marginal utility)* and (b) that the *marqinal utility qfincome* does not vary.

The individual is in equilibrium when the utility gained from consuming one more unit of a commodity is just equal to the loss of utility involved in spending money on that commodity. Given equilibrium, a fall in price of the commodity will induce the individual to purchase more of that commodity since utility per unit of expenditure will be increased. The conclusion which Marshall drew from this is that the demand schedule for all individuals will be negatively sloped in general. Marshall introduced the concept of *elasticity* of demand to describe the responsiveness of quantity demanded to a change in price.

Marshall was also concerned to compare intergroup utilities both through time and in a static framework. The former led him to develop a theory of *time preference* based on marginal utility; and the latter to a discussion of the concept of *consumer's surplus.* Marshall was aware of the limitations which the assumptions imposed on his demand theory. Marshall envisaged equilibrium in a market as the result of price formation arising from the point of intersection of the downward sloping demand curve, and a supply schedule. The supply schedule shows the price at which individual firms are willing to supply the commodity. The value of a commodity is determined by the forces of demand and supply acting like two blades of a pair of scissors.

Behind demand is marginal utility determining the

demand price of buyers, behind supply is marginal effort and sacrifice determining supply price of sellers. This view although similar to the Austrian School version is distinguished by Marshall's conception of the cost of production. Marshall distinguishes between real cost of production' and 'expenses *of* production'.

The former consists *of* the disutility of labour, and the sacrifice or waiting involved in providing capital, He argued that the market valuation of two unequal real costs (expenses of production) might be the same. Actual prices may not reflect the real costs of production. Marshall was well aware of the limitations which a static framework placed on his analysis. He emphasized the changes in production and consumption decisions which may occur over time. Principally he distinguished between the different time periods over which the forces tending to establish equilibrium are operative. He considered: (a) a period where all supplies are fixed and prices correspond to market values; (b) the short period when productive elements are free to vary and supply can be increased up to the point of maximum capacity feasible with the current capital stock; and (c) the long period when all determinants of supply are free to vary given the existing technology, and (d) Marshall seems to have considered the very long period where technology is a variable. In the short and long periods prices tend towards what Marshall calls normal values and the earnings of factors tend towards their real costs of production. The use of time in Marshall's analysis allowed him not only to apply theory to concrete problems where constraints on adjustment operate, but also to formulate a theory of income distribution which differed from the marginal productivity theory insofar as the availability of factors is a variable through time, and the quantity supplied is determined by price. In the short run for example, the incomes of many factors are in the nature of rent or what Marshall calls quasi-rent.

Marxist Economics: A school of economic thought which seeks to analyse the social and economic development of the capitalist economic system. Modern Marxist economists are a diverse group ranging from the more dogmatic followers of the works of Karl Marx to those, sympathetic but critical, economists who are prepared to modify the tenets of orthodox Marxism. In particular the revival of Marxist analysis in the 1960s and 1970s was largely due to the partial integration of Marx's economic thought into mainstream economic theory, Many Marxists have recognized the significance of modern economic theories of aggregate demand growth. Adaptation of Marxian economic theory by such prominent Marxists as P. Baran and P. Sweezy to include Keynesian economic elements and, the real world changes of the capitansT system have brought about increasing recognition of the contribution of Marx to economic thought.

Material Forces of Production: The term used by Marx to define the real economic foundation of any society. The forces of production are the factories, equipment, tools, production skills, scientific knowledge, techniques of production, education of the labour force etc. and they differ according to the state of development attained in any society. These forces of production are the major determinants of the social relations of production.

Matrix: A rectangular array of numbers. A matrix of order m x *n* has m rows and *n* columns. The typical element of a matrix is often denoted as *aij*, which implies that it occupies the *i* th row and *j* th column. Matrices are often used to simplify notation when dealing with large numbers of simultaneous equations.

Maturity: The date upon which the liability of the issuer of a *bond* is due to be extinguished. The date for the repayment of the *principal*.

Maximum Likelihood: A term descriptive of a general econometric *estimation* technique which involves the maximization of the likelihood function of the sample observations with respect to the values of the *parameters* of the equation(s) being estimated. It chooses these values of the parameters which are 'most likely' to have generated the sample observations.

Mean: A commonly used measure of the central tendency of a variable which can be calculated either for a sample or for an entire population.

Median: A measure of the central tendency of a variable. The median of a sample of observation on a variable is that value above 50 per cent of the observations lie. It is often used instead of the mean where the distribution of observations is highly skewed, since under these circumstances it gives a clearer idea of where the distribution is centred.

Median Location Principle: A rule for finding the location at which the total amount of transport involved in serving a group of physical dispersed markets is minimized.

Median Voter Theorem: A theorem concerning collective choice in a democratic society which predicis that poloiticians will most closely represent the views of those voters at the centre of political or social spectrum.

Mediation: Intervention in an *industrial dispute* by an independent and impartial third party who examines the argument of both sides and makes a recommendation for resolving the dispute. The parties are, however, under no obligation to accept this recommendation.

Medium of Exchange: Any asset or instrument which serves an intermediary function in the exchange process. i.e. something which a seller of goods or services accepts in exchange, not for itself but in the knowledge that it can be used in further exchange to buy whatever he wants. As such, a medium of exchange facilitates the act of exchange, eliminating the inconveniences and search costs of barter. To act as a medium of exchange is a prime function of *money,* but historically many objects and commodities have served this purpose.

Merchant Banks: In the UK denotes one of a group of institutions that carry on a very varied range of financial or finance related activities. Amongst these the acceptance of commercial bills and the financing of overseas trade are prominent and the major merchant banks are all accepting houses. The term originated in the last century with institutions that came to combine overseas trade financing with actual merchanting, but which mostly dropped their trading activities to specialize in finance and especially acceptance business. Later, arising from their overseas connections, the larger houses became prominently involved in raising long-term finance for foreign governments and large-scale overseas enterprises. In this century this expertise in raising capital has been largely directed to the home market and most merchant banks have become issuing houses, arranging security issues for domestic users of capital. In recent decades they have moved into the broadening area of corporate financial advisory work-assisting in capital reconstructions, advising on mergers and acquisitions--and the similarly expanding business of portfolio management, especially on behalf of pensions funds. As bankers they take deposits mainly in large sums and for defined periods, and lend mostly to corporate borrowers. They are active as foreign exchange dealers, operate extensively in the eurocurrency,—markets. Different houses combine these activities in differing proportions; some of the smaller ones, financially speaking, retain connections with, or are offshoots of, trading enterprises.

Merger: An amalgamation of two firms where the respective shareholders agree to combine their equity capital to form a single new company. Agreement between the shareholders involves the receipt of shares in the new company in exchange for shares in the old companies at some suitably determined rate.

Merit Bad: A commodity, the consumption of which it is argued should be discouraged or prevented even though individuals choose to consurne it. In such cases it is claimed that through ignorance or inability, the individual is not the best judge of his or her welfare.

Microeconomics: The term used to describe those parts of economic analysis whose concern is the behaviour of individual units, in particular, consumers and *firms,* rather than with aggregates such as *unemployment,* the price level, *national income* etc. which are the subject of *macroeconomics.*

The economic analysis of individual behaviour concentrates on *consumer demand theory* and to a lesser extent on the *theory of the allocation of time*. The analysis of firm behaviour concentrates on *production* decisions and price theory.Much of the, analysis is related to the type of market in which the firm operates, in particular, with the degree of competition.

Minimum Wage Legislation: Such laws represent an attempt to improve the standard of living of workers by setting a floor on the hourly wage rates that can be paid by firms. The *marginal productivity doctrine* states that the effects of such legislation will be to reduce the equilibrium level of employment in covered industries, *ceteris paribus*. In ideal circumstances, however, the minimum wage is set so as to increase both the wage and the level of employment by eliminating monopsonistic *exploitation*. In practice, minimum wage legislation has been shown in almost all cases to have had an adverse effect upon employment, particularly that of teenagers. This demonstrates the ifficulty of formulating a specific wage hat eliminates exploitation without causing unemployment. Two- tier minimum wage structures might protect teenage employment; teenagers might then be hired at a rate below the general minimum for a limited period of time during which they could be trained and their productivity raised to normal levels.

Minority Control: Refers to the ability of an individual or organization to gain effective control over a *company*, despite possessing less than 51 per cent of the ordinary voting stock of that company. This can occur in circumstances where there are dispersed and inert stockholders, which facilitates the use of proxy machinery by the minority group to gain control over a majority of the voting shares. Proxy machinery enables the owners of voting shares in a firm to exercise the right of choosing whom to nominate as a proxy at annual board meetings.

Mint: The place where money in coin form is made. Since earliest times the state has controlled the minting of money.

Mixed Estimation: Estimation which involves the use of extraneous information.

Mixed Market Economy: A system which combines competitive private enterprise with some degree of central control. While the allocation of resources between alternate uses is largely determined by individual actions through the price mechanism, the authorties play some role in determining the level of aggregate output by means of monetary and fiscal policies, and in determining the distribution of income by means of progressive taxation and welfare legislation. In some cases the government may take control of sectors of the economy by nationalizing certain industries. Such a blend of private and public control characterizes most of the industrialized capitalist world.

Mode: A measure of the central tendency of a variable. The mode of a sample of observations is that value which occurs with greatest frequency.

Monetarism: A school of economic thought which argues that disturbances within the monetary sector are the principal cause ofinstabifity m the economy. The term 'monetarism' was inroduced by Karl Brunner in 1068 and is mwst commonly employed to describe the school of thought which argues that changles in the level of aggregate money income are due essentially to prior mutiey stock changes. The monetarism is now considered of such importance must also be attributed to the failure of the Keynesian orthodoxy to explain the emergence of high and sustained levels of unemployment and inflation in many Western industrial countries in the late 1960s. In its earliest phase monetarism rested on an elaboration of the simple quantity theory of money which had explained the determination of the general price level in classical economics. Thus it argued that in the long run changes in the money stock influenced the value of nominal variables but had minimal effect on the quantity of output or employment. The central propositions of monetarism as it emerged in the late 1960s could be summarized as follows.

First, the demand for money function was more stable and better defined statistically than many of the components of aggregate demand. This implied that the income velocity of circulation in the quantity theory of money was relatively stable although it was now admitted that this was a function of several other economic variables, one of which was the interest rate.

Second, the unique properties of money were emphasized, It was argued that money was a commodity which was substitutable for a wide range of other commodities and financial assets. As a result monetary policy would have a direct impact on aggregate demand in contrast to Keynesian analysis which emphasized that the initial impact would fall on financial assets with only a weak and uncertain impact on aggregate demand.

The direct link hypothesized by monetarists is often called the real balance effect. Linked to the notion of real balances, is the idea of an 'optimal' or 'desired' level of real money balances. Exactly how this desired level of money balance is determined is' one of the theoretical weaknesses of the monetarist position, but it follows from this that if an individual's holdings of money are increased through monetary policy, then the individual will attempt to bring actual and desired money balances into line by spending the excess money.

Monetarist ideas also extend to the case of the open economy. Unlike the Keynesian view which emphasizes that balance of payments theory is a problem in the market for goods, monetarists see it as a theory of reserve changes, closely linked analytically to the *gold* standard. A balance of payments surplus will ceteris paribus lead to an inflow of money and thus an increase in the *high* powered money base. This follows from the argument that the demand for money will grow in line with income growth and this demand may be met by either the government increasing the money stock or through an inflow of money. This result appears intuitively plausible as it suggests why fast growing economies have balance of payments surpluses while slow growing economies have chronic deficits. The three weaknesses in the Monetarist approach may be considered to be:

1. its failure to provide a theory explaining why people should hold money at all. It is not sufficient merely to observe that they do hold it

2. the problem of a satisfactory definition of money and therefore of the precise nature of the transmission mechanism;

3. the fact that once some substitution between money

and financial assets is allowed for, and short run impacts on output are admitted, then distinctions between Monetarist and Keynesian views become a matter of degree and less of substance.

The revival of interest in monetarism during the 1970s has done much to clarify the issues that divide monetarists and their critics. Thus it has emerged that the early attempts to summarize the position of monetarists and their critics within the framework of the ISLM analysis is inappropriate, and that the real debate between monetarists and nonmonetarists has little to do with the relative potency of monetary and fiscal policy—Friedman had acknowledged that fiscal policy could affect real output in the short run and the price level in the long run, as early as 1966. The chief area of- disagreement concerns the principal source of instability in the economy.

Monetarists argue that the private economy is basically stable and that fixed policy rules are necessary to insulate the economy against ill-conceived and badly timed government actions which are the principal source of instability, while noumonetarists have argued that the principal source of instability is to be found in the private sector. The latter emphasized: the instability of private investment decisions in particular and generally support an active government counter-cyclical policy in order to achieve stability.

Monetary Base: A term often used in terchangeably with *high-powered money* to denote those assets largely public sector monetary and short term liabilities, which in the traditional theory of *credit creation* are held to detcrrno'ie the total supply of money through *credit (or* money) *multiplier.* The term can be used in a more distinct sense to designate any group of assets which the monetary authorities might seek to control, either rigorously in the short-term or in a looser, long-term way, with the object of con trolling some chosen money aggregate, e.g. M3. Whether or not such control is possible without considerable structural changes in money and security markets, or without causing undesirable instability of interest rates, is a matter of debate. At present, no monetary authority appears to aim at anything approaching a tight, short-term control of a monetary base.

Monetary Management: This term is sometimes used in a very broad sense to embrace the whole range of modern mon*etary policy.* It is also used, in the UK context, with an implicit emphasis on the more narrowly technical aspects of dayto-day management of' the London Money Market, the *gilt-edged* market and the level and structure of *interest rates.* Given the objectives of policy regarding interest rates and the control of the money supply current at any given time, the *Bank* of *England* operates routinely in the London Money Market to smooth out the effects of discontinuous flows of funds between the public and private sectors of the economy.

Beginning in 1980 the Bank moved from a system combining purchases and sales of bills at its own initiative, conducted with the *discount houses* and certain large *banks,* with *lender-of last-resort* loans to the discount houses to a system placing greater emphasis on truly open-market operations in bills at rates which the Bank determines with regard to an 'unpublished bond'. These operations, and the rates at which they are conducted, now give more weight than formerly to market factors, though there is no indication that this implies a passive attitude towards interest rate policy. This change in monetary management operations led to a wider set of changes in monetary control involving the suspension of *Minimum Lending Rate,* and the revision of the reserve requirements for banks and other institutions, announced in August 1981.

Monetary Policy: That branch of economic policy which attempts to achieve the broad objects of policystability of employment and prices, economic growth, and balance in external payments -through control of the monetary system and by operating on such monetary magnitudes as the *supply of money,* the level and structure of *interest rates* and other conditions aflecting the availability *of credit.* Like other arms of policy. monetary policy operates ultimately through its influence on expenditure flows.

Monetary Theory: This term refers to the branch of *macroeconomics* which studies money in all its aspects; how it affects the national economy; what part it plays, it covers issues such as supply of and *demand for money, inflation, central; banks, branch banking, credit creation* and financial institutions.

Monetization of Debt: The process whereby government debt is repaid on maturity, or is for policy reasons 'bought in' without a counterbalancing issue of new non-monetary debt, so that the money supply increases. This situation may arise in consequence of difficulties of debt management, or as a result of a policy to stabilize interest rates which imposes on the government obligations to buy in all its own debt offered to it, at a constant price.

Money: Anything which is widely accepted in exchange for goods, or in settling debts, not for itself but because it can be similarly passed on, has the character of money since it serves the primary function of money, i.e. a means of payment. As a means of payment money is an entity which is transferred when a payment is made; as such it acts as a medium of exchange, a function essential to any economy other than the most primitive. The term 'money' is also used in the sense of 'money (or unit of account': this denotes a system of abstract accounting units in which values are expressed or debts defined. Practically such a system is a necessary precondition of a price system since it reduces relative values to a manageable number of money prices. In modern monetary systems the principal means of payment are debt instruments, namely banknotes and bank deposits. Besides serving as exchange media, such means of payment are held as part of the holder's stock of assets, i.e. they act as ,stores of value.

Money at Call: In official statistics, this denotes loans made by banks mostly to the London Discount Market, on terms which allow recall at any time of the working day. Such loans, which are secured against bills and other securities, were between 1971 and 1981 classed as I eligible assets' for the purpose of calculation of the reserve assets ratio. Prior to 1975 the term 'money at call and short notice' was used, as the item then included loans to the Discount Market subject to recall at varying periods up to seven days. More generally short-term money is lent with or without security, by a variety of institutions, in various markets, on terms ranging from overnight' and 'call', up to seven days' notice and longer.

Money Balances: The amount of *money* held on average by individuals in the form *of fiat money* and/or *bank deposits*. At *equilibrium,* money balances are that amount of money which will remain unspent, but which represents latent demand for commodities and/ or financial assets.

Money Market: A term used in at least three senses, to be judged by the context. In its narrowest and most specific sense it appears as 'the London Money Market', when it signifies the market in short term, secured, loans, most of them 'at call', in which the borrowers are the London *Discount Houses* and a small number of money brokers and *jobbers*, and the lenders are principally the commercial banks, though they include other financial institutions and some companies. In London the terms 'Money Market' and 'Discount Market' are used more or less interchangeably, indicating that even in this narrow sense the money market is to be regarded as embracing the market in bills, in which the Discount Houses are predominant. Secondly, the term is used to denote any market in highly liquid assets which is supported by an identifiable and active set of operators.

Monopoly: In the strictest sense of the term, a firm is a monopoly if it is the only supplier of a homogeneous product for which there are no substitutes and many buyers. Such conditions are sometimes termed absolute monopoly and the *demand curve* for the firm's *output* is the *market demand curve* for the *product*. As with *perfect competition*, absolute monopoly does not occur in real life and actual market structures vary between the two extreme of nearly perfect competition and near monopoly.

The simple economic analysis of monopoly relaxes the assumption of no *substitutes*, but assumes that the monopolist faces a relatively stable and predict able downward-sloping market demand curve and that *perfect competition* exists in the markets in which the firm buys its in *puts.* Under such conditions a profit maximizing monopolist will set *marginal cost* equal to *marginal revenue* and sell a lower output and charge a higher *price* than would pertain under perfect competition.

Monopoly Power: Monopoly power is the ability of a firm or group of firms to influence the market price of the commodity or service it sells. The following are conditions which can give rise to some degree of monopoly power. (1) *Minimum efficient scale of plant is so large in* relation to market size that only one firm can operate efficiently. (2) *Product differentiation. (3) Barriers to entry which* put potential entrants at a cost disadvantage to established firms. (4) *Patent rights* which give exclusive use to a technique of production. (5) High transport costs which encourage local monopolies.

Mortgage: A legal arrangement in which a form of ownership of some asset is made over or conveyed to the lender of funds by the debtor as a gualrantee or see against the loan. When the loan is ownership reverts to the debtor. The debtor retains, within limits set by the mortgage agreement, control over theasset and may sell it in order to repay the loan.

Multilateral Trade: Trade among several countries, whose exports and imports are not in balance between pairs of countries, though countries will tend to be in balance with regard to their total foreign payments and total foreign receipts. Such trade usually conforms to *comparative advantage,* with countries buying in the cheapest market and selling in the dearest.

Multinational Corporation: A large enterprise having a home base in one country but operating wholly or partially owned subsidiaries in other countries. Such corporations expand on an international scale to take advantage of vertical and horizontal *economics of scale* as well as benefits from enjoying near monopoly status.

Multiproduct Firm: A n enterprise which combines factors of production to produce a range of products. With such firms the concepts of a physical volume of total output and unique price are less applicable.

Mutually Exclusive Projects: Refers to a situation where two or more projects cannot all be executed because they all require an input which can only be utilized on one project. For example, a piece of land could be used for an office block or a block of flats but not both. In this situation it is necessaay to rank the projects. Generally ranking by *net present value will* produce the maximum return to the owners unless there is a capital constraint.

Multiple Taxation: When the same tax on the some basis is imposed by more than one authority in a country, it is called as multiple taxation. It makes the taxation inconvenvent as well as inequitable. So, the government usually try to ensure that such a possibility of double taxation is not allowed to prevail.

Multiplier and Accelerator: Multiplier explains the relationship between the investment and the resultant income from the investment number of times the initial investment. This is one way relationship. The investment giving rise to income is called the multiplier effect.

N

National Capital: That part of national wealth which helps in raising of production and of national income is known as National Capital. It is the sum total of all the capital that belongs to all the individuals.

National Capital and National Income: Capital is the fund while income is the flow. National income's dimension depends on several factors. One very determinant capital. As per prof. Brown income is the rate of low of the stream of goods and services, capital is the stock of useful things or qualities—which could be revealed by an instantaneous photograph—supposing qualities could be photographed."

National Income: A measure of the money value of the goods and services becoming available to the nation from economic activity. There are three approaches to measuring this: first, as a sum of the incomes derived from economic activity, these broadly divide into incomes from *profits* and incomes from employment; second, as the sum of expenditures with the main distinction being between expenditure on *consumption* and expenditures which add to the capital stock *(investment)*; finally, as the sum of the products of the various industries of the nation. These three measures, the income, expenditure and output (product) approaches, give rise to several different ways of describing the various aggregates employed in compiling the national accounts and these are described and illustrated in the table below.

The income approach to measuring national income does not simply aggregate all incomes. It aggregates only those of residents of the nation, corporate and individual, which derive directly from the current production of goods and services. It aggregates the incomes of factors of production, factor incomes and excludes all incomes which cannot be regarded as payment for current services to production (transfer incomes).

The sum of all factor incomes gives total domestic income which once adjusted for stock appreciation gives gross domestic product at factor cost. If we then add on net property income from abroad we have obtained one measure of gross national income or as it is more commonly known gross national product. The expenditure approach aggregates consumption and investment expenditures to obtain total domestic expenditure at market prices.

However, since final expenditures at market price include both the effects of taxes and subsidies and our expenditures on *imports* while excluding the value of our *exports,* all these have to be taken into account before we obtain gross national product by this method.

Finally, the output approach aggregates the sum of the *values added* at each stage of production by the industries and productive enterprises in the country. The sum of these values added gives gross domestic product at factor cost which after a similar adjustment to include net property income from abroad gives gross national product.

National Insurance Contributions A form of tax on labour, levied in the UK on both employers and employees. Contributions levied are generally related to incomes though there are variations in payments dependent upon employment status (for example, as between employed and self-employed) and entitlement to benefits. The payments are earmarked to finance payments of National Insurance benefits but they do not provide the full revenue required for this purpose.

National Insurance Fund: A fund into which National Insurance Contributions are paid and from which Social Security benefits are paid out. Although the National Insurance Contributions are the main source of revenue for this fund they are not sufficient to meet its expenditures thus 'topping-up' payments are made from general government revenue.

This fund is an insurance fund in name only since its revenue does not meet its payments, the level of payments is not determined by the earnings of the fund and contributions are not based on any actuarial assessment of risk. The fiction of the fund is perhaps maintained in order to 20 remove the stigma of 'charity' from National Insurance benefits.

Nationalized Industry: An industry which produces output for sale to consumers and other producers by way of *markets* but which is solely owned by and under the control of the government. Nationalized Industries may thus be distinguished from government departments (such as the British National Health Service) which provide goods directly to consumers rather than selling their output. Besides these wholly owned enterprises, governments often have significant holdings in private companies though these are not regarded as nationalized.

National Research Development Corporation: An independent public corporation established in 1949 to encourage the development and exploitation of new technology. It provides finance for technical innovations by industrial companies and exploits inventions developed by government establishments, research councils and institutions of higher education.

National Savings Bank: Formerly called the Post Office Savings Bank, this is a state *savings bank* operating through Post Office branches. Funds may be deposited in 'Ordinary Accounts' where they attract a low rate of interest but may be withdrawn up to a certain limit on demand, and above that limit at a few days' notice. Or they may be placed at higher rates in 'Investment Accounts' where they are subject to one month's notice of withdrawal. A current account and cheque service is not offered.

Natural Rate of Growth: The rate of growth of the effective tabour force in the Harrod- Domar growth model. With a fixed coefficients production Junction the natural rate is the maximum sustainable rate of growth of real income. The natural rate (GN) is composed of the rate of growth of population (n) plus labour-augmenting technical progress (also known as Harrod- neutral technical progress).

Natural Rate of Unemployment: The rate of unemployment implied by the present structure of the economy. That rate of unemployment determined by the structural and frictional forces in the economy which cannot be reduced by raising *aggregate demand*. The *vertical Phillips curve* suggests that any attempt to hold unemployment below its natural rate will result in accelerating *inflation*. *Friedman (1968)* has provided the most often referred to definition of the natural rate of unemployment stating that it is 'the level that would be ground out by the *Walrasian* system of *general equilibrium* equations provided there is embedded in them the actual structural characteristics of the tabour and commodity markets, including market imperfections, *stochastic* variability in demands and supplies, the cost of gathering information about job vacancies and labour availabilities, the costs of mobility and so on'. In simplified terms it may be regarded as that level of unemployment which nonetheless remains at full employment. It has also been described as the warranted unemployment rate, the normal unemployment rate and the full-employment unemployment rate.

Negative Income Tax: An income maintenance scheme in which individuals or households with an income which falls below some 'break-even' level receive payments, the level of payment being related to the level of income. Those with no other income thus receives a guaranteed minimum. The guaranteed minimum income level may be calculated from the break-even level of income and the rate which relates the negative tax payment to income. This type of scheme is formally identical to the *tax credit* system since it is composed of the same elements: (1) a guaranteed minimum (2) a tax rate (3) a break-even point.

Neo-classical Economics: A body of economic theory which uses the general approach methods and techniques of the original nineteenth century marginalist economists. The term neo- classical derives from the view that the originator of the so-called 'marginalist revolution' were extending and improving on the basic foundations of the classical economists used marginal analysis (the concepts of marginal utility and marginal productivity) to analyse the pricing of goods, services and factors of production in competitive markets. They emphasized that the market prices of goods and factors were related to their scarcity. In particular they studied the possibility of a set of market prices which ensured the equality of supply and demand in all markets. The idea of a perfectly competitive economy in equilibrium, which may be attributed especially to Walras, is central to the neo-classical scheme.

Neo-classical Synthesis: The argument that the existence of an *unemployment equilibrium* was to be attributed to the Keynesian assumption of rigid money wages. A synthesis of the Keynesian integration of the real and monetary sectors of the economy, to show the simultaneous determination of money income and the interest rate, and the classical views that the tendency to full- employment equilibrium could only be thwarted by rigidities in the system.

Neo-imperialism: According to socialist and *Marxist* writings the control of the economies of less developed countries by giant corporations with headquarters in developed capitalist countries.

Net Investment: The addition to the economy's total capital stock, i.e. the amount of investment net of depreciation.

Net Present Value: The sum that results when the *discounted* value of the expected costs of an investment are deducted from the discounted value of the expected returns.

Net Profits: That portion of total profits which remains after the deduction of taxation payments and depreciation provisions.

Net Property Income from Abroad: The difference between *profits, dividends* and *interest* received on assets held overseas by domestic residents and profits, dividends and interest paid abroad on *assets* held in the domestic economy by overseas residents.

'New Classical Macroeconomics': Essentially a restatement in a more rigorous form of orthodox *classical economics.* This restatement rests on the notion of resources *rational expectations* combined with a natural rate of unemployment which emerges as a result of efficient market clearing. Accordingly it is argued that the economy will settle at the natural rate and attempts to disturb this equilibrium, say to reduce unemployment below the natural rate, will be fully anticipated and neutralized by economic agents.

Any attempt to stabilize output or employment below or above the natural rate by fiscal and *monetary policy will* prove ineffectual and will not alter the value of real variables in either the long or the short run, The essence of this view is captured in the proposition that there is no trade-off between inflation and unemployment even in the short run, i.e. that both the short-run *aggregate supply* curve and the short-run Phillip's *curve* are vertical.

New Economic Policy: A term used describe the workings of the economic system in the USSR in the 1920s.

New Inflation: The notion that the current inflation that western economies have experienced since World War II is of a different nature or origin to previous inflations in history. The basic argument here is that trade union *pushfulness* constitutes the 'vital parameter; or 'motive force' of the current inflation.

New Issues Market: The primary market not very clearly

defined, in which newly created securities, or securities not previously listed and hence not traded on the stock exchange, are sold: by open offer to the public at large, to existing shareholders in the case of 'rights issues', or to selected individuals and institutions in the private 'placing' of the securities of private companies or of unquoted public companies.

The core of the market consists of the financial institutions and operators engaged in some way in floating new issues, These include the *issuing houses*, *issuing brokers* and the financial institutions, e.g. insurance companies, pensions funds and investment trusts which sub underwrite new issues, i.e. guarantee to buy any part of an issue not taken up by the public or by existing shareholders in the case of rights issues. A new issue is not always made to raise fresh finance for the issuer: it may consist of the sale of existing shares on the conversion of a private to a public company, or simply represent the capitalization of existing reserves.

It should also be noted that the initial (primary) sale of a security previously unlisted on the stock exchange does not take place on the floor of the exchange, even when the security is to be 'quoted' on the exchange, but it may be 'placed' with buyers by the stockbrokers to the issue.

New Microeconomics: The name given to a body of economic literature which has sought to identify the microeconomics of macroeconomics; specifically, to provide a firm microeconomic rationale of the mechanisms underlying the aggregate relationship between price changes and unemployment The new microeconomics builds upon the natural rate (of unemployment) hypothesis, and abandons the notion of fully and costlessly informed market participants. Beyond exploring the implications of the natural rate hypothesis (e.g. accelerating inflation where the actual rate of unemployment lies below the natural rate and accelerating deflation, after some point, where unemployment exceeds the natural rate), the new microeconomics seeks to explain the existence of a positive natural rate of unemployment and the negative shortterm Phillips Curve relation between wage/price change and unemployment.

The new microeconomics models are not identical, but all attribute output changes to price 'surprises'. Thus, unanticipated increases in aggregate demand lead to unanticipated inflation; prices or wages begin rising faster than agents believe they are rising elsewhere in the economy. However, once agents discover the rise in prices and wages to be quite general and not specific to their particular markets, output and employment will return to their previous levels.

'New-new' Microeconomics: The name given to model building exercised which attempt to explain wage and price contracts in terms of microeconomic optimizing behaviour. The existence of wage and price contracts means that prices will react sluggishly to underlying changes in aggregate demand and that the latter will predominantly induce quantity changes in the short run. The casual sequence is from changes in aggregate demand to changes in output and employment which then lead to changes in price and wage inflation.

The new-new microeconomics is commonly contrasted with the new microeconomics, which attributes output or quantity adjustments to price 'surprise'. The new-new micro-economics developed partly in response to perceived limitations of the new microeconornics and in particular, the alleged failure of the latter to provide an explanation of layoffs, here viewed as an involuntary phenomenon) and the counter factual prediction, of a pro-cyclical behaviour of quit.

Recent developments have indicated these criticisms to be less damaging than first thought and so the new-new microeconomics is best regarded as an extension of rather than a replacement for the new microeconomics. By introducing the institutional features of tabour and product markets it is possible to extend the predictive reach of the latter. Two principal variants of the new-new microeconomics exist in the form of idiosyncratic exchange and implicit contract models.

Non-Profit Institutions: Institutions who either explicitly or implicitly do not exist to make a profit, for example, many health care and educational institutions. It is argued such 'firms' face different constraints and to pursue different *objective functions* from those enshrined in conventional theories of the firm.

Normal Cost Pricing: Thus, when output and costs fluctuate in response to cyclical or other factors, price will not be adjusted. If, on the other hand, the costs of producing the normal' level of output change (due to, say, a rising trend in unit tabour costs) then prices will change accordingly. Much controversy surrounds this hypothesis, principally because wages are usually found to be responsive to excess demand inter alia.

Normal Profit: Is the nominal or minimum profit that accures to an industry or to an establishment. If the rate or returns is to fall below this minimum normal level, the entrepreneurs may leave such and industry and join some other industry. With such an exit, the output falls and normal level. In case excessive profits over the normal profit to its normal level. In case excessive profits over the normal profit accure at one particular time or period.

Normal Value: Is the face value of the share or bond which is stamped over it at the time of its issue. when undertaking shows good profits, the share and bonds of such undertakings sell at premium. In the stock exchange market, these may be bought and sold at prices which are far higher than their nominal value.

O

Obsolescene: Is a problem that is becoming predominant because of a constant advances in the technique of production and machinery. While sufficient life may still be left for the machinery and equipment installed, the producer may have to scrap it and instal a new model of scrapping the asset.

Occupational Wage Differentials: Differences in the average levels of pay of groups of workers classified according to the occupation in which they are employed. *Adam Smith* provided the earliest explanation of occupational differentials in competitive labour markets. He argued that while competition would ensure that in the long run the net gains of any employment would tend to equality, the composition of these would vary between occupations for five main reasons. He argued that while the net advantages of all employment would tend to equality, rates of pay were only one of these advantages and therefore they would differ between occupations for any one or all of the following reasons.

First, rates of pay would vary between occupations according to the different costs of acquiring the skills necessary to enter the occupation: the greater the costs of training the greater the subsequent wage needed to attract people into this occupation. Second, rates of pay would differ to compensate for the inherent agreeableness or disagreeableness of particular occupations. Third, rates of pay would differ to compensate for the differing social standing of occupations.

Fourth, they would differ according to the dispersion of pay levels within the occupation, for Smith supposed that the average would be lower in those occupations which offered a very few individuals the chance of a very large reward e.g. pop stars. Finally, he suggested that wages would on average be higher in those occupations which suffered a greater variability in the pattern of employment e.g., the seasonal nature of building work.

However, Smith's analysis assumes that all workers have the same tastes and abilities. If this is not the case we may observe on the one hand substantial *rents* to scarce natural talents, such as footballing skills, and on the other much smaller differentials for what might be considerable undesirable jobs, such as hangmen, for some individuals may exhibit a taste for these occupations.

Oligopoly: A market structure within which firms are aware of the mutual interdependance of sales, production, investment and advertising plans. Hence manipulation by any firm of variables under its control is likely to evoke retaliation from competing firms. These features are commonly ascribed to markets in which the number of sellers is few. There are a number of' models of oligopoly in economic theory.

These range from theories in which each oligopolist acts independently and bases decision making upon some assumption regarding rivals' reaction, to those in which rivalry is overcome by means of co-operation and collusion.

Oligopoly Price Determination: Fixation of the price Oligopoly is very different from all other market situations of monopoly, duopoly, monopolistic competition and perfect competition. In case of oliogopoly, there is no one system of pricing. In case of perfect Oligopoly without product differentiation, the price and the policy of one firm is very likely to affect the others; for the number of dealers is limited to a few and the product is standard.

Open Market Operations: Sales or purchases of marketable *securities* conducted in the open market by the *central bank* as an instrument of control over the monetary system. The immediate objective of such sales may be to influence the quantity of reserve assets held by the banking system, with the further purpose of affecting the volume of banks' lending and holdings of other assets: open market sales will contract the reserve base and compel a reduction in banks' loans and other assets. The further effect of this is to change the quantity of bank deposits and so the money supply.

Opportunity Cost: Perhaps the most fundamental concept in economics, the opportunity cost of an action is the value of the foregone alternative action. Opportunity cost can only arise in a world where the resources available to meet wants are limited so that all wants cannot be satisfied.

If resources were limitless no action would be at the expense of any other—all could be undertaken—and the opportunity cost of any single action, the value of the 'next best' alternative, would be zero. Clearly, in a real world of scarcity opportunity cost is positive.

Optimum: The 'best' situation or state of affairs. To achieve an optimum is to, optimize' and a situation which is an optimum is said to be 'optimal'.

Optimum Output: Is the output at which the average Total Cost (ATC) is at its minimum. such an ideal point is reached whe the average total cost is at its minumum. It is graphically illustrated below:

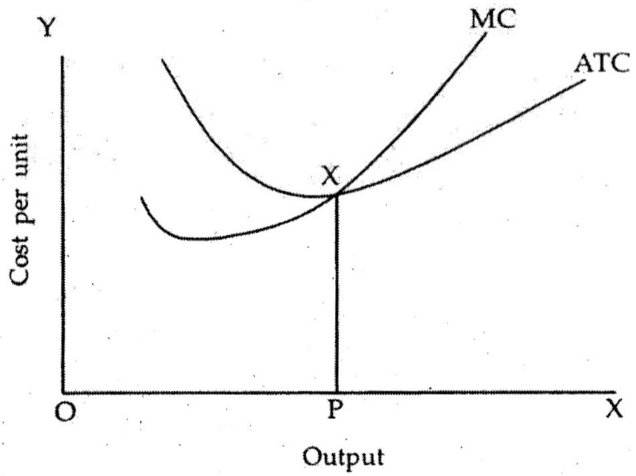

Ordinal Utility: In any ordering of goods etc., that with the highest utility is ranked, above the good with the next highest utility and so on. This ranking or ordering is ordinal if it is not possible to say by how much utility differs between the first and second ranked good and, say, the second and third ranked good. Ordinal utility is the cornerstone of neoclassical consumer demand theory.

Output Budgeting: A system of accounting which classifies costs according to the outputs in the production of which they are incurred rather than in term of the inputs which are purchased .

Over-employed Workers: These are workers who optimally would seek to work fewer hours than the standard working week permits. The over-employed worker might resort to absenteeism as a device to reduce working hours to the optimum income-leisure position. However, this practice threatens the distinct possibility of job loss and will thus not be resorted to by those over-employed workers who desire long-term job attachments.

Note that unlike the typical worker who will always accept overtime at premium-rates, the over-employed worker may decide to reject this option. Whether or not he follows this course depends on the relative slopes of the indifference curve (the magnitude of the marginal rate of substitution of income for leisure) and the overtime budget or income constraint at the standard working week. The steeper the latter and the flatter the former, the more likely the over-employed worker will accept additional hours of work, and conversely.

Overnight Money: Money lent in one or other of the money markets, at the very shortest term of recall. From the lender's point of view it is money which he expects to require, if not the next day, then within two or three days at most.

Overpopulation: A subjective term used to describe a situation when the density of population in a defined area is considered too high. This can be for various reasons; in a developing country the reason could be that there is insufficient food for the number of people, or insufficient employment opportunities.

P

Paid-up Capital: That part of the issued capital of a company which the subscribers have been required to pay. When issuing securities the issuer may require only part payment of the issue price. The remainder is the uncalled capital, and may be called at any time as the financial needs of the company dictate.

Paid up Policy: When on assured who has taken up a life assurance policy, for nay reason decides not to continue it, he can get the policy paid up. The paid up value of the aforesaid policy would be paid to him at the time of maturity. Paid up value is higher than the surrender value of the policy that is paid at the time the assured stops the payment of the premiums.

Paper Money: General term for money in the form of bank-notes. Under a gold standard these are convertible into gold coin or bullion; otherwise they are inconvertible. The term is occasionally used as a term of disapprobation for the money, in whatever form, of modern inconvertible systems.

Paper Profit: When an asset increases in value in nominal terms, this is called paper profit; for example, if a house would sell now for a larger nominal sum than the price for which it was bought, a paper profit has been made. This may or may not represent a real profit which depends on the rate of inflation.

Parabola: Usually in economics the U-shaped, or inverted U-shaped graph of a quadratic equation.

Paradox of Voting: The possibility that the system of simple majority rule voting may fail to give an unambiguous choice between alternatives. Consider the table below which illustrates the preferences between issues X, Y and Z of a community composed of A, B and C. If issues are considered in pairs, a majority vote would choose X above Y and Y above Z but Z above X; this pattern of choice is said to be intransitive. If voting is allowed to continue without limit a process of cycling is generated as one policy defeats another in an unending cycle. If however, some limit is placed on the voting process, the problem of path dependency arises in that the alternative chosen will depend upon the order in which alternatives are considered. In the above case, for example, if X and Y are first compared Y will be rejected, then X will be compared with Z and Z chosen. However, if we began by comparing Y and Z, Z would be rejected and X would be chosen over Y. It has been demonstrated by Duncan Black that if voters' preferences are single-peaked the problem of cycling does not arise. Preferences are single- peaked if there is some scale along which every individual's preferences can be ranked such that each individual moves to a lower level of preference the further he moves from the best or most preferred alternative.

Parameter: A quantity which remains constant in a given context. Thus, for instance, in the equation

$$Y = a + bX$$

where X and Y are variables, and a and b are constants, *a* and *b* are the parameter, of the equation.

Pareto Conditions: A set of rules devised in welfare economics which if fulfilled will give rise to a Pareto optimum. Briefly, these rules are that (1) the marginal rate of substitution in consumption between any two commodities must be the same for all consumers (2) the marginal rate of technical substitution between any two factors of production must be the same wherever those factors are used

Pareto Improvement: A reallocation of resources which makes at least one person better off without making anyone worse off.

Pareto Non-comparability: It when choosing between two states of society some individuals prefer one and some the other, the two states are said to be Pareto noncomparable, In order to be able to attempt a ranking of such Pareto noncomparable states some economists introduced the notion of compensation tests.

Pareto-optimal Redistribution: Transfers of income or wealth from one individual to another which increase the utility or satisfaction of both donor and recipient, thus bringing about a Pareto improvement. Pareto-optimal redistribution is possible if one individual experiences some benefit from giving to another individual- say as a result of humanitarian sentiment. Welfare economics is traditionally based on the Pareto Principle which requires a change to make at least one person better off and no-one worse off before it may be regarded as an improvement. Consequently issues of redistribution, which generally involve one group gaining at the expense of another, have been difficult to analyse in the context of welfare economics. Pareto-optimal redistribution can, however, be analysed in that framework. Nevertheless, many economists would regard the Paretooptimal analysis as being far too restrictive an approach to issues of distributive justice.

Pareto Optimum: When the economy's resources and output are allocated in such a way that no reallocation can make anyone better off without making at least one other person worse off then a Pareto optimum is said to exist.

The concept was proposed by and is named after Vilfredo Pareto A reallocation of resources which makes at least one person better off while making no-one worse off is said to be a Pareto improvement. Much of welfare economics is concerned with analysing conditions under which a Pareto optimum may be achieved. Despite its analytical importance, the Pareto criterion is highly restrictive since it provides no guidance to choice between alternatives which involve one person becoming better off at the expense of another. Since almost any economic policy will act to someone's disadvantage, this is a serious restriction.

Par Rate of Exchange: The expression of exchange rates in terms of gold or US dollars.

Partial Adjustment: A process by which behaviour is adjusted imperfectly towards some desired level, usually defined by the relationship

$$X_t - X_{t-1} = (X_t^* - X_{t-1}) + u_t$$

where X_t represents the current level of the variable,

X_{t-1} represents its value one period ago,

X_t^* represents the current desired level of the variable,

u_t is a stochastic disturbance term, and

l is the reaction coefficient, and that 0 <l< 1.

Note that if l is close to unity, adjustment is almost perfect, whereas if l is close to zero, very little adjustment takes place. For econometric purposes, the desired component X_t^* is usually specified in terms of some observable variable(s), and the equation will contain a lagged endogenous variable.

Partial Derivative: In functions involving two or more independent variables, the derivative with respect to one of the variables, treating all other independent variables as constants. The partial derivative has the same interpretation as the simple derivative, and bears the same marginal to total relationship as the latter.

Thus, for instance, the first partial derivative of the production function

$$Q = f(K, L)$$

with respect to capital, is interpreted as the marginal product of capital. The partial derivatives of the function

$Y = f(X_1, \ldots X_n)$

Partial Equilibrium: The study of a market for a commodity in isolation. Given the prices of all other commodities the conditions for equilibrium in a single market are examined. This technique used by A. Marshall ignores the effects of changes in the price of a commodity on all other related market prices including the prices of factors of production. These changes may have feedback effects on the original market which can only be analysed in a system of general equilibrium.

Partly Rational Expectations: The formation of expectations on the future value of a variable based only on previous values of the variable concerned, while rational expectations take account of previous values of the variable and other relevant variables. Partly rational expectations are often used, as they are much easier to deal with even if they do entail a loss in efficiency compared with expectations which are full rational.

Par Value: The nominal or face value of a share or security. A share stands above par if its price on the stock exchange exceeds its nominal value.

Patent Rights: The granting by the Patent Office of the exclusive right to a process innovation. Patent rights are a source of monopoly power, however. The theoretical case in their favour is that in their absence markets provide insufficient return to the innovator.

Path Independence: Where a choice between a number of alternatives are compared, the choice is said to be Path Independent when the alternative chosen is independent of the order in which the alternatives are considered.

Pauper Labour: The argument advanced by labour in rich countries that the import of goods from countries with low wages will undermine wage levels and employment in rich countries. The argument may be considered to be refuted by the consideration that low wages are usually the reflection of low productivity, and that price is the outcome of wage and productivity. The theory of comparative costs also demonstrates that it is impossible for a country to be undercut in all lines of production, It is possible for labour which is immobile to be harmed by imports.

Pay-back Period: A traditional accountant's method for appraising investment projects. It is the time required for an investment to generate sufficient increments of cash to recover the initial capital expenditure. It thus takes into account the capital expenditure on a new project and relates that to the net cash flow of that project. Projects are ranked according to the length of the payback period with preference being given to those which have the shortest paybacks. The method has been subject to severe criticism by economists. It takes no account of cash flows emanating after the payback period and it does not take account of the pattern of flows within that period.

Pay Ceiling: An effective upper-limit on the size of pay settlements. A pay ceiling may come to be regarded as the norm or the going rate.

Payment-by-results: Systems of payment under which the worker is paid according to the volume of output he or the work group or plant of which he is part produces.

Pay-off: The net benefit that occurs when a particular course of action is taken. The pay-off in a gambling situation is obviously the sum won if the bet pays-off.

Payout Ratio: The percentage of the firm's net profit which is paid out as dividends.

Peak-load Pricing: The peak-load pricing problem arises where the demand for the output of some public enterprise is subject to considerable variation. Overtime and the storage of the output is impossible or very costly, for example, as in the production of electricity. The solution involves charging different prices during different time periods, the prices depending on the demand or cost conditions pertaining.

Peak Period Labour Demand: The level of demand for

labour at its highest point, this term usually refers to agricultural employment, which is cyclical by nature with peaks occurring especially at harvest time. There are various methods of coping with this: one is when harvest time coincides with vacations for students and school children who can then be employed temporarily. In developing countries where this does not always happen, there are some groups of migrant workers who move about finding work where there is a high demand. However, it is often the case that the rural sector has to support the number of people required by such peaks in demand and although some may have additional occupations as tradesmen or small manufacturers of handicrafts etc., there are many who have little to do for the rest of the year.

Pecuniary External Economy: Describes a situation where the profits of a firm depend not only on its own inputs and outputs but also on the inputs and outputs of other firms. These should not be confused with non-pecuniary or technological external effects which describe interdependencies between production and/or utility functions.

Pension: Pension schemes are of two broad types; one, the capital-reserve system, involving redistribution over the lifetime of an individual, is based on workers saving to accumulate capital which is then consumed during retirement, and the other, the pay-as-you-go system, involves redistribution at a point in time between individuals so that those still at work support the retired.

Pension Funds: With the rapid growth in employees' pension schemes in recent decades, the pension funds of the larger public and private sector employers have become major financial institutions, investing large sums annually, and holding at the end of 1978 total assets approaching £25,000 millions.

Per Capita: Per head, e.g. per capita national income-the average level of national income for each member of the population.

Percentile: A measure of location of sample data or distributions. The nth percentile is that value below which n per cent of the observation on the variable concerned lie.

Perfect-competition: A market structure is perfectly competitive if the following conditions hold; there are a large number of firms each with an insubstantial share of the market. These firms produce a homogeneous product using identical production processes and possess perfect information. It is also the case that there is free entry to the industry, that is new firms can and will enter the industry if they observe that greater than normal profits are being earned. The effect of this free entry is to push the demand curve facing each firm downwards until each firm earns only normal profits, at which point there is no further incentive for new entrants to come into the industry.

Perfect Information: The possession by market participants in a competitive economy of complete knowledge and foresight with regard to the array of present and future prices as well as the location of goods and services. An, divergence from such circumstances can be regarded as a state of imperfect information and is commonly cited as a source of market failure.

Permanent Consumption: The average level of consumption that the individual or household plans to carry out over a period of years.

Permanent Income: The average income that the individual or household expects to receive over a period of years while retaining his wealth intact.

Permanent Income Hypothesis: The hypothesis that the consumption of the individual depends on his permanent income. Permanent income may be thought of as the income an individual expects to derive from his work and his holdings of wealth during his lifetime. The hypothesis suggests that the individual consumes a constant proportion of the present value of the income flow from his work and wealth while maintaining his holdings of wealth intact. It is most significantly in this latter respect that it differs from the lifestyle hypothesis.

Personal Income: The flow of income that accrues to the individual or household. The income may be a result of the sale of his labour and/or his ownership of assets or it may take the form of a transfer income.

Personal Loan: Type of loan made by banks and certain other financial institutions to personal borrowers, for the purchase of consumer goods, home improvements and so on, and repayable by regular amounts spread over a period. The borrower's account is credited with the full amount of the loan at the outset, and the interest payable is calculated on the initial amount of the loan.

Personal Saving: That part of personal income which is neither paid out in taxes nor spent on goods and services

Perverse Migration: Migration of individuals, particularly workers, from areas of relatively good economic performance to areas of poorer economic performance. Economists usually explain movement of workers from one area to another as a response to improved employment prospects or higher income levels in the receiving areas. However, in reality a certain amount of movement is observed to take place from high to low income areas and from low to high unemployment areas. This is said to be perverse migration. Such movement may be explained in terms of the influence of non-economic factors such as physical environment.

Planned Economy: An economy where crucial economic processes are determined to a large extent not by market forces, but by an economic planning body which implements society's major economic goals. In such a system the greater part of production activity is determined by obligatory input and output targets generated by vertical signals from an administrative hierarchical body. The advantages of such a system over the pure market economy include the reduction of uncoordinated economic activity which may lead to an inefficient utilization of available resources and the production of undesirable commodities.

Population Explosion: The name given to the ever increasing growth rates of population in the world, especially in developing countries. Population grew fairly slowly until about 1800 when it has been estimated there were just over 1 billion people in the world as a whole. However, by 1930 it had doubled to 2 billion and projections of' 8 billion by the year 2000 were forecast and much publicized, with many expressing doubts as to whether the world could support such a level. Recent figures show a slowing down in growth rates with the annual excess of births over deaths peaking at 69 million in 1970 and falling to 63 million by 1975.

Population Trap: rate of population from 1.95 per cent per annum in 1975-80 to 1.93 per cent per annum in 1980 85, while a US Aid Agency predicts it will fall below I per cent per annum by 1985. The result is a prediction for some 6.2 billion people in 2000.

Population Policy: A government may set up a specific policy in respect of the level of the population it governs. This is more common in developing countries where the ratio of population to necessary resources for survival causes much concern. Policy measures which are usually designed to control the increase of the population usually involve education programmes on the subject of birth control, widespread advertising, marketing and distribution of contraceptives, and offering free sterilization operations.

Point Elasticity of Demand: Slope of a demand curve does not indicate elasticity, for elasticity is different at different points of curve, as is shown in the following curve.

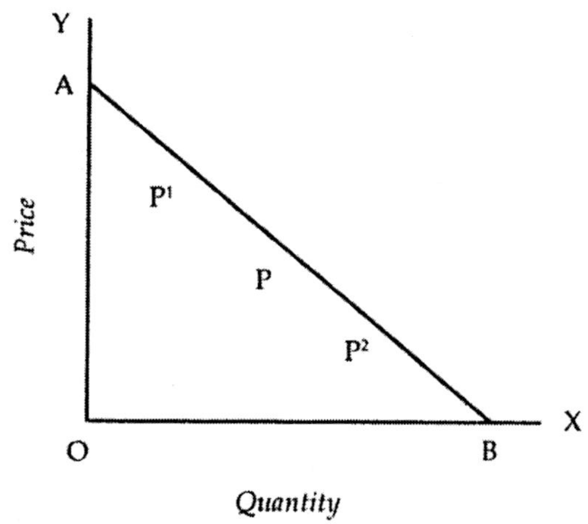

In the AB demand curve, in the two extreme cases of 2 points A and B where it coincides with OY and OX respectively, at part A elasticity becomes infinite while at point B it becomes zero. At point P which is equidistance between A & B and lies on the middle of the demand curve, elasticity is 1, while at P_1, it is more than 1(+) and at P_2 it is less than 1(-1).

Population Trap: An economy with a very low level of income per head may well find that the rate of growth of population exceeds the rate of growth of real income. If so, this equivalent to saying that the real income per head will decline. Only where the income growth exceeds the population growth can real incomes per head actually increase. In the diagram, the rate of growth of income is greater than the rate of growth of population up to point T but after T the situation is reversed and incomes grow less fast than population. As such the economy moves back to point T as per capita incomes decline. Efforts to move away from T are thus doomed to failure because of the effect on population growth being more pronounced than the income growth. T is thus the 'low level equilibrium' or the 'population trap' from which the economy cannot initially escape, Only if it is possible to 'jump' to point K can the process of raising per capita incomes on a sustained basis be achieved. This suggests either measures of control over birth rates in the developing economy, or a means of shifting the growth of income curve upwards. The latter might be achieved by technical progress. A combination of fertility control and technical change is obviously a safer policy still. Empirical evidence for the existence of population traps is not substantial.

Portfolio: The set of assets held by an individual or institution. It generally refers to financial assets, but there is in principle no need to regard it as excluding real assets.

Portfolio Balance Approach: An approach to monetary analysis which emphasizes the significance of decisions basset- holders about the composition of their portfolios.

Positive Economics: That part of economic science which concerns itself with statements that are capable of verification by reference to the facts. In principle all positive statements should be reducible to some form which is testable by reference to empirical evidence.

Price Control: Generally associated with the fixing of prices by government statutory order. By restricting prices considerably below their equilibrium level, a system of rationing becomes necessary. In the post World War II era price controls have been used as part of anti-inflationary policy, though it is widely recognized that these controls are not by themselves a cure for inflationary conditions.

Price-cost Margin: Empirical measures of the profit margin where accounting data are used and therefore the economic definition of profit cannot be directly observed.

Price Discrimination There are two major forms of price discrimination: firstly, the practice employed by firms of charging different prices to different groups of buyers, and secondly, that of charging the same consumer different prices for different units of the same good. In the case of the former, where each group of buyers has a different price elasticity of demand the firm can, by equalizing the marginal revenue generated by each group, earn a higher level of profits than would be the case if a uniform price were to be charged.

Price Index: An index number showing how prices of a 'bundle' of goods have changed from one period to the next. Typically, such an index will not be a simple average of prices, but each price will be weighted by the proportion of total expenditure taken up by the good in question. This weighting may vary depending on which period is chosen for the analysis of expenditure.

Price Leadership: Is said to occur in an industry where one firm takes the initiative in making price changes and the other firms then follow. Three forms of price leadership can be identified: dominant firm, barometric and collusive price leadership. The first, dominant firm price leadership, occurs within industries dominated by one large firm which sets price as a monopolist after due account is made for supply from the competitive fringe of small firms at each price. This fringe of firms are individually so small as to accept the price set by the dominant firm. Barometric price leadership is distinguished by change in the identity of the leader. Whether or not the price initiative is followed depends upon how closely the change reflects market conditions common to all. Collusive price leadership characterizes oligopolistic markets in which the few established firms have similar market shares as well as demand and cost conditions. With such features price initiatives by any one firm will reflect the wishes of the others, and their implicit acceptance comprises the collusive element of this form of leadership.

Price Mechanism: Used with-reference to the free market system and the way in which prices act as automatic signals which coordinate the actions of individual decision making units. By means of this role, the price system provides a mechanism whereby changes in demand and supply conditions can affect the allocative efficiency of resources.

Price-push: The name given to a type of inflation, similar to cost-push where entrepreneurs are blamed for causing inflation by charging unnecessarily high prices in order to make large profits.

Price Revolution: The name given to the influx of gold and silver from the newly discovered countries in America during the fifteenth and sixteenth centuries which caused prices to quadruple. This is considered to be one of the initial causes of the rise of capitalism and beginnings of the industrial revolution In the Western World as these high prices were an incentive for speculation, accumulation of capital and establishment of new industries.

Public Finance: The traditional name for the revenue and expenditure activities of government. Conventionally there are at least three functions, namely the allocation function, distribution functions and stabilization Junction. A more meaningful description of public finance would be the principles and problems of the public sector. The subject matter has been greatly extended with the development of topics such as cost-benefit analysis and output budgeting.

Public Good: A commodity or service which if supplied to one person can be made available to others at no extra cost. A public good is thus said to exhibit non-rival consumption; one person's consumption of the good does not reduce its availability to anyone else. It may be contrasted with a private good where one person's consumption precludes the consumption of the same unit by another person, The extreme, or 'polar', case of a 'pure' public good has been defined by Paul A. Samuelson as a good which is:

— non-rival in consumption

— has the characteristic of non-excludability—that is, if the good is provided the producer is unable to prevent anyone from consuming it.

This latter characteristic prevents private markets from functioning since a seller would be unable to ensure that only those individuals who paid for the good could obtain it. Since the good could be obtained without payment no-one would be willing to pay for it.

Public Sector Borrowing Requirement (PSBR): This refers to the amount by which the revenue of public sector organizations falls short of expenditure. For purposes of the definition of PSBR, coverage includes central government, local authorities and nationalised industries. The relevant revenues include taxes on both current and capital accounts, trading surpluses and rent, interest and dividends. Expenditure includes grants, spending on goods and gross capital formation and debt interest. The public sector financial deficit plus any net financial lending gives the PSBR. The deficit is financed by sales of securities to the non-bank private sector, increases in currency, borrowing from overseas and bank lending to the public sector. The effects of borrowing are more likely to be inflationary if the financing takes the form of new currency coming into circulation than it-genuine' borrowing from the non-bank private sector takes place, as the money supply is obviously increased by the first process but not by the second.

Public Issue: A method of making a new issue of securities in which the issuing body, e.g. a company or a local authority, offers the securities directly to the public at a stated price. A broker to the issue will have to be employed if, as is normal with a public issue, a Stock Exchange quotation of the securities is desired. An issuing house may also be involved in an advisory capacity and to assist with underwriting arrangements.

Public Sector: That part of the economy which is publicly owned as opposed to privately owned. It thus includes all government departments and agencies and all public corporations such as electricity boards, water boards and so on. The public sector is thus defined in terms of' ownership. It should not be defined as the sector which produces public goods, although, typically, public goods will be provided via the public sector.

Public Utility Regulation: The control by government regulation of public utilities who possess elements of monopoly power, the aim being to harmonize business conduct with the public interest. Regulation can cover the level and structure of prices, the quality of service, exit from and entry into the industry and the financial structure of the regulated firms.

Purchasing Power Parity: A theory with little practical validity which considers the equilibrium exchange rate between two currencies to be when they have equivalent domestic purchasing power.

Q

Quadratic utility function: A utility function whose algebraic form is that of a quadratic equation. Most typically applied to portfolio analysis in which such a function is required if the investor in a portfolio is to be assumed to be influenced only by the mean and variance of the probability distribution of returns.

Quantity theory of money: A theory of the demand for money which formed the most important component of macroeconomic analysis. This same theory is now enjoying a revival in more sophisticated forms.

Quartile: A means of location of sample data or distributions. The lower quartile is that value below which 25 per cent of the observations on the variable concerned lie. The upper quartile is that value above which 25 per cent of the observations lie.

Quasi-rent: The return to a seller of a good or service over and above its opportunity cost when the good is temporarily in fixed supply. The concept was applied by Alfred Marshall to the determination of the price of capital in the short run when the supply of capital is fixed. The owners of capital receive a payment which differs from the opportunity cost of using that resource by the amount of quasi-rent. In the long run when the factor can be augmented or depleted the equilibrium price will reflect the cost of alternative uses. Quasi-rent exists because prices in the short run are not in equilibrium. Marshall used this concept as an element in his explanation of the rate of profit.

Quick assets ratio: This is the ratio of liquid assets to current liabilities, Liquid assets are cash, most term investments which can be quickly realized and accounts receivable where an allowance is made for bad debts. Stock is not included as it may not be readily realizable. This concept is a refinement on the working capital ratio but still does not present an entirely up-to-date picture of the current situation. It also ignores the inflows and outflows of cash which are of great importance to the liquidity of a company.

Quits: Employees who voluntarily leave their current employment either to change jobs or to leave the labour force.

Quota: An imposed limit on the quantity, of goods produced or purchased. Import quotas can be used to restrict the purchase of goods from foreign origins, while export quotas have been used to stabilize the export earnings of countries producing primary products by restricting supply, and thereby sustaining prices. Quotas may also refer to the minimum required level of production, particularly in the context of planned economies.

R

Random variable: A variable which takes on values according to its probability distribution. Thus, for instance, a normally distributed random variable will take on values in a certain range with the probability given as the integral under the normal distribution curve lying between the limits of that range.

Random walk: An example of a time series model in which the current value of a variable is equal to its most recent value plus a random element.

Range: A measure of the degree of dispersion of a sample of observations, or of a distribution, calculated as the difference between the highest and lowest values of the variable.

Rank correlation: A measure of the degree to which two variables are associated with each other, not necessarily in value, but in rank. The measure involves the assigning of a rank to each of the observations on each of the variables according to decreasing value. Thus the highest observation for each variable would be assigned the number 1, the second highest 2 etc. The calculation of the rank correlation coefficient involves computing where D is the difference between the ranks assigned to the ith observation on each of the variables and N is the sample size.

Rank of a Matrix: The maximum number of linearly independent rows or columns of the matrix. Thus, if there are no linear dependent rows or columns in a matrix of order *m* ´ *n*, then the rank of the matrix is either *m* or *n*, whichever is the lower. A square matrix of order *n* is said to have full rank if its rank is *n*. If it has less than full rank its determinant will be zero, and it is a singular matrix. The rank of the matrix of cross products and sums of squares of independent variables in a regression analysis must have full rank in order for least squares estimates of the parameters to be obtainable. Similarly, the matrix of coefficients of a set of linear simultaneous equations must have full rank for a unique solution to exist.

Rate of return: A general concept referring to the earnings from the investment of capital, where the earnings are expressed as a proportion of the outlay. The term is applied to a wide variety of situations in economics. It can refer to the earnings from the investment of physical capital, money capital and also to the return to investment in human capital. The term is most frequently applied to the rewards from capital expenditure by businesses. The definition employed unfortunately varies among users. Accountants and businessmen have traditionally had a different definition compared to economists, but there is now a tendency for the economist's definition to become more widely accepted. The traditional approach of businessmen and accountants is to define the term as the ratio of profit to capital employed. Profits have been defined in various ways for this purpose, but the most sensible is net profits after taxation and depreciation. Profits can refer to the initial year's profits or to the average over the lifetime of the project. The initial year's profits may be quite unrepresentative and average profit is clearly more sensible. Capital has been defined as either the initial capital expenditure on a project including working capital, or average capital employed over the project's lifetime. The latter definition is superior.

Rate of surplus value: In the Marxian scheme the ratio which surplus value bears to variable capital. Marx regarded this as an expression for the degree of exploitation of labour by capital, for the rate of surplus value indicates how many hours the worker labours creating profit for the capitalist for every hour he labours creating the value equivalent of his own subsistence.

Rates: The only significant tax currently available to local authorities. The tax is based on the rateable value of land and buildings. Rateable values are based on annual rental values.

Rate support grant: A mechanism for transferring funds from the national government to local authorities. This intergovernmental grant now forms the main source of income for British local governments. The amount of grant allocated to a local authority is calculated on three main elements.

Recession: Like boom and depression, recession is another phase of a trade cycle. Recession may be deformed and understood by comparing it to depression. While depression becomes a sharp and a prolonged decline in the business and economic activity, recession brings such a fall which is of less intensity and lasts also for a shorter period.

Redemption Date: Is the date on which the securities are to be converted into cash.

Redemption Yield: Is the cash amount which is realised against the securities at the time of redemption.

Re-exports: Are the goods that are imported with the idea of exporting them in the same state and condition. The importing country of such products does not put any custom duties of these.

Register of Companies: Register is the government official whose prior permission has to be taken before the limited company can be incorporated or start its business thereafter.

Reserve Assets: Are the assets that the banking institutions keep with them in order to meet the demand of their customers for cash as and when it arises. Financial institutions run a trust and it is essential that certain assets are kept in liquid form.

Resources: That help in the raising of goods and services.

Return: Whenever any enterprise is run, it is with a view to obtain good returns out of it. It is calculated by finding out the ratio of the total net profits to the total capital that is invested. Return is expressed in terms of a percentage.

Roundaboutness: The term used to define more time-consuming and usually more productive methods of production. Fish can be caught directly but inefficiently by hand. If a fisherman were to spend some time constructing a rod, he would be more successful in catching fish as a result of this roundabout process. A still greater time spent making a net, a yet more roundabout process, would lead to even greater catches. An increase in roundaboutness is also described as a lengthening of the period of production.

The notion of and the greater productivity of roundaboutness is a central tenet of the Austrian school in its discussion of capital. This notion or its synonym, the average period of production, is criticized on the ground that since it involves measuring capital as an amalgam of magnitude of input and duration of input, it is not possible to obtain a unique measure for roundaboutness. Furthermore it is not empirically necessary that every increase in roundaboutness, if it could be measured, should lead to increased productivity, or that productivity can only be raised by increasing the degree of roundaboutness.

Royalty: This is a tax paid to the government by organizations exploiting minerals as all mineral rights are vested in the Crown. Royalty is the share accruing to the landlord from the exploitation of a resource in his property.

Rule-of-thumb: A simple formula or procedure which provides the basis for decision making by economic agents.

Runaway Inflation: Is the galloping inflation the last and the most damaging state and the stage of inflation.

S

Safe Custody: Is one of the miscellaneous functions of a commercial bank. If offers the facility of lockers of varying sizes for the safe custody of valuables on nominal changes. Thus, the customers are relieved with regard to the safety of their documents shares, bonds and valuables like jewellery.

Sackings: Discharges from employment for cause. Employees who have lost their job through some fault of their own. One element in labour turnover.

Salary: The remuneration of almost all non-manual and some manual employees in exchange for the supply of labour services. Frequently payment is made at intervals of one month and, in contrast to manual workers' wages, does not vary with the number of hours worked or the intensity of effort during those hours provided some minimal contractural obligation is honoured.

Sales Ledger: Is one of the books of account kept to record the sales or turnonver of the businessman.

Sales Promotion: It refers to various devices by which the businessmen and traders raise their sales and attract customers for their products. With this aim in view, they resort to various methods of advertisement and attractive salesmanship. Modern business concerns spend huge amounts even in million or dollars, pound sterling and rupees for promoting and raising their sales and extending the market for their products.

Sales maximization hypothesis: Due to W. J. Bau-mol: the hypothesis is in the spirit of managerial theories of the firm. Baumol's model considers the maximization of total sales revenue subject to a profit constraint as typical of an oligopoly. The profit constraint is specified as that minimum profit level necessary to secure shareholder acquiescence. If this constrained maximiza*tion* problem is to be solved by choice of output level alone, then it can be shown that with increasing marginal costs, price will be lower and output higher than would otherwise be the case if the firm chose a profit maximizing level of output. Once advertising is also included as a *choice variable* either advertising or output must be higher than profit maximizing levels, but not necessarily both.

Sales tax: A tax levied on a market transaction. There are many types of sales taxes but they may be divided between those which apply to a large range of expenditure and those which apply to the sale of a specific good or service. Thus a *value-added tax,* a retail sales tax, a *turnover tax* and a comprehensive *expenditure tax* are examples of general sales taxes. Customs, excise and protective duties are examples of taxes on specific goods.

Salvage value: When considering capital *budgeting,* the value of the capital assets at the end of the project life has to be taken into account. This is known as salvage value or scrap value.

Sample: The word sample is used in a sense more than one. In one sense sample is a method of extending the area of market to a physical contact between the buyers and the seller is rendered superfluous. The trader merely sends a few samples (say of cloth) of different qualities, colours and designs. On its basis, the prospective customers make the selection.

Samuelson, Paul A: American economist professor at the Massachusetts Institute of Technology, and winner of the Nobel Prize in Economics in 1970 for raising the general analytical and methodological level of economic science with the aid of mathematical tools.

Samuelson's work, which encompasses almost the entire field of economics, has appeared mostly in article form in journals. In *dynamic, economics* he has investigated how an economic system behaves outside *equilibrium* and how an economy develops from period to period in a chain of development phases. He has specified the conditions under which an economic system is stable conditions which often coincide with the requirements for static stability. The intimate, formal dependence between comparative statics and dynamics Samuelson called the Correspondence Principle. In his Interaction between the Multiplier Analysis and the Principle of Acceleration, he analysed the process which has become a mainstay of *trade cycle* analysis. In the debate on capital and growth in the 1960s with Cambridge, England, he up-held the neoclassical concept of' capital but without complete success as became evident in the controversy over *reswitching*. Samuelson has also elaborated the conditions for economic efficiency overtime, in particular in his *turnpike* theorem, which defines conditions for maximal growth.

In consumer demand theory his approach has been the opposite to that most commonly adopted, i.e. the development of theorems about consumer behaviour based on deductive methods, for he has defined preferences on the basis of observed behaviour or 'revealed preferences' as they are called. In welfare economics he has established the Samuelson tests as criteria for judging whether welfare will be improved by some change; all other criteria are but special cases of his tests. In international economics Samuelson has made many definitive contributions. With Stolper he developed the theorem which bears their name and which states that free trade reduces the income of the scarce factor of production. He has gone on from this to elucidate in a Heckscher—Ohlin framework the conditions necessary for factor price equalization. His treatment of the transfer problem and of the gains from trade are both rigorous and classic statements of the current position.

Samuelson test: According to this test one situation is potentially superior in welfare terms to another if for every distribution of the commodity bundle in the first situation there exists some distribution of the second commodity bundle in which at least one person is better-off and nobody is worse-off. This implies that the point utility possibility curve for the second bundle lies entirely out with that of the first.

Satiation: The phenomenon of having enough: of a *good.* More formally, the *utility* attached to an extra unit of' the good beyond its satiation level is zero or negative, i.e. it creates zero utility or *disutility.*

Satisficing behaviour: Conduct aimed at achieving satisfactory aspiration levels of the objectives of decision-making and which may not therefore involve maximizing anything. The concept of satisficing behaviour is an integral feature of behavioural theories of the firm.

Savings: All income not spent on goods and services which are used for Current Consumption. Both firms and households save.

Savings and loan associations: Corporations organized either as mutual or capital stock institutions to accept savings from the public and to invest their funds primarily in mortgages.

Savings banks: Banks originally established by philanthropists, and later by governments, to encourage thrift by providing a secure repository, with some interest incentive, for the savings of' people of limited means.

Scale of Production: Is the scale on which the businessman turns out the output. Scale of production may be small or large. Large-scale production results in certain economies internal and external. Hence large scale has become increasingly popular.

Secured Creditor: Is one against whose loans, bonds and debentures, the company has earmarked certain specific properties. Its claim for repayment of the loan comes prior to that of the insecured creditors. Such a loan is considered more secure from the re-payment point of view.

Shadow Price: Is the price deduced from the concept of opportunity cost of the productive resources that have been used in its manufactured.

Single Tax: Is that system of taxation where only one tax is imposed on the people of the country. Single tax has remained a discussion for the theoble nor practicable.

Stolper-samuelson theorem: Using the Heekscher-Ohlin framework Stolper and Samuelson have shown that on certain restrictive assumptions international trade necessarily lowers the real wage of the scarce factor of production without it being necessary to specify its pattern of consumption. A corollary to this proposition is that protection necessarily raises the real wage of the scarce factor.

Stop-go: Action on the part of the government to curtail aggregate demand due to a balance of payments deficit, soon followed by action with opposite effect to ameliorate the rise in unemployment caused by the first policy intervention.

Supply-side economics: A body of thought which emphasizes that the principal determinant of the rate of growth of national output in both the short and long run is the allocation and efficient use of the tabour and capital in an economy.

Surplus units: Any economic unit whose assets are greater than its liabilities, and is therefore willing to lend money, extend credit or purchase financial instruments.

T

Tail Price: Restrictive Practices Court states that any agreement on the restraint of trade is null and void, but, if it can be proved that on balance the advantage is greater than the detriment to the public interest the restraint to trade would stand.

Tap Issue: When the Treasury instead of resorting to the market, issues the government bills direct to the government, it is called tap issue.

Target Price: Is the price that is aimed to prevent for most of the products that have been included by the European Economic Community in pursuance of the common agricultural policy. It is one the crucial elements in the CAP. In order to ensure that the price does not fall below a certain point, it effects purchases and stores in its buffer stocks.

Tariff: A tax imposed on a good imported into a country. A tariff may be specific, when it is levied as a fixed sum per unit of the imported good, or *ad valorem*, when it is applied at a percentage rate with reference to the value of the import.

Tariff factory: A change in the location of production of a good from a low cost situation to a higher cost location in another country, where the inability to sell in the latter country, over a high tariff wall, makes necessary the creation of a 'tariff factory' to supply the market in that country.

Tariff Structure: The overall pattern of tariff rates. Tariffs are not usually applied to all imports at a uniform rate. A typical structure may allow duty-free entry to raw materials, a positive tariff on semi-manufactures and a still higher rate on finished goods. Such a structure results in an *effective rate of protection* in excess of the nominal rate.

Tatonnement: The bargaining process by which equilibrium is reached in the Walrasian market. The direct translation from the French is 'groping'. A set of prices is called by the auctioneer which then rise or fall according to excess demand or supply situations and a further set is called; by this process, an equilibrium is reached.

Tax: It is defined as a compulsory levy on the citizens of the state without any quid proquo. While special assessment is an adhoc imposition by the Government on certain people when the value of their properties rise without any effort made by them, a tax is a regular routine feature.

Taxable income: Gross income minus allowances and expenses. In theory taxable income should include all accretions to spending power within the taxable period. The concept of total accretion has been accepted by many economists as a sound basis for defining taxable income. This definition would include all factor earnings and all gifts and windfall gains. They are included whether they are *realized* or not. All reductions in wealth such as capital losses and wear and tear are allowed for. Market values are used to determine the value of assets. In practice income tax systems generally do not operate on the basis of accrued values but on realized values. This causes a distortion in that it gives an incentive to postpone sales of assets. In principle taxable income would be measured in real terms, thus the value of net worth at the end of the period in question should be deflated to take account of inflation. Similarly allowance should be made for losses suffered by holding debt at a time of inflation. For corporations a period of inflation means that replacement cost rises and *capital allowances* based on historic cost do not allow the company to recover the rise out of its expenditure. In principle all assets and liabilities should be adjusted for inflation but piecemeal adjustments are unlikely to improve equity overall.

Taxable income can consist of *transfer payments* as well as *earnings* by factors of' production. In principle the source makes no difference to the appropriate definition for tax purposes.

The definition given above takes no account of the possibility that income might accrue at irregular intervals. This becomes important under a progressive income tax and means that a person receiving his income at irregular intervals would pay more tax than someone receiving the same income on a regular basis. In practice averaging provisions for people such as authors and artists help to maintain horizontal equity

The appropriate definition of income should take into account all income whether it results from market transactions or not. Thus food grown and consumed by farmers should be included. Imputed rent accruing to an owner-occupier should be a part of taxable income. Income should be defined in net terms. Thus the cost of acquiring an income should be allowed as a deduction. In practice the appropriate costs are often a matter of dispute.

Taxation: Compulsory levies on private individuals and organizations made by government to raise revenue to finance expenditure on public goods and services, and to control the volume of private expenditure in the economy. Taxes are classified in various ways. Some are called direct taxes, examples of which are income tax and wealth tax. Others are called *indirect taxes.* These are taxes on transactions especially expenditure.

Tax Base: Whenever a tax is imposed, it is on some base—it may be income of the person the price of the goods.

Tax credit: This is a credit given directly against a tax: the tax payable is reduced by the amount of the credit. It can apply in several different situations. In some countries: personal income tax credits are given instead of personal allowances against gross income. When an income tax credit is raised all taxpayers benefit equally unlike the situation with personal allowances under a *progressive income tax* system where an increase would benefit high income earners and tax payers more than those in low tax-paying positions. Another example relates to *value-added tax.* Under the system employed in the EEC a tax-paying organization is liable for VAT on the selling price but is allowed as a tax credit the amount of VAT which has been paid on purchases of inputs.

Tax credit scheme: An *income maintenance* programme in which everyone Is guaranteed a minimum income, while income above that level is taxed. When a certain income level is reached, the tax paid will be just equal to the guaranteed payment—this is the 'break-even' income level. This type of programme is formally identical with the *negative income tax* though there are differences of emphasis in presentation. Both types of scheme are characterized by (1) a minimum guaranteed income, (2) a 'break-even' income level, (3) a tax rate if any two of these are known, the third element may be calculated. Thus a guaranteed minimum income of' 4,100 plus a break-even level of 1,100 implies a tax on income of 10 per cent. Proposals for such a system were put forward in the UK by the 1970—4 Conservative government but were never adopted. A negative income tax system has been operated in New Jersey, USA.

Tax disincentive: An income *tax* may cause work effort to be reduced, Its existence makes leisure relatively more attractive, as it is not subject to taxation. This is termed the *substitution* effect of the tax. The tax will also encourage someone to work longer hours to earn a higher gross income so that his net income is not reduced so much as a result of the tax. This is termed the income of the tax. The two effects thus pull in different directions. In general it may be argued that the substitution effect operates more strongly the higher the *marginal rates of tax* and the income effect may operate more strongly with high average rates. Much empirical work has been done to discover the effects in practice. In general the disincentive effects have not been found to be strong for the majority of taxpayers. There is some evidence that the effect may be significant for married women.

There has been a considerable debate about the effect of taxation on *investment.* The view that income taxation reduces the return to investment, and thus causes a disincentive to investment has been found to be too simple, When the uncertainty of the outcome of an investment and the fact that most income tax systems have loss-offsetting *provisions are* taken into account the existence of income tax may not reduce the mean expected return from an incremental project: the government becomes a partner which shares in both the losses and the gains from the new project. In fact, because of the risk-sharing investment could actually be increased as a result of the tax. The outcome depends on several factors, such as the attitude of investors towards risk and the variety of assets available to investors.

Tax expenditure: A term used to describe the various allowances which may be used to reduce tax liability -generally liability to income tax. Examples include tax relief on, payments of mortgage interest and dependants allowances. Tax expenditures are so called on the grounds that they should be seen as analogous to direct payments or subsidies provided by the government. This is said to be so in three ways; first, the granting of a tax allowance increases the recipient's income just as a direct payment would have done, second, the existence of a tax allowance will influence the pattern of expenditure and third, granting a tax allowance reduces government revenue and thus alters the government's net deficit or surplus in the same, way as would an increase in expenditure. Thus it is argued that analysis of the effects of public expenditure should include the effects of tax allowances.

Tax Progressive: When with the increase in income the rate of tax increases, it is called progressive tax. It is more equitable. It has been universally adopted in the sphere of direct taxation.

Tax-push inflation: This is related to workers' interests in maintaining after-tax real wage growth and is one of the factors alleged to have made wage changes less responsive to business cycle conditions. On this argument, then, there is a significant tendency for nominal wage demands to be raised to catch-up a past short-fall of real or desired after-tax earnings compared with their normally expected' increase. Tax thresholds that are not inflation indexed will result in a growing claw-back of income to the state and threaten the desired increase in net earnings. Nominal wage claims will be notched-up accordingly and the rate of wage inflation increased. This is a controversial hypothesis.

Tax shifting: The phenomenon whereby those on whom taxes are levied are able to pass the burden either partly or fully on to others.

Tax yield: The revenue collected from a tax. The relationship between collection costs and revenue from a tax is often a matter of discussion. The elasticity of the tax yield in response to a given increase in income is often analysed especially in less developed countries where a growing tax yield is particularly important.

t-distribution: A probability distribution often used in hypothesis tests in small samples, and where the variance of the variable concerned has to be estimated from the data. It is a bell-shaped distribution, with mean equal to zero, the dispersion around the mean being dependent on the degrees of freedom dictated by the sample size. The t-statistic is the most commonly used test statistic in quantitative economic analysis; and is defined as the ratio of a Normal Variable to a Chi-square variable divided by degrees of freedom. In Me case of tests of significance of parameter estimates in regression analysis, the calculation of the t-statistic involves dividing the estimate of the parameter by its estimated *standard* *error.* The distribution of the t-statistic approaches that of the standard normal variable as the number of degrees of freedom approaches infinity.

Technical progress: A central element in economic growth which enables more output to be produced for unchanged quantities of the inputs of labour and capital to the production process. In the simplest growth models no particular transmission mechanism is specified: rather, technical progress is 'disembodied' and assumed to fall 'like manna from Heaven'. More sophisticated models allow for *embodied technical progress,* to be included in new capital stock. Classification is usually into labour saving, neutral or capital saving technical progress.

J. Hicks and R. Harrod were among the first economists to take up this task of classification. Hicks' procedure was to compare points in the growth process at which the capital to labour ratio is constant while Harrod considered points at which the *capitol -output ratio* is constant. The Hicksian view was to 'classify inventions accordingly as their initial effects are to increase, leave unchanged or diminish the ratio of the marginal product of capital to that of labour. We may call these inventions "labour saving: "neutral", and "capital saving" respectively'. The neutral' type has become known as *Hicks-Neutral Technical Progress.* Harrod defined 'a neutral advance as one which, at a constant rate of interest, does not disturb the value of the capital coefficient' and which 'leaves the distribution of the total national product as between labour and capital unchanged. This second neutral type has become known *as Harrod Neutral Technical Progress.* Since innovations which are Harrod Neutral do not affect the capital coefficient in the production function the result is labour augmenting technical progress, which can be seen as equivalent in effect to an increase in the supply of labour or to an increase in labour efficiency.

Hicks' definition of' neutral technical progress is much less amenable to use in growth models with steady growth than is Harrod's definition which was specifically designed for such models.

Technological dualism: The process of combining capital-intensive heavy industry with labour-intensive methods elsewhere to utilize the excess labour. The heavy industry leads the move towards modernization and the other projects employ the excess labour while the basic capital infrastructure is built up.

Technological external effects: An alternative name for externalities. The adjective 'technological' was included originally to differentiate such effects from pecuniary external economics.

Technological progress: Most theories of' economic development emphasize the necessity for technical progress, and often an increase in the rate of technical progress.

Theory of Distribution: Seeks to explain the manner in which the joint produced wealth is distributed amongst the factors of production.

Tight Money: It refers to the tightness of the money market—The comparative scarcity of the loanable funds and a consequently the high rate of interest that tends to prevail.

Trust: As a term of law this applies to various legally defined and regulated arrangements under which assets belonging to an individual or a group are placed in the custody of trustees who, depending on the type of trust, may actually manage them for the benefit of the owners. For various reasons, including tax advantages, trust arrangements are widely used by private individuals and by institutions.

Trustee savings banks: These are savings banks first established in the UK in the early nineteenth century, with the object of encouraging thrift and providing a secure repository for the funds of small savers. The laws regulating trustee savings banks for long restricted the type of deposits they might accept and the kinds of assets they could invest in-these being gilt-edged securities and local authority mortgages. However, from the mid-1960s their powers and operations have been radically transformed. In 1966 they were permitted to open *current accounts and* issue *cheque* books.

t-Statistic: A statistic which follows the *t-distribution*. t-statistics are commonly used in *hypothesis tests* to determine the *statistical significance* of the *parameters of econometric models,* and are calculated as the ratio of the estimated parameter value to its *standard error.*

Turning point: The point in the business cycle when an *expansionary phase* of the business cycle is replaced by a *contractionary: phase* or vice versa. Peaks and troughs are known as turning points.

Turn Over: Refers to the sales affected by a firm or a company. The aggregates value made by the undertaking in one accounting years is called the turn over.

Turnover tax: Sometimes known as cascade tax. This is an early form *of sales tax.* It is normally levied as a given percentage of the sales value. It is levied on each occasion that a transaction takes place and the base of the tax includes any tax paid on transactions at previous stages in the production and distribution process. The effect of this tax is thus to encourage vertical integration in industry and commerce, as a reduction in the number of times that a transaction takes place reduces the amount of tax payable. The inefficiency of this type of tax has been realized and in recent years many countries have changed over to a value-added tax which does not have these inefficiencies.

U

Unavoidable Costs: Are the costs that can not be avoided irrespective of the scale on which the production takes place. If even the production is temporarily closed these costs continue to be incurred. It is the other name for the fixed costs.

U-form enterprise: A company in which decision making is centralized around a top board of executives whose functional responsibilities are applied to all company products. This form of organization is common to small and medium-sized firms; large firms adopting the U-form organization tend to suffer control- loss.

Unanimity rule: A procedure for collective choice which requires that before a policy can be adopted it must be approved by all of the members of the community affected by the decision. If this rule is adopted we can be sure that any policy adopted will be a Pareto improvement. However, in practice use of the rule would be difficult and time consuming. The use of this rule is analogous to the voluntary exchange model of public finance.

Unanticipated inflation: That proportion of the actual level of inflation which people did not expect; actual minus expected inflation. If people expect the rate of inflation to be 5 per cent per annum but in fact inflation is 10 over that period the unanticipated inflation rate is 5 per cent.

Uncertainty: A situation in which the likelihood of an event occurring is not known at all. That is, no probability distribution can be attached to the Outcomes. If the event in question is an investment in a project, uncertain returns would mean that the conceivable returns will be known but their probability of occurrence will not be known. In such circumstances it is necessary to resort to some rule based on the investor's attitude to the balance of gains and losses in the event that a particular choice is taken and a particular set of circumstances occur.

Undated Securities: These securities bear no date assigned on its face for its redemption. Hence undated these are also called irredeemable securities.

Underdeveloped countries: A term for developing countries which is now used infrequently, in favour of less perjorative terms.

Underemployed workers: The mirror image of over-employed workers. The underemployed worker is thus one who values income more highly and leisure less highly than the typical worker or, in other words, one whose marginal rate of substitution of income for leisure is less. An underemployed worker would prefer to work a larger number of hours than that offered to him by the standard working week. Indeed he would be willing to offer more hours at a rate possibly substantially below the established wage. Underemployed workers will actively seek overtime and if this is denied them in sufficient quantities, they will seek part-time work elsewhere in addition to their principal job. This latter phenomenon is known as moonlighting or multiple job holding. The propensity to moonlight is a negative function of' income and a positive function of family size. Also, moonlighters must have principal job schedules which permit them to take second jobs. Classic examples are postal workers, milkmen and school teachers. In the US approximately 5 per cent of all employees are moonlighters. In less-developed economics under-employment of workers is commonplace.

Underemployment: According to the dual tabour market hypothesis, the secondary tabour market consists of many workers who either already possess skills that would enable them to function satisfactorily within the primary market or who could be trained for skilled jobs at no more than the usual costs. Given the barriers to entering the primary sector, however, they are forced to take up unskilled secondary sector jobs and are in this sense underemployed.

Undervalued currency: A currency which, due generally to a balance of payments surplus is below its free market equilibrium level. To correct this, revaluation is necessary.

Underwriter: An underwriter is someone who agrees to bear a risk, or some part of it, in return for a payment known as an insurance premium. Issuing houses also underwrite new issues of shares such that if the whole issue is not taken up by the public, the underwriters are left to take up the remainder of the issue.

Undistributed profits: That proportion of total profit not distributed in the form of dividend payments to owners of equity capital or released in the form of tax payments. These funds are an important source of finance for corporate sector investment plans.

Unearned income: A term which usually refers to any type of non-wage income, which could be in the form of profits, interest or rent. It is differentiated usually for taxation purposes as most 'earned' income i.e. wage income is taxed at source, but unearned income often has to be declared and taxed separately.

Unemployment: The stock of all those individuals who are not in employment and who are either in the process of moving to a new job or who are unable to find work at the prevailing real age rate. The unemployed may be classified by cause according to a modern Keynesian view.

Unemployment benefit: A payment made to an individual who is unemployed. These payments are made from the National Insurance Fund and are related to the level of national insurance contributions made by the individual, prior to unemployment. There are other forms of transfer payment made if an individual is not eligible for unemployment benefit. The purpose of such payments is to ensure incomes do not fall below subsistence level during periods of unemployment.

Unfavourable Balance of Payment: Refers under 'B' balance of payment unfavourable and favourable. It is a phenomenon where exports of a country are less than the imports.

Unit Tax: Is a tax that is imposed per unit of sale or output for example 40 P of tax positive on petrol sold is a unit tax.

Unit trust: The term used for an institution, resembling an investment trust, which enables investors to spread their risks by purchasing an interest in a portfolio of securities. By buying 'units' in such a trust the investor in effect acquires ownership of the trust's securities in proportion to the number of units held. Unit trusts are run by managers, who include many of the major banks and insurance companies and who usually run several trusts each specializing in particular ranges of securities. The managers are obliged to sell and buy back units freely at prices related to the current market values of the underlying securities: if sales exceed repurchases, the portfolio expands, so that unit trusts are 'open-ended'.

Unvalidated inflation: An inflation rate which is not accompanied by a similar rate of increase in the money supply.

Urban economics: That branch of economics which applies the tools of economic reasoning to the analysis of economic activity in, and the economic problems of, cities and towns. Much of urban economics is concerned with analysing the pattern of location of economic activities in and between urban areas-thus it has strong links with regional economics and with location theory. Other topics include the issues of optimum city size and analysis of the economic growth of towns and cities-this latter indicates a connection with regional macroeconomics.

Urbanization economics: Cost which arise when economic activities are concentrated in urban areas are a particular form of agglomeration economies. The existence of urbanization economics helps to account for the growth of urban industrial and commercial centres.

User cost of capital: The implicit rental value of capital services, or the price firm should itself pay for the use of the capital stock it owns or is considering acquiring.

U-shaped cost curves: Curves showing how the average costs of a firm or industry vary with the level of output. They are an integral feature of the theory of perfect competition, where it is assumed that the long-run average cost curve of the firm initially exhibits increasing returns to scale which pertain up to the Point of minimum efficient scale.

Utility Function: Is a device by which a mathematical ratio is worked out between the quantity of a product that is consumed during a given period of time and the aggregate satisfaction that is so derived out of it.

Utility Theory of Valuation: As per the valuation theory, price of an article depends on the utility that a consumer derives at the margin. The Austrian school of economic thought advanced this theory in the sphere of price determination. It tried to restore the balance between the forces of demand and supply.

V

Vacancies: Employers' unsatisfied demands for additional employees. Vacancies for most manual workers and some non-manual workers are notified to the public employment service and are systematically recorded. As a result monthly statistics on the level of vacancies and the vacancy rate are published. In contrast vacancies for professional and senior non-manual employees are most frequently advertised in the national press and professional journals. They are not notified to and recorded by the public employment service since this does not constitute the traditional channel of job search for this class of workers. Published vacancy statistics therefore under-record the level of vacancies outstanding in the economy at any one time although changes in vacancies probably provide a reasonably accurate indication of changes in the demand for extra employees.

Vacancy rate: An index of the demand for labour at the prevailing wage rate. This is computed by expressing those vacancies notified to the public employment service as a proportion of vacancies plus the total number of employees in employment.

Validated inflation: Inflation which is allowed to persist because the government allows the money supply to expand at the same rate as inflation.

Value: Is the power of an article to command other article in exchange. Values prevailed in days of barter when goods were directly exchanged with goods.

Value, money, a standard of: One of the functions of money is that it acts as a store of value.

Value, theory of: The intrinsic worth of commodity. If defined in terms of money value determines price.

Value-added: The value of the firm's output minus the value of the inputs it purchases from other firms.

Value-added Tax (VAT): Conceptually this is a tax based on the value-added in a country. The thinking behind the tax is that it is an equitable way to tax the value of sales.

Variable: Variable in economics we broadly such divide under two parts independent variable and dependent variable. When a change in the price of a product brings a change in its demand, demand is a dependent variable, while price is the independent variable.

Variable capital: In the Marxian scheme that part of capital, represented by tabour power, which undergoes an alteration of value in the production process.

Variable costs: Costs which vary with the level of output e.g. tabour costs.

Variable labour costs: The costs of employment that vary proportionately or more than proportionately with hours worked.

Variance-covariance matrix: The matrix of variances and covariances of a set of jointly distributed random variables, the variances forming the diagonal elements while the covariances occupy the relevant rows and columns. In econometrics this term normally applies either to the matrix of variances and covariances of parameter to that of the value of the stochastic disturbance term in regression equation.

Venture Capital: Is the capital that is exposed to risk at one particular time in a particular venture.

Visible Trade: Is the trade in merchandise products. When a nation exports and imports merchandise goods, it is called visible trade. In contrast, invisible trade is one in which item other than visible goods are exported or imported such as capital or services of foreign shipping companies or of foreign exchange bank or of foreign marine insurance companies.

Voting Shares: Are those shares the holders of which have a right to cast their votes in the selection of the directors of the company.

W

Wage: Is the amount agreed to be paid to the worker for the work to be done by him. This work or labour of his may be physical or mental. The payment may be made daily, weekly or monthly. In India, the mode of payment is monthly except for the causal labour that is paid daily.

Wage Boards: Wage fixation has aroused lot of controversy and tussle between the employers and the employees. With a view to ensure industrial peace, it is essential that the mechanism by which wages are determined should be mutually decided by the representatives of the two main parties employers and the workers.

Wage contour: A set of *key rates* across several different *internal labour markets*. Contours may be bounded by the specific product market in which the firms populating the contour operate or they may be confined to a specific *labour market* or sphere of influence of a trade union. Across the contour wage settlements will display a marked degree of uniformity.

Wage contracts: Formal and informal agreements between employers and either employees or their representatives about the number of hours to be worked, the quality of work, and the remuneration that is to be received in return. Frequently these contracts take the form of a basic *wage rate or salary* in return for a standard number of' hours per week, the *standard working week.* Thus the contract averages employment conditions over some period and reduces the uncertainty of both employer and employee which is associated with continuous recontracting.

Wage differentials: Differences in the average levels of pay of groups of workers classified according to the industry or location in which they work or according to the occupational or racial group to which they belong. In its narrower sense this term is applied to differences in the pay of groups of employees in a single negotiating group.

While the concept of the *wage structure* is concerned with the relative ranking of groups of workers along one of these dimensions the concept of wage differentials is concerned to measure the differences in pay between groups on some common scale. Occupational and regional wage differentials are perhaps the most frequently employed. In the former the relative pay of workers who differ only in respect to the occupation in which they are employed is compared while in the latter case a single group of workers differing only with respect to the region in which they work are compared. When analysing occupational wage differentials it is necessary to control for differences in industry region, sex and race as well perhaps as other intruders, In practice it is of course extremely difficult to do this and for this reason differentials are seldom observed in their pure form.:

Wage drift: An increase in the effective rate of pay per unit of labour input by arrangements that lie outside the control of the recognized procedures for scheduling rates. In practice this is frequently interpreted to mean a rise in standard weekly *earnings* in excess of the rise in nationally negotiated wage rates, e.g. it' standard weekly earnings rise by 15 per cent in one year and wage rates by 10 per cent wage drift would on this view be 5 per cent. This is not, however, correct because recognized procedures for scheduling rates might still account for part of the difference between these two variables. Formal *plant and company bargaining,* increased payments for shift-working or increased bonus or productivity payments may account for the difference. 'True' drift arises from informal arrangements between employers and workers to allow pay to rise or the required labour input to fall and most frequently occurs under *piecework* systems.:

Wage fund: According to classical economic doctrine, a fund available for the payment of wages. At any given time the fund along with the given supply of labour determined the average wage. In the long run both the fund and supply of labour were variable, since the fund could be augmented by savings while the supply of labour was thought to be determined by some 'minimum of existence'. While classical doctrine was clear that wages were advanced out of capital, it failed to explain satisfactorily the division of capital between the wage fund and physical capital.:

Wage inflation: A rise in money wages over time. This may be due, but need not be, to *wage-push inflation.*

Wage leadership: A single settlement, or the general level of settlements within a specific sector serves as a point of reference for all subsequent wage claims.

Wage-price spiral: The notion that wage increases lead to price increases, via the increase in production costs, which in turn feed through into wages, as workers seek to preserve the purchasing power of their wages, and so on. The interpretation of the wage-price spiral as a mechanical sequence is intimately linked to the *cost-push* view of inflation.

Wage-push inflation: A variant of *cost-push* which attributes the origins of the inflationary process to trade union pressure in the labour market. There are a number of versions of the argument ranging from the exertion of trade union monopoly power, through models of union bargaining power based on objective economic variables through to non-economic models of trade union militancy.

Wage rates: The rate of payment an individual receives for the supply of each of the minimum number of hours specified in the *wage contract*. Often referred to as basic hourly wage rates, they specify some minimum level of remuneration of the individual can expect for each hour of the *standard working week*. The wage rate should be distinguished from *earnings* which vary with the length an intensity of the input of labour

Wage round: The hypothesis that substantial linkages exist between the settlements of all negotiating groups in the economy and that in consequence settlements conform to certain patterns each year. Deen suggested to take the form a bunching of settlements in certain months, an orderly and repetitive sequence of settlements and a marked similarity in the size of all settlements.

Wages boards: Statutory bodies similar to *wages councils but* controlling the pay and conditions of work in the agriculture industry.

Wages councils: Statutory bodies powered by the government to make proposals about the pay and hours work in certain industries in the UK. Established in 1909 and modified in 1945 these bodies were introduced into industries which were thought too weak to support voluntary *collective bargaining in* an attempt to eliminate low pay.

Wage structure: The ranking of pay levels of different groups of workers classified according to the industry or location in which they work or according to the occupational or racial group to which they belong. While the concept of *wage differentials* is concerned to measure the differences in pay between groups on some common scale the notion of a wage structure is concerned only with the relative ranking of groups of workers. Since groups of workers who differ on one of the above dimensions are unlikely to be the same in all others, in practice, it is extremely difficult to describe a ranking along any single dimension. Nonetheless the notion of a *regional wage structure,* and of an industrial wage structure still attract attention.:

Wage theory: Neo-classical theory is today the dominant scientific paradigm in the analysis of wage determination. However, the predominance of neo-classical labour theory has by no means been continuous and was itself preceded by the classical treatment. The cornerstone of the latter was the Malthusian principle of population and the concept of the wages *fund.* The classical economists firmly believed that wages tended to oscillate around their natural or subsistence level. This pessimistic view of the long-term prospects for the working class led to the designation of economics as the 'dismal science'. The classical economists were aware that wages varied between occupations and although their main concern was to explain the general level of labourers' wages and the movement of tabour's share in the national product with population growth they did give attention to these variations and much of their analysis of differentials remains valid today.

Gradually the approach to the theory of wages changed. Among later classical economists, especially J. S. Mill, the wages fund doctrine fell into disrepute, although the classical school continued to cling to the Malthusian principle of population. The latter half of the nineteenth century was characterized by dissatisfaction with classical analysis on two principal fronts, First, the development of Marxist theory provided a radical departure from the classical analysis, particularly in respect of' value theory. From the manpower perspective of wage theory, however the Marxist *labour theory* of *value* and the prediction that the wage rate under capitalism tends toward the subsistence level were in fairly close conformity with early classical analysis.

Warrants: Warrants are securities that give its holder a privilege to subscribe to a share at a given price from a given time. The price so offered is lower than the one that rules the stock exchange market.

Wear and Tear Allowance: Is the allowance for depreciation made in case of the fixed assets.

Winding up: Liquidation

Without Profit Policy: Insurance in which a person in insured for a fined sum.

Work in progress: Production that remains uncompleted at the end of the accounting period.

Working Capital: Is that part of capital which helps in the day to day running of the enterprise.

Work-leisure model: This constitutes a straightforward application of the theory of consumer behaviour to the allocation of time question. The individual worker is assumed to devote time both to market work and to non-marketable activities called leisure. He maximizes his *utility* by choosing combinations of goods and leisure hours subject to time and price constraints, which can be combined into a single budget or income constraint, the slope of which measures the wage rate. Equilibrium exists where the *marginal rate of substitution* of leisure for goods in consumption is equal to the slope of the budget line. The effect of a rise in the wage rate can be decomposed *into income* and *substitution effects* although the direction of the total effect cannot be determined *a priori* but depends on whether the negative income effect: out-weighs the positive substitution

Work sharing: A means of maintaining employment levels by reducing hours of work per employee. Although worksharing was at one stage much favoured by trade unions, it now appears that unions prefer layoffs as a means of accepting reduced labour costs in the cyclical down turn while resisting cuts in nominal wages. This development is explained in part by the disproportionate influence of senior workers on union councils.

Work to rule: A partial form of strike, resulting in a slow-down of production rather than complete cessation. Workers insist on producing only in accordance with the strict rules of some written job description or departmental rule and can usually manage seriously to impair productive efficiency. Adherence to some written rules avoids the application of sanctions by employers.

World Bank Group: Is an organisation formed specifically with an object to ensure that the complementary functions of the World Bank, the International Development Association and the International Finance Corporation are brought together.

X

X-efficiency: A situation in which a firm's total costs are not minimized because the actual output from given inputs is less than the maximum feasible level. This outcome is also termed a situation of technical inefficiency. X-efficiency is a direct function of monopoly or market power in which competitive pressures are weakened. The term was originally applied to the manager-worker relationship but can be extended to deal with the manager-owner relationship.

Y

Yaoung conventions: After two years of negotiations, a convention of association between the *European Economic Community* and the Associated African and Malagasy States was signed at Yaounde, the capital of Cameroon, in 1963. This convention, known as the Yaounde Convention, established a series of reciprocal and non-discriminatory trade policies, outlined rules governing international payments and capital movements and extended financial and technical co-operation programmes. *Tariffs* and *quotas* were gradually eliminated on most goods traded between the EEC member countries and the associated states. Provisions on establishment services, payments and capital transfers were based on the principle of reciprocal non-discrimination against individuals and firms. The convention also increased the volume of economic aid for development and technical co-operation programmes provided by the *European Development Fund* and the *European Investment Bank* in the form of direct grants and *soft loans.* In addition, an executive council, parliamentary conference and court of arbitration were established to implement the provisions of the convention. A second Yaounde Convention, which largely renewed the terms and conditions of the first convention, came into being in

1969 and operated until it was replaced by the *Lome Convention* in 1975.

Y-efficiency: The effectiveness with which existing profitable market opportunities are exploited. It is conceivable that the lack of competitive market pressures induces a failure by firms to supply potential customers who are willing to pay a price which yields a profit. Thus though firm may be minimizing the cost of producing a given output, and therefore be *X-efficient,* it can be failing to maximize profits due to this slackness with regard to market opportunities. Though in principle this could be the case, Y-efficiency and X-efficiency are likely to occur together given their similar origins.

Yen: The currency unit of Japan divided into 100 sen.

Yield: The annual return on a security calculated as a percentage of its current market price. In the case *of equities,* there is a distinction between earnings yield and dividend yield, the former being calculated on net profits and the latter on declared dividends. The dividend yield is normally below earnings yield because of retained profits.

Yield Cap: The difference between an average *yield* on *equities* and a corresponding yield on long-dated fixed-interest securities. Traditionally equities were on the upper side of this gap reflecting the risk element involved, but since the late 1950s a 'reverse yield gap' has existed with the dividend yield on equities falling below that of debt securities. This was caused first by the expected growth element in equities, then increasingly by the effect of inflation in raising the nominal yields on debt.